Africa Solo

www.penguin.co.uk

Also by Mark Beaumont

THE MAN WHO CYCLED THE WORLD
THE MAN WHO CYCLED THE AMERICAS

and published by Corgi

AFRICA SOLO

My World Record Race from
Cairo to Cape Town

Mark Beaumont

CORGI BOOKS

TRANSWORLD PUBLISHERS
61–63 Uxbridge Road, London W5 5SA
www.penguin.co.uk

Transworld is part of the Penguin Random House group of companies
whose addresses can be found at global.penguinrandomhouse.com

First published in Great Britain in 2016 by Bantam Press
an imprint of Transworld Publishers
Corgi edition published 2017

A CIP catalogue record for this book
is available from the British Library.

ISBN
9780552172479

Typeset in 10.12/13.96pt Times NR MT by Jouve (UK), Milton Keynes
Printed and bound by Clays Ltd, Bungay, Suffolk

Penguin Random House is committed to a sustainable future for
our business, our readers and our planet. This book is made from
Forest Stewardship Council® certified paper.

MIX
Paper from
responsible sources
FSC® C018179

1 3 5 7 9 10 8 6 4 2

In loving memory of
Jessie Holmes MacLeod, aka Granny
4 May 1923 – 2 February 2016

Mummy to three, Granny to eight, great Granny to nine
With two more in our midst, who are waiting their time.
But for my generation, I can speak for us all:
She was Queen of all Grannys and ever so small.

Cherry meringue slice, lemon pudding, pancakes and more,
Who ever knew what that cupboard, those tins had in store?
And always a bowl to sample, a mixture to prepare,
For the sweet-toothed amongst us, our baker extraordinaire.

Thornly Park, Westsyde Farm and tales of the war,
Land Rovers and ponies, what a perfect memory, bedtime
    stories galore;
1 Milton Cottages, cloaked in clematis, with its old creaking stair,
Beds so tightly tucked in layers of sheets, ready for us and
    Granny Bear.

Old-fashioned letters and neat, thoughtful cards
Have kept us all company, made us smile and remember
    her words.
'Oh, how wonderful to hear from you' she would answer
    the phone
Making us always feel loved when we were many miles
    from home.

For our first memories and our fondest memories
Our thanks and our love
To Jessie, to Granny, who now looks down from above.

Contents

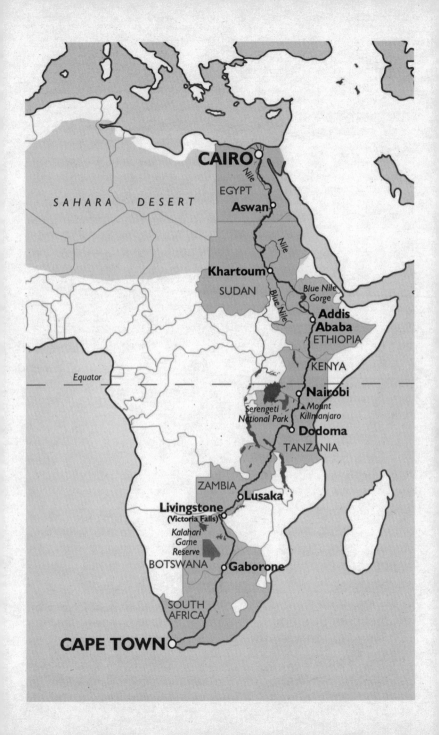

Prologue

Facing a Watery End

Treading water in high seas hundreds of miles offshore gives you a new perspective on life. I had been in serious scrapes before, but 31 January 2012 was the first time when I clearly thought I was about to die.

On a cheerier note, it is what brought me back to the bike.

It was 10.55 a.m. and I was rowing hard in the final five minutes of my shift. Ian, as always, was in front of me, Yaacov behind, and we were going fast, just over 500 nautical miles from our destination in Barbados. The swell and winds were coming from the east and it was a large but fairly predictable sea. I was completely dry, which is as good a gauge as any for how big the waves were. My thoughts were on what I was going to eat during my two-hour break and I was looking forward to a short sleep, too. None of us had slept for more than ninety minutes at a time in the twenty-seven days since we had set out from Morocco.

Despite huge fatigue after four weeks of very hard rowing, spirits were high. The trade winds had finally reached us and for the last forty-eight hours our speed had picked up considerably. We were tantalizingly close to world record pace – just another six days.

I didn't see it coming. I didn't hear it coming. *Sara G* pitched up without warning, the stern cabin in front of me lifting quickly as a large wave sped under us. She then pitched wildly to my left. I instinctively let go of the port-side oar and held on to the metal safety rail like it was a monkey bar. There was an awful moment in equilibrium as we perched perfectly on our side. In all the huge seas we had seen she had never been this far over, yet I still thought she would self-right. I can't remember anyone calling anything, I can't remember much at all except I was then upside down, in the water and fighting to get my shoes out of the rowing straps. They were stuck. I managed to pull my feet free, leaving both shoes tied in, and kicked for the surface.

For Aodhan it was worse. He was lying down in the bow cabin. Thrown to the side, he struggled to the hatch door as it swung open and water flooded in. He quickly realized that *Sara G* wasn't going to self-right and had to pull himself out and swim for the surface. Simon and Matt also had to swim out. The timing couldn't have been worse. With both hatches open for those few minutes during the change of shift, both fore and aft cabins were flooded and there was no chance she would right herself, as she was designed to do. She was completely capsized, and taking on more water. For the first ten minutes we didn't know whether or not she would sink. Holding on to her upturned hull, we had very little time to act. If she went down before we set off an emergency beacon or salvaged a life-raft then our chances of survival were nil.

Every emergency you ever train for allows for a short period of time to prepare – get lifejackets, pull the life-raft, get the grab bag of supplies. Our reality was clinging on to an upturned vessel with nothing. Anything was progress from that point.

Within five minutes Ian and Matt had ducked under the waves and salvaged the EPIRB (emergency beacon) – setting that off would at least let the UK coastguards know that we were in a Mayday, fighting for our lives. Salvaging the life-raft wasn't as easy. It was in a hatch on the rowing deck of the boat, which was now upside down and submerged. Worse still, an air pocket was holding it firmly in place. It took Aodhan, Matt and me nearly twenty minutes to wrestle it free. The whoosh of air as it auto-inflated was the first moment of great relief – we now had a chance.

So as not to puncture the life-raft on the riggers of the upturned hull, we tied it off on a long line before swimming over one by one and climbing in. Yaacov had swallowed a lot of water during the capsize and had been hyperventilating since surfacing. Feeling weak, he struggled with the swim, but managed to pull himself along the slack line to safety.

We counted the small blessings: it was daylight, and being so near the Caribbean the water was fairly warm. Even so, after so long treading water and holding on, I was shaking with cold. Simon had spent most of the first half hour lying on top of the upturned hull looking after the emergency grab bag, which was such an important lifeline. It had in it the first aid, some fresh water and foil blankets that would keep us going for a few days.

Inside the life-raft it was incredibly cramped, not that this mattered initially. We took stock of our situation. Everyone was uninjured, very much alive. The raft had a cover so we closed ourselves up to stop waves coming in. The floor space was very wet and we set about the fairly futile task of sponging it dry, while figuring out what to do next.

Water was the main priority. We could be in the raft for twelve hours or twelve days. Within the first hour Ian and Matt swam back to *Sara G* and managed to retrieve two of the water bottles that were clipped on deck. We now had another litre and a bit. Ian came back to the life-raft joking and jovial, a thin veil for how shaken he was.

It is hard to remember how long anything took over the following hours. It is hard enough to remember what order they happened in. Most of the team closed their eyes for periods, either falling asleep or doing their best to pass the time quickly.

We had no idea how long we would be there and speculated about whether a plane would fly over to spot us, or how close any ships could be.

It was clear that to get rescued quickly would mean going back to *Sara G* to find other emergency equipment. And if we weren't rescued quickly we would need to go back to find more food and water. In the first moments of the capsize I had ducked back under to close the stern hatch and discovered I could see clearly. This amazed me, especially as I wear contact lenses. Matt knew he couldn't see in the salt water, but wanted to come with me to assist.

During the afternoon we made two return trips. At first we were concerned that by reopening the hatches *Sara G* could take on even more water and sink further. My other concern was that to get to the hatches meant swimming underneath the safety rails and back up into the upturned boat. Having never been a strong swimmer, I wasn't confident about holding my breath long enough to do anything useful. Luckily, the boat had settled just high enough to allow a small air pocket in the footwell. I could turn my head into this and try to keep my lungs full. The swell kept closing this space off without any warning, but it was enough to work with.

We needn't have worried about the cabins flooding further: they were already full and the hatches opened easily. But finding anything useful was difficult in that dark, flooded, upside-down world. The first time I resurfaced I brought with me a fire extinguisher. Despite our situation, Matt joked at the absurdity. The next trip was more successful. I will always remember Matt's relief when I broke the surface holding a GPS tracker beacon. This was the lifeline we needed – rescuers would now know exactly where we were.

The second trip back was mainly to find the desalinator so we could make fresh water. As much as we fought with the hatch and hacked it with an axe we couldn't open it, so we had to give up. Diving back underneath, I instead tried to find another emergency bag. Feeling weak after a long period of finding nothing useful, I was about to give up when my hand fell on a handle. I knew it was on a waterproof case. Grabbing it and thrusting it out to Matt, I swam for the surface. It was the laptop case that also contained a satellite phone.

That last trip back to the boat was by far the worst. Matt and I had already agreed that we were too weak to return when we set out for the raft. Matt went ahead and I could see he was struggling. The line was constantly slack from the swell and I fought to keep my head above water. Every time I looked at the life-raft it seemed no closer. Halfway across I saw some wooden slats I had thrown out from one of the cabins. They were less than a few metres away and I reached for them to help me float. But as much as I kicked and stretched out, the swell kept us apart and I eventually had to give up. The relief when I reached the raft was immense, and I stayed next to it for a minute before Aodhan helped me climb back in. I immediately had to lean back out to be sick after all the salt water I had swallowed.

The battery on the phone was almost dead but there was enough charge to call the UK and say that we were all fine. Matt's wife was able to keep brilliantly calm and reported back that a vessel was on its way and should reach us by 1 a.m. We were going to be rescued. The conversation aboard the raft fell to everyone back home and the relief of being able to tell our families that we were OK.

From then on it was a very slow waiting game. As the evening drew in it got colder, and soon it was dark. The seas picked up a bit and we huddled together, occasionally checking *Sara G*.

By 11.30 p.m. we were all extremely uncomfortable and playing silly word games in order to stay awake. After dark we had decided not to go to sleep as it would have been very easy for us all to slip into a shock-induced slumber and miss the rescue ship. Matt made another call on the VHF radio, just in case there was a vessel within distance. Incredibly a call came straight back. It was the captain of the *Nord Taipei*, a Taiwanese cargo vessel. Since gone 11 a.m., only a few minutes after our initial Mayday, she had redirected and covered 120 nautical miles to reach us. We scrambled to look out of the life-raft and couldn't quite believe the sight of the white navigation lights on the horizon.

But while we could see it, there was no way it could see us, a tiny speck on the dark ocean waves. After punching the raft and shouting in excitement, Matt set about lighting a few rocket flares to guide the *Nord Taipei* closer. We all knew that the rescue would be very dangerous, especially at night and in choppy seas. It took three passes before the captain was able to bring the *Nord Taipei*'s vast 177-metre hull near enough so her crew could throw lines down for us to catch. The second time we missed, the life-raft drifted under her vast bows. Simon aptly described it as something out of *Star Wars* – a vast mother ship dwarfing us in the darkness. The waves that broke off the bulb at her waterline threatened to flood the raft and we all understood it would be a disaster if we were hit or flipped.

Third time lucky, though, and one by one we were able to grab hold of and climb a rope and wooden ladder that had been dropped over the side. The Chinese crew pulled incredibly hard on our safety lines so that I hardly felt like I was climbing at all. They practically lifted me up that ladder and a few strong arms dragged me over the rails and on to the deck. Before joining the others on the ground, huddled under a blanket, Yaacov and I looked back down and saw Matt clinging on to the lowest rungs of the ladder. We were all safe.

For the next ten days we recrossed 2,500 nautical miles of Atlantic Ocean to Gibraltar, where friends and family would meet us.

We had plenty of time aboard the *Nord Taipei* to think back over what had happened. After an ordeal like that, it no longer mattered about the world record or the Atlantic crossing on which we had focused so obsessively for so long. We all knew how close we had come to not surviving so returning alive was all that mattered. We also realized what a tough time it must have been for family and friends back home. The level of support from the public and our sponsors had been staggering.

I cannot speak highly enough of the Taiwanese and Chinese crew that saved us and then looked after us so well. The captain and first officer were particularly generous. I think they found it very odd that they rescued six hairy, unwashed men, most of whom were dressed only in boxer shorts – and, remarkably, the only items we had with us were a satellite phone, two laptops, a GPS tracker and a VHF radio!

Our saviours were taking a cargo from Venezuela to Cairo, and had rerouted by over a day to rescue us, at an eye-watering cost of over $100,000. Thankfully there is insurance for such things; more fundamentally, thankfully there is a 'Good Samaritan' legal obligation to render assistance at sea, unlike for land lovers, where there is only a moral obligation.

These mariners have it seriously tough, nine months onboard and then three months off each year. I spoke to a number of the crewmen about their families back home and the lives they lead. They were all motivated by a better life, not necessarily for themselves but for their children, or for their parents. Even the captain, who lived in relative luxury, talked about the sacrifices he had made to allow his children to go to university. There was no gym on the ship, no social area outside the galley, which had prison-like metal furniture and trays of food. One old television sat in the corner. We spent most of our time in front of it working our way through a box-set of fifteen Jean-Claude Van Damme films and season two of *The Walking Dead*.

Seeing as these men had saved our lives, we should have remained grateful for everything that came our way. But it took only a few days before one of the team broke rank and said what we were all thinking: 'How do these guys survive on this?' The food was meagre, tasteless, and we were all struggling to do nothing on the rations, let alone work twelve-hour shifts like the crew.

A few days from Gibraltar I went up to see the captain, to ask about plans.

'We will need to anchor outside the harbour wall and a pilot boat will come and take you all ashore,' he told me.

'And will it just be the six of us?'

'No, there will be eight: my chief engineer is leaving, and also the chef. They are finished.'

'So they are both having some time off?'

'No,' he replied. 'The engineer is going home for a holiday, but the chef is fired – he is no good!'

We'd set out to try to be the first to row across the Atlantic in less than thirty days – the first sub-month ocean row. That soon became impossible without help from the trade winds, but up to and including day twenty-seven we never gave up hope of breaking the world record. When our luck ran out, it was simply a case of surviving. The training we had all undergone paid off and it is thanks to having such a resourceful team that we managed to survive the closest scrape of our lives. We did survive, so ultimately the expedition was a success. No regrets. Then again, I knew the Atlantic wasn't a place I'd be returning to any time soon.

It was time for dry land again. I didn't know it as we docked in Gibraltar, but my future lay just across that narrow strait of water, in Africa.

Part One

The Dream of the World

My road back to cycling wasn't that simple, however.

In fact, I retired from sport. It had taken so many years to convince myself this was actually a career, it seemed rather grand and premature to be retiring aged twenty-nine. And it wasn't planned. The fact was that I returned from the Atlantic and everything had changed.

Just eight weeks later I stood at the front of a gigantic teepee, with two bikes either side decorated beautifully in spring flowers. The hessian canvas let through a warm golden light that bathed my friends and family as they sat patiently.

I can set out on half-year expeditions into the unknown with steely resolve yet here, on my wedding day, I was a bag of uncontrollable nerves. During the soundcheck an hour earlier our chosen entrance music, 'Wild Mountainside', had reduced me to tears. My best men clearly didn't know how to deal with this unprecedented show of emotion and reacted in the only way they knew how. Whisky.

It is important to mention that my marriage to Nicci was not a kneejerk reaction. Far from the Atlantic being a catalyst for marriage, it was seen more by my family as an elaborate ploy to avoid the planning phase. I had asked Nicci to marry me during a short trip to Barcelona in late October 2011. And with the wedding the following April, it was a short engagement even without my absence. But there was certainly no way I could meddle with plans while mid-Atlantic and the day was all the more successful for this. Over Christmas, one of the many final decisions I made before leaving for Morocco was that our favourite caterer's menu was a long way outside our budget and so was scored off the shortlist. It was with some surprise, then, that I sat down on my wedding night to that exact meal.

In contrast to me, Nicci was the picture of composure and took my breath away. I could hear the celebrants' words, but they seemed very far away. I struggled to remember the short phrases I had to repeat, despite having written them myself. I was aware of a slight reaction from the guests. Afterwards my mother-in-law asked about these long pauses, which I assured her were not for dramatic effect.

Your wedding day should have immense gravity, but I was definitely still very shaken by what had happened two months earlier. While not wishing to talk shop, I mentioned the accident briefly in my wedding speech and the fact I felt very lucky to be there at all, and how the day meant even more than I had imagined. There is nothing like a near-death experience to make you appreciate what you have. If nothing else, this was a useful tactic to reduce one of my best men to tears, taking some of the wind out of his sails before he started telling tales on me.

The truth of the matter, though, was that while my personal life was on an absolute high, my career was in the doldrums. I faced a complete mental void in terms of what to do next with my professional life and felt lethargic, troubled. My Atlantic memories went round and round my mind, tormenting me and causing some odd emotional swings. I reached the stage where I spoke to a psychologist, needing reassurance that this was normal, and would soon pass.

There is always a big mental comedown after an expedition, a period of emptiness before it gets filled with plans for a new adventure. However, this time it was different; everything I had been working towards for six years was forgotten. The big goal had gone, and nothing filled its place. Only this void remained. Unlike before, I wasn't feeling particularly ambitious and I couldn't find the motivation to care about much.

During that spring of 2012 I hosted a dinner in Piccadilly for LDC, a private-equity firm that has supported my expeditions from the outset. Around the table sat twelve senior executives, all suited, relaxed but formal. As I started talking about the Atlantic capsize my throat clammed up, and tears came from nowhere. I fought to hold them back and ploughed on, hoping the images and my story, with a few well-needed pauses, would distract the audience. Rob, the marketing director and a good friend, afterwards teased me, saying he thought I was going to need a lie-down. So I guess I didn't get away with it. I was probably not the most convincing inspirational speaker this audience had heard, but I was certainly memorable.

The Atlantic accident was not the sole cause of this profound lack of direction. Over a week before the capsize I had emailed Nicci from the boat to say that I wouldn't be taking on any more oceans. I know this must have been an incredible relief to her, but to me it was a major turning point. I'd always thought that if I ever backed down from my dreams then I would live in regret. But making this decision, over a thousand miles offshore, was one of the eureka moments of my life. And having made it I kept rowing with renewed vigour, thinking only of this one journey, only of reaching dry land.

While still at Glasgow University I read *Pedalling to Hawaii* by Stevie Smith, the madcap adventure of a bored, happy-go-lucky twenty-five-year-old office worker who in 1998/99 joined his then best friend Jason Lewis to cycle, pedal-boat and inline-skate from England around the world. Stevie 'only' made it to Hawaii, and at a painstakingly slow pace, but for me it sowed the seed for unbroken man-powered journeys.

In 2007/08 I cycled 18,296 miles in 194 days and 17 hours. My journey was televised by the BBC as *The Man Who Cycled the World*. Fresh out of university, I had never raced before and was a complete amateur. But this effort took eighty-two days off the old world record, which had been broken only five times before and was barely known. Since then it has been amazing to watch the developing renown of the world cycle; there have been regular attempts and the record now stands at a slightly humiliating eighty-eight days faster. However, I am proud that my circumnavigation, subsequent documentary series and book seem to have been a catalyst for so many pedal-powered journeys.

I watched with interest as ultra-endurance racing quickly evolved from five-pannier touring on trekking bikes into frame-packing on carbon race bikes. Mike Hall, one of the riders who led this revolution, met me at a talk I gave in 2010 in Durham and told me of his plans. He went on to cycle the world in 107 days, completely unsupported. So if I in some small way inspired his amazing ride, his ultra-light set-up certainly inspired me.

However, even before this explosion of interest and before I lost my world record, it bothered me that I hadn't really completed a circumnavigation. The line of the equator is 24,901 miles long, yet land-based circumnavigations are only 18,000 miles. If you speak to primary-school children, which I often do, about cycling around the world, you can be assured that one of the first questions will be about crossing oceans. Most 'sensible' adults have lost that logical observation, accepting that you have to fly.

Except you don't have to. You can row. Sailing isn't man-powered and pedal-powered boats tend to be painfully slow. Ocean rowing is about as niche a sport as there is. By 2012, when

I was taking on the Atlantic, only 283 people had successfully rowed it, and only thirty-one had rowed the Pacific or Indian Oceans. Compared to the 3,142 people who had summited Everest or the 2,671 people who had swum the English Channel, this was a sport in its infancy, despite an explosion in ocean-rowing expeditions in the last decade.

The fastest man-powered circumnavigation. As simple and as big as dreams get. How fast can I get around the world from this point to an antipodal point and back? Any journey is going to end up at considerably further than those 24,901 miles, and because over 70 per cent of the world is water, it will involve a number of massive ocean crossings. But as ocean rowing is relatively slow compared to cycling, the best route would prioritize land over sea. The more you look at a globe, considering all the influencing factors, the more this 'best route' baffles you. And I spent years working on it.

Still, this dream became the motivation behind every expedition, each of which was a building block to make the circumnavigation happen. Cycling from Alaska to Argentina, climbing Denali and Aconcagua on the way, rowing 800 miles north of the Arctic Circle in the Nunavut Territory of Canada, and then the Atlantic, were all designed to build experience for what I was now calling the World. These were each stand-alone BBC documentaries and expeditions in the eyes of the public, but in my mind they were working towards one goal.

Rowing the Arctic in the summer of 2011 was a fascinating, beautiful and tough journey from Resolute Bay, an Inuit community and the second most northerly inhabited settlement in Canada, to the 1996 location of the North Magnetic Pole. I was the film-maker and presenter on a six-man team, trying to take a rowing boat further north than ever before. It was a bittersweet success, highlighting a moment in time when you could row to a place where before you could only ever walk or ski. The film was about capturing this historic change, and every day of this journey through an archipelago of islands and vast ice fields was different. Our companions were polar bears, beluga whales and Arctic birdlife.

Fifteen weeks after returning from the Arctic I set out from Tarfaya, in southern Morocco on the border with Western Sahara, destined for Port St Charles, Barbados. After a flying start through very rough conditions – most of the six-man team were seasick for a few days – we settled into the torturous routine of two hours on, two hours off, never sleeping more than ninety minutes.

Physically I was in great shape, giving it my all to smash another world record. But mentally I was feeling desperate. I have always relished the toughest times on expedition, enjoying being up against it. Yet here, living in the closest possible proximity with five other men, I felt desperately alone and bored, unable to focus on anything but getting through my next shift. This was not a reflection on my team-mates, who showed great camaraderie throughout.

Before the Atlantic in January 2012 I had always thought that what motivated me was simply pushing myself mentally and physically, trying to test my limits and comfort zone. I had completely underestimated the importance of the world around me, taken for granted that constantly changing tapestry of culture, people and places. On all my exploits I had always thrived off that excitement for tomorrow, the buzz of the unknown. That had always kept me from boredom, or loneliness, even when alone for weeks at a time.

The middle of the Atlantic is best described as big waves and little waves; almost nothing changes and your journey is entirely about you. Mariners and ocean rowers whom I know talk wistfully of the ocean's allure, but I found myself on an adventure without any of the reasons why I do adventures. And for that simple reason I gave up on the dream to cross the Pacific and the Indian Oceans. To quote Jim Rohn – and I have always tried to live by this – 'If you don't like how things are, change it. You are not a tree.'

But letting go of a dream that had become an obsession for over five years was an unsettling process. Making the decision and telling Nicci initially felt like a massive weight taken off my shoulders. Then, a week later, on the twenty-eighth day out from Morocco, we capsized. It was the nail in the coffin for my ocean-rowing days, metaphorically and so nearly literally.

Having hung up my oars, and bike, and crampons, but having loved making documentaries, I decided I would be a TV presenter. It seemed like a sensible and far safer career. My timing proved immaculate, as the same team at BBC Scotland whom I had worked with for the world, Americas and Arctic projects were looking for someone to lead the coverage of the build-up to the 2014 Commonwealth Games in Glasgow.

Eleven days of sport, seventy-one nations and territories, and all in the city of my alma mater. Glasgow was where I dreamt up the plan to cycle around the world, and it was wonderful that such a celebration of sport was coming to a city I loved and knew so well. However, life had now become a bit more complicated.

Six weeks before starting another journey of a lifetime, the story of the entire modern Commonwealth, I was dressed in surgery scrubs standing at Nicci's bedside in Ninewells Hospital, welcoming Harriet Beaumont to the world. Before then it had seemed like a tough but sensible decision. Of course I had to go; I justified it by reasoning that at least I'd be at home for the birth, and I would only be away for nine months. Nicci and I had been through nine-month projects before and we had our families nearby. This single man's thought process doesn't relate well to the emotions of parenthood which, as any young dad will bore you by telling you, are indescribable, unexpected and quite overwhelming. My responsibility was now at home. Yet I was leaving.

After departing from Buckingham Palace on 9 October 2013, the Queen's Baton Relay darted its way around the planet on an erratic flight plan of 118,000 miles over those nine months. We landed first in Delhi, where the Games were held in 2010, before taking in the rest of Asia, Australasia and the Pacific Islands, the eighteen Commonwealth countries in Africa, and then the Caribbean. The home leg was up to Canada, where the Games were first staged in 1930, and then the Mediterranean run of Cyprus, Malta and Gibraltar, before coming back to the British Isles in Jersey.

It was a whirlwind trip, arriving in a new country every three or four days, creating a weekly programme for the BBC, putting the spotlight on the thousands of athletes preparing to descend on Scotland. Well used to living out of bags, I wasn't so accustomed to life in hotels and airports. And while I kept running and swimming whenever possible, this frantic, non-athletic life meant that I was soon in the worst shape of my life. I started to really miss what had often previously felt like torture: training.

More significantly, I spent nine months meeting remarkable, driven young people on a daily basis, and this soon started to change the way I reflected on my values, and my ambitions.

Osika Finau, a twenty-two-year-old boxer from Tonga, had no gym and trained outdoors with a broken bag, a set of gloves and a skipping rope. 'I have two legs, two arms and one heart, just like them,' he told me defiantly. If things were going well he could afford a few meals a day. The Commonwealth Games would be his first time leaving Tonga. I could see the youngsters around him looking up at him, inspired by his belief . . . as well as by his tattoos and lightning speed.

Nijel Amos, a twenty-year-old 800-metres runner, drove me

to his Gaborone training track in the clapped-out BMW convertible he had recently bought. His showmanship and the welcome by everyone we met reminded me of Prince Ali in *Aladdin*. An odd comparison, but perhaps not so ridiculous. Until six months before London 2012, Nijel was training with his Geography teacher on the grass track at the back of his school in rural Botswana. In the Olympic final he collapsed over the line and had to be stretchered off. He took home silver, second to the great David Rudisha of Kenya. It was the first Olympic medal for Botswana in any sport. Awarded six head of cattle by his government – a very high accolade – he went on to fundamentally change sport in his country. At Glasgow he went one place better and beat his hero Rudisha. Young people now believe if he can, they can.

Kent Gabourel, known to all his friends as Bob, was the Belize national football captain. After retiring at the age of thirty, he decided to become the country's first international triathlete; however, there were a few challenges facing this likeable father of two. Bob lives on Ambergris Caye, an island ninety minutes by boat from the mainland, a strip of white sand with a mangrove swamp in the middle, no more than a mile wide. In order to train, Bob borrowed a road bike from a friend on the mainland, but the only stretch of tarred road was the airstrip, about 1,500 metres long, where he would do circuits in the early hours, before 6.30 a.m. when planes started to land. I asked Bob how he was training for the plunge into Strathclyde Park, which on a very good summer's day might scrape 14°C, half the temperature of those equatorial parts. He assured me that he had that covered, sometimes training offshore at 3 a.m. in the morning, when the Caribbean Sea was, he said, freezing. Bob definitely didn't understand the scale of his ambition. But he wasn't going to Glasgow to win gold. He called himself a sporting social worker, using his story to stop the kids on his island from falling into gangs and drugs. And this isn't a pipe dream: he spent his entire time training and inspiring young people.

For nine months I heard enough tales like these to make the laziest human alive want to dig out his trainers. Still finding my direction after seven years pushing myself as an athlete, I was given a toxic dose of jealousy and inspiration. I even started wondering if I could somehow make the grade and compete myself in Glasgow, in any sport. I hadn't been too bad at lawn bowls in Norfolk Island, had I? Niue didn't have a cycling team; maybe if I applied for New Zealand citizenship straight away, I could be eligible. It was a fleeting ambition, a clutching at straws that entirely disrespects and underestimates the time and dedication required to compete at this level.

When the Queen's Baton Relay reached Scotland near Coldstream, I was tasked with rowing a small fishing boat at dawn down the Tweed, the river border between Scotland and England, with a local ghillie holding the wooden handle and metal latticework aloft, and a drone camera buzzing overhead, sharing the homecoming with viewers on *BBC Breakfast*. After we'd landed on English soil, Daley Thompson ran through a procession of young people holding all seventy-one flags of the Commonwealth and met Eilidh Child, the Scottish 400-metres hurdler, on the brow of a small stone bridge.

'Hasn't Linford Christie changed?' a local elderly lady called to her friend just as I went live to the nation, standing right next to Thompson.

I was back in Scotland after nine months, which brought me incredible joy and an immense feeling of relief. It was good to be home.

The finale to this journey, forty days later, was being allowed to bring the Queen's Baton into Glasgow. Through some TV wizardry, they had me soaring in a seaplane over Loch Lomond, coming in to land on the River Clyde and then emerging on live television through a gauntlet of fireworks. Cut. I jumped rather unceremoniously into the front seat of a Ford Galaxy and drove across Glasgow. Re-emerging on live TV to 1.5 billion viewers around the world, I ran the final few metres into Celtic Park. Inside the stadium a few minutes later, Sir Chris Hoy placed the baton back in front of the Queen.

During the competition, as a Chieftain of the Athletes' Village, my role was to welcome to Glasgow many of the competitors I had met in their home countries. From Usain Bolt to my friend Bob from Belize, I shook hands with hundreds of hopefuls, all primed to perform, all of them in my favourite city to put their names in the annals of sporting history.

When the Games came to a close I resolved to get back to writing my own story rather than telling others', as wonderful a journey as it had been.

It is sometimes hard to place the origins of an idea. It is also tempting to claim that your ideas are original, very much your own and born of pure inspiration. But our lives are far too inter-connected for that to be true and we are too prone to being shaped by experiences and, most importantly, the people we meet. Still, vague ideas don't grow to be acted upon without being nurtured.

At 6,750 miles, Cairo to Cape Town is three times the distance of the Tour de France, twice the distance of the Race Across America and with exactly ten Everests of climbing. I wanted to do it solo and unsupported. After being home-schooled in rural Scotland on Wilbur Smith adventures and David Livingstone's explorations, I could claim it was only a matter of time before I turned my attention, and my bicycle, to Africa. I had certainly dreamt of the circumnavigation, the Pan Americas and the Cairo to Cape Town as the ultimate hat-trick of cycle journeys ever since pedalling around Europe during my university days.

Another personal motivation, one I have faced criticism for, is my desire to race against the clock. Surely the point of these massive cycles, people say, is to explore the world, be immersed in other cultures, discover and share experiences? I agree with that, and at the speed at which a bike goes you can remain connected and in tune with the world around you in a way that would be impossible by vehicle, or even with company. But the kid inside me still wants to go fast, to prove something to others and myself. And the hardest part to explain is the deep pleasure I derive from pushing my limits, being up against it; I feel utterly alive despite, or maybe because of, discomfort. I have the rest of my life to go slowly and explore better, with company.

In recent years there has been a lot of talk about the great Tommy Godwin record, set in 1939: he cycled 205 miles a day for a year – 75,065 miles in twelve months. This has to be one of the greatest feats of human endurance ever. Indeed it is difficult to fully comprehend. Speaking as an endurance cyclist who has a better understanding of the impact of daily distances like these, the fact that Tommy completed this feat during wartime, in Britain, on a steel bike with four gears, is truly staggering. Others are now attempting to go further and I doff my helmet to them, but this is not what motivates me to ride. There is a significant difference between cycling from your front door each day in order to accumulate huge miles and cycling huge miles across continents. That interaction with the world, with its unknowns and daily contrasts, is vitally important to me, as I discovered when rowing the Atlantic. So I could never be motivated by what drives Steven Abraham and other contenders to the Godwin throne. Equally, I am not as motivated by the idea of nomadic global pedalling as championed by the likes of Al Humphreys, Emily Chappell, Pete Gostelow and Rob Lilwall. But therein lies the joy of cycling: there is no right or wrong reason to ride.

There were instead some seemingly incidental events which

shaped my decision to cycle Africa solo. In the autumn of 2011 I was sitting next to Michael Kennedy at the annual Saltire Foundation black-tie dinner. It was my own internship with the Foundation in 2005 that had been a turning point for me – no longer plunging headlong into an accountancy career but confident enough to take that first step into turning my real ambitions into a career. Michael is not an adventurer by trade but retired young after a very successful business career and has since racked up an enviable list of endurance achievements. His first, which still hangs in pride of place in his Edinburgh home, was being part of the group that set the initial Cairo to Cape Town Guinness world record. Michael, David Genders, Chris Evans, Paul Reynaert, Jeremy Wex, Steve Topham, Scotty Robinson, Andrew Griffin and Sascha Hartl – an eclectic bunch of amateur racers ranging from cabinet-maker to lawyer, software architect to cook, minister to estate agent – pedalled the inaugural Tour d'Afrique in 119 days, 1 hour and 32 minutes between 18 January and 17 May 2003. Of the thirty-five starters, only these nine completed the entire route and at the time it was marketed as 'the biggest bike race ever'. Later I would reflect on how Michael's account of the ride was testament to how much had changed on the continent in just twelve years. On the night, as we shared adventure stories over dinner, the seed of an idea must have been planted.

Then in January 2014, when I landed in Nairobi with the Queen's Baton, I was met by Dr Christian Turner, the young and energetic British High Commissioner. The relay from his residence through the city's leafy suburbs was one of the best attended, and having visited Sierra Leone, Ghana, Cameroon, Nigeria and now Kenya I was building a great affinity with Africa which would grow as I passed through the rest of the eighteen Commonwealth countries on that great continent. So there was definitely an urge to return and explore from the grassroots level. I was under no illusion that jet-setting around was allowing me to see only what each country wanted me to experience.

Christian was keen to run the longest leg of the Queen's Baton Relay and was joined by hundreds of members of the public and athletes, including several from the Kenyan cycling team led by their captain David Kinjah. David is best known as the man who first coached Chris Froome, but he has also competed at the Olympics and Commonwealths and was the first black African to be signed by a European cycling team. Now a charity worker, he runs the Safari Simbaz cycling club out of his tiny house in the village of Mai-I-Hii, north of Nairobi. In 2013 he pooled his winnings from a year's mountain-bike races, the equivalent of £600, to buy a satellite dish, decoder and TV subscription to watch his boy winning the Tour, sharing the inspiration with the children in the club. But David's own athletic career was far from over. While researching this Nairobi relay, I came across news of his ambition, as part of a massive team time-trial, to smash the Cairo to Cape Town world record. My BBC interview on the roadside was entirely focused on the Kenyan team and the celebrations of the day, so in the mayhem of the relay and the TV cameras I didn't get a moment to properly introduce myself as a fellow cyclist, or to discuss his plans.

In September 2014 I sat down with Nicci and discussed, quite carefully, the idea of another big cycling trip. In terms of my career, it was a major U-turn to go back to being an athlete. Harriet, our daughter, had now visited thirteen countries in her first year on the planet, which I was proud of; however, this did not make up for my nine-month leave of absence, so there was a serious parenting debt to balance before I could even gain the credit to leave again. We also had the serious conversation about the business behind the adventures; I would be far more financially secure and at home more if I worked contentedly in broadcasting and the corporate world. Or I could change career entirely, move on. All these options were discussed, for the purpose of being thorough, but in truth I was interested in only one path: getting back on my bike.

There was no major moment of commitment, a firm decision by Nicci and me, but rather an agreement to explore further, do some planning so we could decide on things over the autumn. As is often the case, this theory exercise soon rolled into a practical one without having to have a major parley and show of hands.

My definition of what is important was markedly different at the age of thirty-two from what it was at the age of twenty-two when I first pitched the around-the-world idea to my family. The consequences of failing in Africa were a lot greater than bruised pride. If I had to admit my greatest fear, it was not finishing. How many sporting comebacks have ended in an apologetic performance and someone retiring for good, admitting they should have known when to stop? If I was coming back, I wanted to go beyond what I had achieved before, to set historic records that became significant milestones in the sport.

I am sure many people can relate to the internal dialogue between the security of playing it safe and the excitement of raw ambition. These voices tend to have different volumes at different stages of each day, let alone over the course of one's life. During the early stage of any big project, when I am trying to get family, the team, sponsors and media onboard, I often feel very alone. I face the greatest doubts early in the morning; it can be quite desperate. I wonder what the hell I am doing, risking things in such a big way when there are much simpler paths. Then out training, when the endorphins are flowing, I have often bellowed with triumph so enthused have I become, determination coursing through me.

There are three main areas to any expedition: training and logistics, sponsorship and team-building, then broadcast and media. Training and logistics is where people imagine I spend my time, but in fact fundraising, networking and broadcasting take the lion's share.

Setting my sights on Africa, I started with the fun stuff, strolling into Stanfords of Covent Garden and buying maps, then poring over them at home while stopping to tap place names into Google Earth for a closer look. I then contacted Guinness World Records to register my intentions and to gather the latest information. To my amazement, considering the fame of the route, the Cairo to Cape Town world record by bicycle had only been set twice, once by Michael and friends in 2003 with their time of 119 days, and then in 2011 by Robert Knol of Holland in a time of 70 days. That looked very beatable, even at my world cycling speed of 100 miles a day – but I was naive about cycling in Africa.

The first major factors to nail down were when, how much, and what media? Setting a start date would dictate the amount of focus needed, the *how much* might also influence how long the project took, and *what media* could have a major influence on *how much*, so the three factors were all very much related.

When is normally dictated by climate, and Africa was no different. There were lesser considerations like the rainy season in East Africa but the trump card was the heat of the Sahara. Leave too late in the spring or too early in the autumn and you get cooked in Sudan.

How much was, this time, not very much. It could cost a lot more to fly into Cairo and home from Cape Town than to feed and accommodate myself in between. It was looking as though it would be my cheapest expedition ever. However, that very much depended on media plans.

The *what media* part took six full months to crack properly in terms of set-up and ended up being one of the most interesting, stressful and important aspects of the journey. And when it was over I couldn't guarantee that the risks I was taking would pay off. The documentary hadn't yet been commissioned for net-work TV. Cairo to Cape Town was to be an out-and-out race, with no compromises for filming – no stopping to capture stor-ies or pedalling back down the same road to get the shot. And yet I was determined to film the story.

One month into my cycle around the world, the Foreign Office had advised against my travelling through Baluchistan in south-ern Pakistan; the BBC High Risk team agreed with this and made it clear that if I were to carry on then it was at my own risk. And so from the town of Bam in southern Iran I couriered back my cameras, and from the border carried on under armed police guard until I reached Lahore three weeks later, where the BBC gave me back my cameras. If you watch *The Man Who Cycled the World*, you will notice this entire stretch of the trip is covered using photography, with my dictaphone recordings played over the top. I was not paid by the BBC for this project, they only funded their filming, so the decision to carry on was mine.

When I cycled the Americas, on reaching Panama the BBC High Risk team once again advised against continuing my trav-els because of recent headlines coming out of Colombia. This time I had to comply as this was an in-house BBC project. I completely understand the difficult calls a corporation needs to make when their teams are on location around the world so I am not about to criticize the decision; however, I would have been very comfortable carrying on alone through Colombia. The sort of risks you face as a solo cyclist are very different to those of a journalist, although carrying decent cameras and BBC creden-tials can be as much of an issue as it can be a get-out-of-jail card.

The more I studied Africa and its perceived risks, the more I realized that I absolutely could not hand over control of this pro-ject to anyone. As I was going for the world record, I couldn't have a broadcasting executive prioritizing filming over racing. I met with the BBC a number of times during the autumn of 2014, but the crux of the decision wasn't this issue of control, but rather of legacy. Each of the previous documentaries have been shown on the BBC, but then have sat in the archive for ever more. After putting years into expeditions and filming them to be shared and to inspire, it was becoming disheartening that there were no DVDs available, and nothing downloadable. Members of the public have placed some of the documentaries on YouTube, which is not meant to happen, but at least it allows people still to enjoy these journeys. So the decision was made to film Africa independently.

To be doubly sure I was making the right decision, once sponsors started coming onboard I asked them if they would prefer one showing of a documentary on the BBC or for us to control and have access to that footage for ever. It was a unanimous vote to go it alone. I signed a co-development agreement with a production company to help with post-production and distribution while I got busy learning how to contract cameramen, finding fixers and vehicles, and bringing onboard some advisers for information on how best to film the journey. Used as I was to the organization of an in-house production team, this was a far more complicated project.

With this decision, the budget for the project grew exponentially and I worked hard well into the New Year to pull in the support needed. It had been nearly five years since I had gone cap in hand to sponsors, and that is a game of hard knocks. While I had a long track record of high-profile expeditions, confidence had been lessened by the aborted Atlantic crossing and a failed expedition to climb Cerro San Valentin, the highest mountain in the north Chilean ice cap. I needed to hark back a few years to find an expedition that had gone to plan.

The first backing came from LDC, with whom I have worked since the world cycle, then from Endura, Martin Currie and the Wood Foundation. Drum Property Group and the WEIR group then came onboard as charity sponsors for Orkidstudio and we were in good shape. In truth I was a good way short of my planned budget – enough to fund the entire documentary – but I had what I needed to go and that is what was important. Pulling logistics, sponsorship and training together in half a year was a mammoth task and I relied on a team of volunteers and freelancers to take charge of different parts.

Finally, Africa Solo was born – a name that explains the important distinction from team rides. I knew that David Kinjah was aiming to leave in the autumn of 2015 and that his team was led by an Englishman, Nicholas Bourne, a former Armani model who set the world record for running from Cape Town to Cairo (just 318 days) in 1998. Their aim in the six-man CaroCap supported team time-trial was to complete the route in less than forty days, so my only option was to try and get in ahead of them and set down a solo and unsupported world record. Even if Guinness World Records didn't make an official distinction, I was certain that the press and public would respect the difference. I wished Nicholas, David and the team my best, in fact I helped them with information, and they helped me, but I didn't see it as the same record at all.

The 2014/15 winter in Perthshire was a particularly icy one and training on the road proved nearly impossible for several months. But during the Commonwealth Games I had got to know the Scottish cycling team so I asked if it would be possible to come and train at the new Sir Chris Hoy Velodrome. I would soon learn that you are meant to get your accreditation first, then start working your way up the track leagues. Instead, I boldly turned up when invited to one of the Scottish development squad training sessions and took my place alongside the rising stars of the sport. I had never ridden track in my life and the coaches eagerly watched to see what I could do. Not very much, as it turned out, or at least to start with. On my first outing, holding on to the back of the line of cyclists, desperate not to be dropped, I momentarily forgot to keep pedalling and with an almighty clatter was ejected from the pedals and was left riding a tearaway bike for two laps as my feet flailed wildly.

A few weeks later a new bike arrived from KOGA. All the gear, very little idea. I now had one of the best bikes at the velodrome, whereas these phenomenal young talents, guys in their late teens and early twenties, many of them working menial jobs to pay for their dream to be professional cyclists, often rode second-hand frames, the best they could afford.

Halfway through the session we were practising Madison changes, where one rider gets slung by hand into the racing line of cyclists after riding around high and slow on the track. I was riding right up on the bank, keeping in mind that the corner is about 45°, when I tried to slow down into the corner and drop on to the back of the line. What a rookie's error; the only way to keep grip high on the bank is to keep pressure on the pedals. With a horrid thud the wheels slipped off the wood and I slid in a heap to the bottom. I lost a fair amount of skin down my hip and knee but was too embarrassed to say much. The coaches and riders had a good laugh at my attempts to trash a £5,000 bike on its first outing.

A few weeks later they had me doing my first flying kilo, where you circle the track a few times to build up speed and then do a flat-out four-lap sprint. I put my absolute all into it, feeling the lactic acid tying my legs in knots, my breathing dry and rasping even on the penultimate lap. When I had recovered, Mark McKay, Scottish Cycling's track endurance coach, told me the news – 1 minute 12 seconds.

'Great, that felt about as fast as I can go at this stage,' I gasped.

'No, you can go much faster than that, you just don't know what it feels like to push it that hard.'

He was right; after a short recovery I went faster. Nothing had

changed, except my acceptance of the pain, and my belief because
I had been told I could go faster.

I trained harder and smarter, really pushing the gym, interval
and high-intensity training to build all-round conditioning. I
probably went out on the road bike a few dozen times at most; the
rest of the riding was done on the Wattbike in my office and on the
velodrome, trying to keep up with guys ten years my junior.

In February 2015 I flew to Dubai for a family holiday, but also
to test the newly finished bike through the desert. It had taken
months of conversations and a trip to Holland to oversee and
film both the bike build and wheel build. KOGA built custom
bikes for the world and Americas cycles, along the lines of their
much-loved and -tested KOGA Signature; however, the Africa
build was a completely new direction. We took the KOGA
Solacio carbon frame, thanks to its disc compatibility and quite
comfortable geometry, then turned to Wheel-Tec to build bulletproof thirty-two-spoke wheels.

Final training and testing came during a week in Cyprus in
March up the awesome climbs and on the perfect cycling roads
of the Troodos Mountains. But even then my longest ride was
about seven hours. I was relying on being able to translate a winter of very high-intensity training into the ability to ride 150
miles a day for a month and a half down the length of Africa.

It was an untested theory and a very bold plan from the start.

Part Two

Salaam Alaikum, Africa!

Flying low over Cairo after dark is the perfect introduction to the largest metropolitan area in Africa, which over twenty-two million people call home. The only part not polluted by streetlights as far as the eye can see is the Nile, black in the night and dissecting the urban jungle. As we came in to land I spotted the latticework of lights on Cairo Tower, the official starting point for my race. Looking down on this labyrinth of roads, it looked like a tricky city to leave quickly. Only a few weeks earlier John Hamilton from the British Embassy in Cairo had advised moving the start from Thursday to Friday, reminding me that Friday/Saturday is the Muslim weekend, so as to avoid gridlock from the off.

After a long queue at immigration and customs, Tamer Alaa, a small-framed man around my own age, met us at arrivals. He was an excitable, seriously enthusiastic tour guide from Lady Egypt, the company I had been working with as fixers for the first, and administratively difficult, part of the journey down Africa. His company had been working hard to ensure my safe and speedy passage through Egypt. More time, correspondence and worry had been spent planning Egypt than the other seven countries put together.

It was nearly 10 p.m. when we crossed downtown on the immense 6th October Bridge, a 12-mile elevated highway with views across the city nightscape, then across the Nile to Gezira Island and the west bank suburbs to find our hotel.

Lady Egypt had been able to negotiate with the authorities to act as the go-between between the Tourism Police and myself. The police had initially wanted to escort me through the entire country; this had then been reduced to my carrying an Egyptian phone on which they could contact me at any time to check my whereabouts, as long as I told them ahead of time exactly where I would stay each night; finally, we settled on the police being updated by the Lady Egypt team, who would assume full responsibility for me. These are negotiations I certainly couldn't have done myself. The full name for the force is the Tourism and Antiquities Police – a fitting name for a country that in my opinion looks back a lot more than it looks forward.

Egypt has been paranoid about the safety of its tourists ever since Islamic fundamentalists killed some German tourists in 1997 so they tend to provide blanket security. But this level of control can be more deterrence than comfort. Tourism now accounts for less than 15 per cent of the GDP, a significant drop from a few decades ago, and the vast majority of visitors go straight from the airport to Red Sea resorts and then back home, without exploring anything else in the country. Recently, of course, more political instability and terrorist incidents have made the situation even more volatile, with Sharm el-Sheikh effectively closed for business and deaths too in Hurghada, which lay on my route south.

On our first day in Cairo, I built the bike in my hotel room in the morning and then spent the afternoon speaking to journalists back in the UK, including an interview at the BBC Arabic studios. Tamer dropped us outside a dilapidated-looking building with an entrance hall that seemed to be deserted. After calling to check I was in the right place, we took the tiny lift up, and emerged into modern offices. The BBC obviously wanted to keep a low profile and their headquarters in the UK designated the whole of Cairo a high-risk area in which to work. On 5 April, just two days before I flew out, another bomb blast, this time at a bridge in the Zamalek district of the city, claimed by the militant Islamic group Ajnad Misr, killed a policeman. I asked one of the BBC Arabic reporters about this and the current security situation for the public and for journalists. She acknowledged that on the day of the blast she had had to take a different route to work, but other than that seemed unworried. The perceived risks, even within the same organization, were very different depending on whether you lived with the situation or watched it from afar.

I had asked Jeremy Sutton-Hibbert to come with me to Cairo for a few days as the official photographer, but the unofficial part was that I wanted a friend there as well. It was valuable to have another set of eyes and ears to get to the start line without mishap. The Egyptian capital can in one sense seem controlled but at the same time utterly frenetic. And it wasn't just Egypt; my internal dialogue was oscillating from complete calm and focus to a bag of butterflies, intimidated as I was by the scale of the imminent challenge.

It became clear that Jeremy would need a temporary press card in order to take photographs in public places. A recently passed law criminalized taking pictures of the police, embassies, the military and military sites, with the definition of what constituted those sites remaining open for interpretation. On top of that, journalists had been harassed and even jailed for expressing their opinions. It was not a safe place for the media to operate.

Lady Egypt worked tirelessly to get this press pass sorted, but the level of lethargy and bureaucracy seemed irreversibly high. The support of the British Embassy was reassuring, but we were all struggling to get answers. The high-profile race start at Cairo Tower would be a positive news story for Egypt in the global press – nothing could be less threatening to national security or be less political – yet there was real concern over the rights of my friend to be there with his camera. Jeremy had been given only two of the three permissions he required to shoot on the streets we had requested, and had been told that the authorities couldn't help if he was detained or stopped. He was willing to take the risk.

On our second day in Cairo we also wanted to film some publicity shots at the pyramids with Robbie Wright, an English freelance cameraman. A local for over a decade, Robbie's laid-back approach to life didn't succeed in hiding his worries about the authorities. We drove out past Giza, miles of residential tower blocks, to the fenced park that is home to the Sphinx and the pyramids. What was once rolling dunes is now urban sprawl, like an oil slick threatening a beach. The juxtaposition of the ancient and the modern is jarring, especially the KFC opposite one of the main entrances.

We had to transfer big cases of cameras from our car into Robbie's, and before I realized what was happening we had stopped right in front of a military checkpoint to do this. Not clever. A soldier wandered over, but we moved quickly on.

I was looking for a location where we could film with the pyramids in the background. The police now took a much closer interest in our cameras and us, asking for permits and identification. Jeremy hung back and Robbie and I tried to negotiate, but it was clear from the first sentence that this was a negotiation for us to get away without issue, as opposed to getting into the site.

We retreated and regrouped at Robbie's house, a beautiful smallholding on the edge of the desert. It turned out to be a perfect outdoor location to film some of the pre-start interviews away from prying eyes and away from the bustle of the city. Piling back into his Jeep, we then found some side streets that led out on to rocky sand dunes, with a perfect view across to the great pyramids. There was a great big fence between us and security forces, and a clear view to the gatehouses, which we watched for any activity. We worked quickly, and no vehicles approached.

Like so many of the world's most famous wonders, the pyramids' gigantic reputation means you can't help but be slightly disappointed by their real-life size. They are awe-inspiring when you consider how they were made, but their modern surroundings neither give them the space they deserve nor do anything to help radiate their glory.

As first impressions go, I don't think Robbie was particularly impressed with my bike-riding skills either. His direction to me to 'just cycle along the ridgeline of that dune, looking forward' ended in multiple false starts and then spills. It is harder than it looks to cycle on soft sand and rocks. Spare a thought for those who first cycled Cairo to Cape Town in 2003 and who had this terrain for the entire Sahara, long before the Chinese came and built some of the best roads in Africa.

In the end we got all the shots we needed, and soon it was time to prepare for the start itself. From the moment we arrived in Cairo there had been a sense of exhilaration, compounded by the cacophony of horns and engines. I was immediately a million miles from home. On our first night, Jeremy and I were hungry and asked Tamer for a local recommendation before getting to the hotel. Eager to impress, he stopped at an open-fronted corner kebab shop packed with young people inside and stray cats outside.

'How many would you like?' he asked us.

Not quite knowing what we were ordering I said four, assuming they'd be fairly modest kebabs and we could manage two each. Tamer disappeared into the scrum and reappeared with a bulging carrier bag of food. We checked into our hotel and feasted in Jeremy's room on what turned out to be four large kebabs *each*. Tamer must still think us Scots eat the equivalent of four Egyptians – a legend which I hope is exaggerated with time and retelling!

An early bed would have been sensible before my *grand départ*, but inevitably I was far too preoccupied to switch off. A ceremonial repack for little gains and then simply lying there, eyes open, bike propped against the hotel-room wall, thinking of what lay ahead.

I hadn't trained for over a week and athletes will sympathize with that feeling. You're like a dog that desperately needs a good long walk; a coiled spring. You expect to feel utterly relaxed, but when you are used to full-time training you feel physically frustrated, longing for exercise. Still, there were nearly 7,000 miles against the clock of exercise ahead, and the pause for rest was nearly over.

I jumped up before the 5.30 alarm. Final preparations felt ceremonial. Getting ready for a ride is normally second nature, yet this morning I applied suncream with immense detail, took time over the chamois cream, polished my already clean sunglasses. It felt good to take time physically while my mind rushed around.

Jeremy was downstairs in the dimly lit and empty dining room. As I tucked into eggs, bread and cereal, he sent a picture back to my mum, Una, to assure her that he was taking good care of me. Ever since I was twelve and pedalled across Scotland, Mum has supported my expeditions, and since the world cycle we have pretty much worked full-time together. The projects have got much bigger and more expensive with many more base-camp team members, but Mum remains. When I was younger I was unsure how this working relationship looked, I was keen to look professional, but over the years I have realized it is a very special thing to be able to work closely with family. And as a professional relationship she does well to be Una and not Mum, most of the time.

When she does slip back into mother mode I am no longer embarrassed. She sent Jeremy a long email of information for our journey through Egypt, signed off as Una, and added a PS: can you please remind Mark to have a massage. She would have preferred Jeremy to tuck me in nice and early as well!

The hotel staff were very excited about my plans and had treated me as a celebrity from the moment I arrived. Tamer was waiting with the minivan but our departure was delayed as everyone bundled out on to the pavement for photos. The look of disdain on the face of Jeremy, a consummate professional and world-class photographer, as the receptionist wrestled with a selfie stick was worth the delay.

Months earlier I had reached out through social media to the two main cycling clubs in Cairo to help get me out of the city without delay, assuming one of them would help. Both GBI (Global Biking Initiative) Egypt and Train for Aim were keen to be there but it was immediately clear that they weren't completely happy to share the limelight. There was gentlemanly and well-disguised jostling for start line positions and media interviews as local news crews and Wael Hussein from the BBC soaked up the early-morning atmosphere. The guards on the entrance gate to Cairo Tower had been forewarned by the British Embassy of the event and so gave us the first smiles and welcomes by anyone in uniform that we had met. There must have been around forty cyclists milling around, from fairly serious to enthusiastic but very out-of-shape individuals, most noticeably an eccentric Brit on his Brompton folding bike. There were even a few saltire flags being waved among the crowd of ex-pats who had set their alarms early to be there. I was grateful for any kind of an event in a country where I knew nobody.

Stephen Hickey, the Deputy British Ambassador, was on hand to do the official witness duty, signing, time-and-dating, then rubber-stamping an official start letter. It was a shame not to be able to get anything more than snatched conversations with him and so many others who had made the effort to be there. These crowded moments at the start and end of major events are always confusing to be at the heart of. I am trying to make sure I have everything, that all media commitments have been completed and we stay on time, but inevitably everyone who has come wants to speak to me. I did my best to meet and greet, say thanks and leave a positive impression. The majority of people get it – they sense the pressure I am under – but invariably you meet excited people who wish to monopolize you, normally to tell you their life stories. This happens more with cyclists than bystanders and I politely smile as I am talked at, usually about why they love cycling and everything they have done in the saddle. In time-pressured moments at the centre of a well-wishing crowd I do struggle to engage properly.

Jeremy dashed about doing his professional duties, as well as shouting out the checklist. A good thing he did, as I had forgotten to turn on the GPS tracker. I changed into my cycling shoes and gave him my trainers to take away. Hardly the most thoughtful leaving gift.

As 7 a.m. neared I called everyone's attention and cued up Stephen to start the countdown. Everyone positioned their bikes closer together and got ready.

'Mark, turn around, we're going this way!' one of the cyclists said.

Any tension evaporated as we laughed and turned about-face.

Back in Glasgow while training in the velodrome I thought it would be amusing to get someone to hold the bike and do a track stand – clipped into the pedals, ready to make a racing start – so as to absolutely stomp the first 20 metres of an 11,000km race. I remembered at the last minute and looked around for a suitable 'coach'; but the media was poised, the spectators were cheering, the cyclists were crowded around and Stephen was looking keenly at his watch to get the countdown bang on seven o'clock. Ah well, it might have seemed odd anyway.

After the crowd had completed the 10, 9, 8, 7, 6, 5, 4, 3, 2, 1, I clipped in and pedalled off very slowly indeed, waving to everyone lining the roadside.

Day 1: Friday, 10 April 2015, Cairo to Zaafarana

I didn't have the slightest idea where I was going. I didn't even have a street map of Cairo. However, as planned, I had a peloton of locals protecting me from the traffic and showing me the way. We struck out at a competitive pace. After the first few turns I looked back and realized we had lost half of the riders already, which was a shame, but I hope they at least enjoyed the start. And it also took the media a while to catch us up as they were all on foot at the start and had to run for their vehicles. We rode the first ten minutes without cameras.

It felt unreal to be on my way. The clock was now ticking and wouldn't stop until I reached Mouille Point in Cape Town.

Once away from the buzz of the start, it felt like the beginning of a social ride, public events during which I chaperone and encourage a mixed group of amateur cyclists. Except those around me were now the chaperones and I was warming up to execute the plan of 150 miles a day for the next forty-five days or so. The streets were by far the quietest I had seen, it being early morning on a Muslim weekend, and we rode two or even three abreast, sharing stories. Everyone seemed to know lots about me and I spent the first few hours finding out about them and getting insider tips for the road ahead.

It turned out that the Ain El Sokhna Highway, the main connector from Cairo to the Red Sea south of Suez, had long been a favourite training road for cyclists from Cairo. But last year the authorities banned them, unless they got special permission and paid a weekly fee. It had taken us a few months of negotiations to get a final-week approval, but I was still nervous that the slip of paper I carried would indeed allow me quick and sure passage. I knew that Keegan Longueira had ridden the same road out of Cairo only to be stopped and turned around 40km later at the first checkpoint. This kind of delay was what we had spent a lot of time and some money trying to avoid.

Keegan was the new Cairo to Cape Town record-holder, having reached Cape Town in his native South Africa on 2 March, only just over a month before my departure, in a time of 59 days, 8 hours and 30 minutes.

My local peloton all used to train on this road and they raved about the best tarmac and the quietest stretch of highway near Cairo, which all sounded excellent, if I got on to it. As we left the suburbs behind, one of the young riders, Hatem Kotb, came alongside to tell me that the biggest climb in Cairo was coming up. I looked forward to a gentle spin uphill, climbing out of the city. Twenty minutes later my remaining team-mates, now only five strong, reported that we had made it. Cyclists can get terribly territorial about this subject – 'my hill is bigger than your hill' – but I can honestly report without any agenda that Cairo has no hills. There was a very gradual incline, the type where your speed drops by nothing at all but you can't just freewheel. But it was their big climb, and they were proud of it. And to be fair, we had dropped people by staying at the same speed. Maybe it was my nervous energy giving me strength. I told myself to go easy, to settle down.

Robbie leant right out the back of the Jeep using a camera stabilizer for smooth shots. But the roads were surprisingly good and the lack of traffic meant the press vehicles could stay close by. Jeremy worked away alongside him, until on the outskirts we passed a military zone and army barracks. We hid all the cameras and Jeremy lay back, looking like he wanted to disappear altogether.

We had slipped out of Cairo far quicker than anticipated. The biggest limiting factor on my ride south was daylight. On the equator you have twelve hours of daylight, in the north and south a little more or less, depending on the season, but none of the extremely long days or nights I am used to in Scotland. So my mission was to be riding at first light, knowing it would not be safe to night-ride for most of the journey. I would have left Cairo before 6 a.m. if it hadn't been for my wish to have the good folk from the Embassy and my chaperones there. An anonymous departure would have been harder to convince Guinness World Records about – witnesses are important, even in this age of GPS tracking. Plus it felt right to create something of an event around my departure on what I hoped would be a historic ride.

We were now moving at solid training-ride pace, holding around 35km/h on each other's wheels, and the conversation had dropped off. We also had a gentle tailwind. There were a few comments about this, requests to drop the pace, as when my companions turned they would have a tough ride back into the city. '*Really?*' I bit my tongue, tempting as it was to put these concerns into perspective. Five of us were left now after gently ramping up the speed over the first 40km and taking on Cairo's *epic* climb.

My chaperones were all psyched to carry on, and I was enjoying their company, but I tried to encourage them not to: I know from years of experience on checkpoints and borders that low-key is the way to go. I tried to find a polite way to tell these locals that they should turn round, that I didn't want them to risk us all being turned back, but they took this concern as further encouragement that they were in fact needed to ensure my safe passage. They felt it was their responsibility. Resigned to this, I at least managed to flag down the filming car and tell them to go ahead, to disassociate themselves from us.

Ahead the lanes multiplied, and the Ain Sokhna toll gate came into view. It was only 8.40 a.m. – a stomping start. But the next few minutes were what my team had spent a long time working on and worrying about. Being turned back here would be a devastating blow on day one. The next best alternative route would take me on the Suez road, involving a detour to the north and then east, instead of directly south-east, and adding more than a hundred miles.

I aimed for the right-hand tollbooth, but a soldier saw me coming and signalled us all over to the kerb in the parking area at the roadside. His body language was wholly negative – cyclists aren't allowed on this road. Before anyone could start a debate I held my papers out, and he walked off with them a short distance towards an office block. After bringing an older and I assume more senior soldier over, they scanned my permissions.

At this point my chaperones started chipping in with their thoughts on the matter. I have no idea what was said, but I was left on the outside for about five very tense minutes as a heated exchange ensued. Some of the other cyclists who had been left behind now arrived, and joined in enthusiastically. Tamer then ran back through the toll and tried to take charge, adding to the already heated debate. I really hoped he wasn't telling them how important all this was: bigging me up was a sure way to be detained or turned back. What was happening was exactly what I had wanted to avoid.

The senior soldier barked a final retort and the cyclists backed down. The first soldier shoved the papers back in my direction and signalled to me. I wasn't sure what I was being told, but Hatem reassured me: 'You can go, we have to turn back.'

It wasn't a place to stop, take photos and complete pleasantries, so shouting my thanks and goodbyes, I speedily shoved my papers under the lycra of my shorts and cleared the toll without a backwards glance.

Tamer caught up at a run as I reached the car. Jeremy and Robbie were relieved to see us. We had passed the first major hurdle, and nothing now lay between us and the Red Sea.

Literally nothing. Just an industrial-looking rocky desert, too close to the city to be left untouched, scored with tracks and sparsely littered with scrap.

Soon after the toll I stopped at a roadside restaurant. It was a welcome coffee stop and my first taste of packaged chocolate croissants, which reminded me of France, and would become a staple fuel in Egypt. It was the sort of synthetic pastry that could last for years.

There weren't many people there. I was sitting under the wicker canopy, appreciating the shade, when a girl of around fourteen came over from her family car. 'Can I have a selfie, please?' Although unaccustomed to teenage fans I complied, asking who she thought I was. 'I heard about you on Twitter and we are all following.' I wasn't sure if she was referring to her family or a far greater *all*, but was surprised and flattered all the same.

The tailwind made for euphoric pedalling – you couldn't imagine a better start for the soul. All concerns were put to rest as I was so wrapped in the moment, stretched out on the tri-bars, spinning my legs effortlessly. I knew I wasn't yet conditioned to very long hours in that position, low on the bike, neck craned forward. But it was fast and the cameras were rolling so I lived in the moment, unworried about consequences – not the best mindset for day one of an expedition, and one you pay for later.

The dual carriageway was fairly empty and fast, so I kept inside the hard shoulder, except for when I encountered broken glass, which could only be from bottles thrown from windows, at which points I kept to the inside of the white line. With these huge horizons I wasn't too worried about not being seen.

A motorbike screamed past me, its rider low on the bars, tucked in for straight-line speed. He was going at least four times my speed, and I was flying, so I could see one argument for keeping cyclists off this road. Still, with a wide hard shoulder, there was plenty of room for everyone. If they kept it clear of glass.

A few minutes later I was approaching a flyover when I saw a car in the middle of the road. As I drew closer and sat up on my bars, the scene unfolded. The motorbike was on its side near the central reservation, the rider still lying on the tarmac and the back of the car indented where the two had impacted. Others were already on the scene so I pedalled on slowly.

It was a while before I caught up with the camera car. I wasn't sure if they had witnessed the crash. It had certainly sobered me – a horrid reminder of my biggest fear. You talk about cycling Africa to friends and journalists alike and they ask about terrorism, Ebola and being eaten by lions. But I knew the greatest risks were more mundane: road-traffic accidents and malaria.

The dual carriageway petered out as the Red Sea came into view and I turned right, before reaching the town of Ain Sokhna itself, heading due south for the first time. I had been advised by everyone I'd asked that this coastal route would be faster. On a map it looked slightly silly to go three sides of a rectangle in my first three days on the road rather than follow the Nile straight south from Cairo to Luxor. Close to 100 per cent of Egyptians, over 88 million people, live in Cairo, Alexandria or somewhere along the Nile river and Suez canal. When you consider the country's area is a million square kilometres, that is serious population clustering. I had been warned that the roads along the Nile were of poor quality, seriously busy and with constant speed bumps. Speed bumps didn't sound that menacing, but then I hadn't yet met the Egyptian speed bump. The deciding factor was the promise of a northerly wind nine days out of ten along the coast – a cyclist's best friend.

For the next day and a bit I would have the Red Sea to my left, that infamous stretch of water that links Europe to the Middle East and Asia. Across the Gulf of Suez was the Sinai Peninsula whose southern point is the tourist hotspot of Sharm el-Sheikh. Over that horizon, less than 200 miles away, was the Israeli border.

The road deteriorated badly – not for long, but long enough for me to start worrying. It was much more narrow, rough, and at points rutted along the side, so I slowed and encouraged the crew to look for a place to stop for food. I had blasted the first 160km almost without stopping and it was now early afternoon, and I needed fuel. Our plan was for some photos and filming along the Red Sea and then I would be left alone as they turned back to Cairo.

A loud hiss erupted from my front tyre as I pulled off the road and into a dirt car park. A puncture would have been annoying but easily fixed; a ripped sidewall was devastating. After 100 miles I replaced my front tyre with the only spare I carried. The only spare that was meant to last until Kenya, 3,000 miles down the road.

The rip was small, but enough for an inner tube to bulge through and puncture again without something to reinforce the sidewall. You can use any bit of plastic for this, even a folded-over crisp packet, but such bodge jobs weren't the plan for this custom-racing machine, and certainly not straight out of the starting blocks with the Sahara and the Ethiopian mountains ahead.

Jeremy and Robbie sensed a story and stuck cameras in my face, but I wasn't up for entertaining TV jeopardy right then and gave fairly monosyllabic explanations. I was seriously worried.

I don't want to get you bogged down in bicycle geekery, but it is worth appreciating the magnitude of this sort of issue. KOGA had wanted me to ride tubular tyres, a completely enclosed tyre cemented on to the wheel rim, which are less likely to pinch-puncture on the rims but are messy to fix if they do. Clinchers, normal tyres, are so called because they clinch the rim of the wheel, and are easy to fix. I hadn't followed KOGA's advice and instead chosen the Schwalbe Marathon Supreme – only 310g compared to the 750g bulletproof Marathon Plus that I used on my world and Americas cycles. Saving nearly one kilogram across both tyres, they are built to be a durable commuting tyre with a toughened lining on the rolling surface. But the sidewalls are thinner, saving weight, and this is what had ripped.

Had I made the right choice? I was wallowing in self-doubt. The conditions had been perfect so far, apart from these slightly rougher final miles, but absolutely nothing compared to the dirt roads and mountains that lay ahead. Months had gone into building this bike, with every detail being agonized over. The cost and pressure of sponsors and media sat very heavily on my mind as I worked cross-legged in the dirt. There was nowhere on my route south where I could find suitable spares for this dream machine. And I was unsupported.

By the time I'd finished repairs and caught up with Jeremy and Robbie they were already halfway through lunch. I wasn't great company, and stayed fairly quiet – a heavy fall from the emotional high of that morning. I felt irritated by how relaxed and chatty they both were, which was a negative reflection on me, not them – their job was pretty much done.

It was a touristy spot on a stone-decked terrace, overlooking the sea. Other Europeans, as well as locals, sat nearby as we tucked into chicken and chips. We could have been anywhere on the Mediterranean; it certainly didn't feel like Africa. Idyllic, beautiful. I should have been soaking up these final moments of company: it might be over 10,000km before I saw a familiar face again.

Afterwards, on the roadside, Robbie and I brainstormed what I should say on camera to accompany them turning back. 'Let me just try something and see how it sounds,' I suggested, swinging my leg over the bike.

Shaking hands with Jeremy and Robbie on camera as my TV goodbye, I turned and pedalled off, for show.

I should have turned back and said proper goodbyes. They had supported me brilliantly and I owed them a great deal of thanks, especially Jeremy. But by the time I had cycled 50 metres I didn't want to stop. I barely wanted to glance back and wave. I just kept on pedalling. I don't know how odd they found this farewell, but later I felt sorry about it.

The road hugged the coast, with crash barriers on the left and steep sandy hills on my right. A few gentle turns took me well out of sight of the car and I settled into a rhythm, feeling rude, but beyond the point of return.

My sunglasses were sat on my helmet, their arms poked through the airgaps. I quickly lifted them out and drove an arm straight into my eye. It was a ridiculous accident, and it sounds pathetic, but I was blinded and struggled to bring the bike to a quick stop. The pain was searing, and for the next three days I had blurred vision in my right eye and a very angry-looking eyeball.

At the start of the year I had taken the decision to have laser eye surgery. I went from a minus 6 prescription to perfect vision within seconds – a remarkable operation. However, I had not made a big point of telling the surgeon that I was soon off to cycle the length of Africa. Getting a serious eye infection or trauma was definitely best avoided. The evening of the operation I was told my eyes could be quite sore and to take painkillers accordingly. Nicci and I and some close friends went out for a meal, to an Edinburgh restaurant that happened to have hundreds of candles burning. It proved to be one of the most painful nights of my life.

On the roadside in Egypt, it was a full fifteen minutes before I could pedal on, slowly, with one eye streaming tears. It was immediate karma for pedalling off.

Day 1 was scheduled to be 'only 220km', a concession to the fact

I had no idea how long it would take to get out of Cairo, so I headed for Hotel La Sirena, which is where I had told the police I would stay. My paperwork in Arabic and English explained this schedule, so I couldn't have gone further even if I'd wished to. It wasn't worth the risk of losing the hands-off support of the police. I passed strings of gated resorts, huge hotel complexes and beachside condo blocks. Many of them were partially constructed – grand plans without any demand to be completed.

The second line of La Sirena's address was the town of Zaafarana. It was a sparse place, not touristy at all, with a few travellers' hotels and my first military checkpoint. The soldiers showed a lot of interest in the bike and crowded around, one resting the muzzle of his rifle on the toe of his khaki boot in that nonchalant way they have.

They seemed unsure about the whereabouts of La Sirena, until one remembered and pointed back. After discussion they agreed it was about 10km back. What a blow. I called Tamer to check as it was his company that had arranged my schedule through Egypt. But I kicked myself for assuming the address meant the hotel was actually in the town. Tamer and the guys were already nearly back in Cairo and he apologized; yes, the hotel was further back, but only 5km. That wasn't so bad.

Nineteen kilometres and ninety minutes later, this time into the wind, I reached La Sirena, a well-signposted hotel that I had flown past, like many others. It was a ridiculous start to a world record attempt, and I promised myself it was the only time I would go back in Africa.

The tyre, my eye and these lost miles; I hoped that hat-trick of bad luck on day 1 was not a sign of what was to come.

La Sirena turned out to be a decent but not fancy holiday resort for Egyptian tourists. They definitely weren't expecting a Scottish cyclist. Or at least the security guard wasn't. He ran out from his gatehouse and told me to take my bike to the car park. Declining with a smile, I repeated the word 'reception' and walked around him, along a path, up some steps and over a small footbridge. He took a shortcut and met me right at the reception doors, taking hold of my handlebars to stop me. I gave him what he wanted, and let go of my bike, pushing open the door. He didn't look very happy but we didn't have a common language to communicate in and he wasn't about to do anything silly in front of his bosses. The receptionists were more welcoming, although clearly used to weekly family packages as opposed to lycra-clad travellers. Back in possession of my bike, I was shown to my spacious room and wheeled it inside, which clearly irked the security guard deeply.

I didn't like these wasted hours of daylight – even after a shower and sorting kit I walked back outside and the sun was well above the horizon. If only I had known how fast this initial route was or not had the police restrictions I could easily have pushed on another 50km. But I was here now and I had to bury any regrets, get back in that mindset of only focusing on what I could affect. I reminded myself that this controlled start was probably a good thing: build up, don't overstretch.

Dinner wasn't served until 8 p.m., and it was only five, but there was a pizza booth alongside the hotel and I ordered whatever chef suggested. He seemed to appreciate being given free rein and threw an imaginative pile of meat and veg on a gigantic base. Later I queued up alongside all the Egyptian families for their buffet dinner and enjoyed a huge portion of couscous and then jelly.

I was back on the road, and needed a serious amount of fuel.

Day 2: Zaafarana to Hurghada

I was up and out long before breakfast was served. The only person I saw at 5.40 a.m. was the same security guard in his box, poor chap, looking confused. Or was it he who was looking sorry for me?

There was no need: I felt great, having slept well, and first light is always the most magical time to ride. The demoralizing part was having to cycle this now familiar road for the third time. The wind had come around in the night and was no help at all, but I made it back to Zaafarana itself by seven, in time for a cheese roll and Red Bull breakfast. Not perfect sports nutrition after the Snickers bar and two packaged chocolate croissants that had been my first breakfast.

My mind danced between the excitement of the open road and the sheer intimidation of over 6,500 miles against the clock. I am well used to this odd transition in mindset that happens in the first days of any expedition as you adapt from the planning phase to the doing, when you go from talking about and selling a massive journey, seeing the macro scale, to living it, only focused on the micro details.

Each day on the road feels so full, so thinking a week or a month ahead, hoping you will still be in this zone, still urgent, still racing, can be quite overwhelming. People tend to want to endure hardship only when they can count down to a time when it will be over. These periods of physical and mental commitment become our career- and life-defining moments. But to take that commitment from the scale of running a marathon or something that lasts for hours to journeys that take weeks and months is purely about that ability to stay motivated when you can't count down, because the finish is just too far away. You have to understand the big picture and your ultimate output, but only be motivated by your immediate inputs.

When cycling, those inputs are beautifully simple: what you need to eat, what you need to drink, how much you need to recover and how long to spend on the bike. For the same amount of effort – the sum of these four inputs – you can go 200 miles one day and the next struggle to 100 miles, because of external factors you can't control – border crossings, road conditions, wind direction, etc. So if you base your mindset and contentment on your 'success' each day, you will feel depressed when you under-achieve, and lose motivation when you smash your target as you have put miles in the bank. But if you realize that over weeks and months these daily mileages will average themselves out as long as you put in the same effort each day, you stop worrying about how far you go and become obsessed about getting enough food, hydration, rest and riding time. Nothing else matters. Life on the road can be tough, but it is wonderfully simple.

After 9 a.m. the wind picked up, swinging around to the north, and my speed picked up accordingly. Free miles, that's the joy of a tailwind – pedalling on the flat and barely slowing at all. The road remained fairly straight, hugging the coast, and as the early-morning haze cleared, the Sinai Peninsula came into focus.

Whenever there was a slight change in road direction, not even a proper bend, lines appeared on the road, five of them, repeated three times over a few hundred metres. They had the visual effect of speed strips, getting closer as you crossed them, but the impact of speed bumps – thick lumps of yellow paint. In a car at speed they would have been jarring; on a bicycle they were worryingly harsh. It meant that every time the road took a turn I had to pull on the brakes and gingerly crawl over these sections before building back up to cruising speed. Before long I would learn that speed bumps of every imaginable design are a speciality of Egypt. The first casualty of this jarring was one of my flip-flops. I thought they were strapped pretty tightly on to the top of the bag behind my saddle, but one had disappeared by the time I stopped late that morning.

Checkpoints also became more regular as the road left the tourist strip behind. The first few were negotiated with a cheery wave and without stopping, but in mid-afternoon my luck ran out. As they rushed out, I realized the police had been expecting me. I was waved to a stop, my papers were checked, and despite every conversation about being left to my own devices, I was told to wait while they got some officers ready to drive with me. I protested politely, pointing out this wasn't necessary and that I was in touch with their colleagues about my whereabouts and plans. But this fell on deaf ears and I waited a further fifteen minutes on the roadside as they finished their conversations. There was no urgency to get going so I saddled up and went to cycle off. This got their attention and they told me firmly to wait, but at least it made them get behind the wheel. Shortly afterwards we rolled away. They sat on my tail for the rest of the day.

Having had police escorts before, I have found that it isn't just the language barrier that prevents an appreciation of my need for speed. There is an unavoidable power dynamic when someone is being escorted. It is very difficult, on a bicycle, as a foreign 'tourist', to remain in control of the situation. The control, and therefore the time schedule, tends to be assumed by the local force. There are certainly moments when escorts are necessary and welcome, but in general they are more of a hindrance than a help to fast miles.

It was a 270km day, set by having told the police I would reach the town of Hurghada. I was sitting northwards of 30km/h, so comfortably on target. The Honorary Consul to the British Embassy in Hurghada, a chap called John, was a keen cyclist and had offered to ride with me, which I was looking forward to. Unfortunately I completely missed him at a checkpoint 30km from the town, assuming our rendezvous was closer. It was a shame: some company would have been welcome and I needed some help finding my way into Hurghada as well as trying to find a temporary solution to my broken tyre. I spoke to John briefly after realizing my mistake, and we made plans for him to ride out with me in the morning instead. (Either the 5.30 a.m.

start proved slightly too keen, or I once again missed the rendez-vous, but we never met.)

But I did have the police with me all the way into Hurghada. I assumed they would know their way, but we ended up taking an imaginative route with a few about-turns and some pavement-hopping on my part before eventually finding my hotel. It is always simpler just to ride into town and book somewhere at random rather than try to find a specific place. Once again, Lady Egypt had made these plans and done well to find a cheap but functional hotel on the southern reaches of the town, so I could get quickly back on track in the morning. They also had a local rep, Mohammed, who had been asked to meet me, head into town and find a replacement tyre. I was nervous about heading into the great expanse of the Sahara with a spare that was ripped.

The manager of the Hotel Santa Maria was standing outside expecting me when I arrived, with a big smile and a warm hand-shake; I wondered what they had been told for me to deserve this VIP reception. The police were also in high spirits and I shook their hands, too, and waved them goodbye. They had been impressed with my speed and mileage – obviously not their normal tourist shift – and after the faltering start had not delayed progress. Still, I hoped they would be the last I saw in Egypt.

Mohammed had called the bike shop to check they had what I needed. Every bit of research I had done and everyone I had spoken to had assured me that nowhere between Cairo and Nairobi would stock top-end bike parts, and even in these capital cities the right parts often had to be ordered in. But I had to hope for the best and go on their word. Leaving the bike and kit locked in the room, we drove into town.

After the relative quiet of the coastal road, downtown Hurghada at night was a surprise. There were hoards of kamikaze drivers who viewed street lines and signs as mere suggestions and their car horns as indicators. It took half an hour to go the short distance back into town and I was pleased not to be cycling it. From my first glance of the bike shop I knew ours was a futile search, but so as not to embarrass the enthusiastic rep I went inside and made enquiries. All the tyres hanging from the ceiling were cheap Chinese imports; nothing of the right size and certainly not foldable. I reported the situation back at the car but Mohammed was adamant, repeating that he had spoken to the shop owner and been promised what we needed. He stormed in, asked the same questions and returned, assuring me there were four more shops and one of them had to help.

So we spent the next hour and a half driving around in traffic, repeating this rigmarole of questions and indignation. Meanwhile I was getting very hungry; 170 miles was by far the furthest I had cycled in a single day for a long time. I was fit enough but not yet conditioned to these long hours of endurance. So my hanger – anger caused by hunger – meant my patience and politeness were seriously tested as we immersed ourselves in the traffic for the sixth time and headed back, empty-handed.

It turned out to be a two-hour trip to the cash machine, which mainly served to pay Mohammed for the wasted journey. It also bought a dinner of two burgers, chips and four small chocolate milks. The day's nutrition seemed more of a recipe for cardiac arrest than fuel for an endurance cyclist, but that's the way of unsupported expeditions. Calories must be consumed in whatever shape they come and whenever they present themselves.

For $20, the Hotel Santa Maria had a lobby full of mosquitoes but also good wifi for the first time since Cairo, so I was able to update social media on my progress. The first few days had gone to plan, if you didn't look too closely at the details. I was where I said I would be and bike and body were in working condition – ignoring the bloodshot eye and ripped tyre.

Day 3: Hurghada to Luxor

It had been surprisingly cool so far, no more than 20°C, considering the Red Sea coast can reach 50°C in midsummer. At 5.30 a.m. it was certainly fresh. A well-caffeinated receptionist insisted on posing for photos before I left. The cleaner was dragged over to do the honours but hadn't used a touchscreen camera before, so stabbed at the screen as if it were a button, meaning each photo was blurry. The dingy light didn't help. The receptionist turned out to be a bit of a perfectionist and six or seven attempts were made, accompanied by some fairly curt-sounding Arabic words, especially considering the early hour and the poor chap's untrained promotion from brush to smartphone.

The first 40km continued to hug the coast to Safaga, where I turned inland, and left the flatlands. Apart from looking out for John I was ecstatic to be alone on the open road after eight months' training and planning. But this didn't last long: the police were waiting for me at the first checkpoint after 6km. Apart from that the wind was behind me and the sun climbed quickly. It was perfect. The road would climb spectacularly through arid hills and then descend through the afternoon to meet the Nile. I would soon learn that this tourist route wasn't really Africa.

Another checkpoint, and once again I was stopped. Until around 2009 most foreign vehicles on this 100-mile linking road from the Red Sea coast to the Nile, from Safaga to Qena, had to travel in convoy with armed police. The map suggested little along the way apart from some desert cafés and small villages. My relationship with the Egyptian police was a fairly unhappy one from the start. They didn't want to be with me, just as I didn't appreciate their company. A hundred metres after the checkpoint I pulled over to a restaurant on the far side of the road, lifting my bike across a high central reservation; I had no idea where the next food would be so I had to eat. As I tucked into omelette, bread and tea, the police sat in their car watching and waiting. It clearly wasn't the best use of their time.

A young policeman then came over to take my bike, which I refused to hand over, saying in broken English, 'Road, mountain, go up.' He gestured to the back of the pick-up. I smiled to be friendly, but shook my head clearly in case he didn't understand. 'No, I have to cycle, thank you.' At least the words 'Yes' and 'No' are universally understood.

As the day went on and I kept changing guards, there were a few exceptions, with some friendly policemen – normally those who spoke a bit more English. Late in the day with the wind once again at my back and flying along, the now familiar Toyota pick-up pulled alongside me and a policeman leant out waving a packet of cigarettes at me. I declined with a smile, then quickly looked back at the road. It was meant as a kind gesture, but lighting up at 40km/h on a bicycle would be a feat worthy of another record. I felt this was more a hand of friendship than a genuine offer.

The temperature soared as I cut inland but the road was wide and perfect, and it climbed gradually for many miles into the first foothills. From there I was surrounded by rocky terrain, miniature mountains of the desert ranging from deep ochre to shades of tawny and fawn. A wide hard shoulder and little traffic made for perfect pedalling and I soon settled into the steady rhythm of a long climb, covered in sweat but with steady breathing and heart rate. It was a pleasurable slog.

A few basic ramshackle huts, nomadic-looking shelters and the odd goat herder and some animals were the only roadside presences for a few hours. As the road flattened out – I assumed because I was nearing the summit – I spotted a small open-fronted restaurant set back from the road. The contrast with the morning was incredible: this was a traditional travellers' rest, the first I had seen, and very unlike the establishments on the Red Sea coast which aspired to European norms. The police obviously felt at home there and joined me at a table as I tucked into more omelette and bread, this time with beans.

A loaded assault rifle was placed on the table right next to my plate. I felt this was rude, dirty and unnecessary, like putting your shoes on the table. Was this a power play? It certainly felt deliberate enough, perhaps in order to provoke a reaction from me. I didn't react. The thought flitted through my mind to put it on the ground but I calculated that touching a policeman's rifle wasn't going to keep the peace.

Inevitably this wasn't the summit and the road continued to weave a path of least resistance through the Red Sea Mountains. It was stunning. I have always been drawn to deserts and mountains, so finding both together was perfect. The terrain reminded me of the eastern United Arab Emirates and Oman.

On the Nile side of the divide lay the Maaza Plateau, a vast limestone area bordered by huge scarps and dissected by wadis draining westward to the Nile. The word 'wadi' was one I had come across in the Gulf, a valley or steep-sided gully which becomes a watercourse only in the rainy season. But there are no predictable rains in this part of Egypt. What rain does fall is not annual but happens during violent cloudbursts. Dewfall is a more reliable supply for plants, and along the roadside scraggy low bushes and grasses clung on for life, fighting to produce chlorophyll in their sun-baked leaves.

At the true summit I reached a small village of shops and a mosque, a surprising tourist trap selling pottery and trinkets in the middle of nowhere. It was the only place most travellers would stop, but I didn't need much, so ran in for water and carried on. The climb was never steep and wouldn't have been an issue, but the wind was now against me and it was slow progress. I was relying on being able to reach the Nile, turning left and flying the final 100km in order to reach Luxor by dark. If I didn't speed up then I would be riding well into the night.

A railway line appeared out of the desert from the left, crossed over the road and followed it for a few hours. Despite the gradual descent it remained slow going, riding hard into a hairdryer of a wind.

Ahead was the Nile. It flows like a 4,000-mile oasis right down Egypt, which is otherwise an interminably bleak desert. There is a riot of activity a stone's throw on each side of the river, at most a strip of a few miles, where irrigation allows cultivation of plants and trees. But where the water stops, the transition is immediate. Sand. Egypt has many planned irrigation projects which may spread habitation further inland, but for the most part life in that country is represented by that thin green line. With the river comes life: people, animals, and traffic.

Sweeping into the outskirts of Qena, I turned left and stayed on the east bank of the Nile. If I had seen an option to stop I probably would have, and then called Lady Egypt to explain. But there were no options. It did seem slightly daft that I was still updating the police centrally through Lady Egypt while also having a permanent escort.

I had a few hours until dark and pushed on, slowed by regular speed bumps denoted by signs with big Xs, and occasional traffic jams. We passed a few checkpoints and each of them also obliged me to stop while my policemen chatted among themselves or had a change of guard; they did not share my urgency or worry about the limited remaining daylight. Most of the road was a boulevard of mature trees with a canopy of branches, giving structure and shade to an utterly frenetic roadside life.

The turn-off to Luxor came just after another police checkpoint. Another Lady Egypt rep, Aymed, was meant to meet me there and show me into town. Light was fading fast when I stopped and called him. Aymed was nearby but didn't want to come to the checkpoint, instead suggesting that I meet him around the corner. I don't know why, but he wanted to lose the police. I explained to them that my hotel was nearby and thanked them for their help, but was told that I couldn't leave. So I called Aymed back and convinced him to appear. After a brief conversation I was told to follow him, at which point I had Aymed's car in front of me and a police truck behind, all the way into Luxor. I couldn't understand why the police would go to such lengths; surely an official tour guide was enough. As I cycled in this convoy I also had Tamer calling me to check I had met his contact and to report back to the police . . . who were also with me.

Luxor was a place I would have loved to stop and explore – it is in essence a vast open-air museum. There was an embarrassment of riches, starting with the hieroglyph-lined Karnak Temple (which I pedalled past, less than 50 metres away, yet couldn't even grab a photo or moment to appreciate it) and the tombs of the Valley of the Kings. It was also a beautiful-looking city, which is not something I had thought about Cairo or Hurghada. The Nile glinted on my right in the last light of the day. Feluccas glided to and fro, their iconic-looking lateen sails hanging off long yards at jaunty angles to the mast. Horses and carts lined up by the wide boulevard on the riverbank. It felt a relaxed and gentle place, the first and maybe only I would find in Egypt.

My convoy pulled up outside the Hotel Gaddis on a downtown street parallel to the Nile. Two men stepped out of Aymed's car and introduced themselves as Aymed and Aymed. Aymed needed paying, which was fair enough as he had been hired to chaperone me into town, but I didn't understand the need to pay for all three Aymeds. The police were there as well, looking on expectantly – a little baksheesh for their trouble? I shook their hands and thanked them warmly but wasn't about to hand over money. It sets an unhealthy precedent. I didn't mind paying for services when I'd asked for them, but not for those I explicitly didn't want. This was the first time police had looked for money in Egypt, and I wondered if this was because I was now in a town where tourism had helped establish a tipping culture.

As in Hurghada, I immediately realized that my arrival had been heralded in advance, which is rarely helpful. But while checking in I learnt that this was no one's fault; they had seen me on the news and wanted to give me the royal treatment. The Hotel Gaddis was a snip at $15, but the staff had an odd style of hospitality. Of course a warm welcome is pleasant, but it soon became clear that they saw me as a marketing opportunity.

Inside the rickety old lift hung an emergency phone that was decorated in pink tartan – an amusing link with home. My room was basic and very dated, but perfectly fine, spacious and clean. On expedition I can live without home luxuries; for me it is people who make experiences.

I wondered if I was the only guest as the lobby and restaurant were dimly lit and empty. The young waiter handed me a menu but explained that most of it wasn't available as the chef wasn't in.

'Can I have the kabab halaa, please?'

'No.'

'Can I have the fish tagen with sayadia rice, then?'

'No.'

'OK, what can I have?'

'Chicken.'

'Perfect. Can I have two portions of chicken, please? Roughly how long will that be?'

'Twenty minutes, that is all.'

Experience told me that I therefore had the best part of an hour before dinner was served, so I left the waiter/chef to it and went out to explore.

Back at reception I asked to borrow scissors for some urgent cobbling. Since losing my flip-flop I only had my hard-soled cycling shoes, which were giving me some grief. I thought they were worn in, but they had in fact become painful after only about forty hours' wear, especially under the cleat and at the toes. After taking the insoles out I cut the entire toe section off both, making a lot more room. It wasn't ideal to be doctoring kit so early in the trip, but I didn't have much choice.

Outside the hotel there were more horses and carts, and the drivers touted for my trade as their animals munched their dinner from mangers hung around their necks. I declined with thanks and headed off, my shoes clip-clopping down the pavement. The street was fairly quiet and before I could reach the end I spotted a fast-food restaurant. Motivated by my rumbling stomach I went inside and had a spicy meal deal that was ready before I ordered it. After a quick call home, I thought I had better cut my exploring short and head back for the main course. When I passed the same carts, the drivers knew I didn't need a lift this time so offered drugs instead. I once again declined, with thanks.

The impromptu meal before dinner turned out to be inspired, as the huge pile of chicken that eventually arrived in the Gaddis was as dry as the desert around Luxor. I tried it and failed to finish, even with copious amounts of water between mouthfuls. I am guessing the poor waiter had nuked it in the oven for nearly an hour.

During this attempted second dinner the receptionist, a man in his fifties with a fine moustache, came over twice to ask if I wanted to use the swimming pool. It was a kind thought, but the outdoor pool was in pitch darkness out back so the thought of a refreshing swim didn't really appeal. Instead I stocked up with biscuits and yoghurts for breakfast from the small shop across the road and headed off for an early night, exhausted but in good spirits after three days on the road.

It had been nearly thirteen hours on the go that day and my biggest yet at 280km, with a serious increase in climbing which, together with the headwind on the inland leg, reduced my average speed by more than 5km/h. The excitement of the start had subsided and I was physically and mentally adjusting to the daily routine.

I was in bed at 9.20 and had just switched off the light when there was a loud knock on the door. I quickly threw on a T-shirt and padded over. It was the receptionist.

'Could you come to the restaurant, there is a journalist here to speak to you.' It was more of a statement than a question.

'No, I am sorry, I am in bed and must sleep.' I didn't entertain the idea of an interview even for a second. I closed the door politely before anything else could be said.

At 10.30 I was fast asleep when there was another loud knock. Disoriented, I jumped up and found the light. This time I stood behind the door and called, 'Who is it?' Opening a door to strangers had got me mugged in Lafayette during my world cycle and I wasn't about to make that mistake again.

It was Manuel's Egyptian brother again, but this time – I discovered when I opened the door – he was accompanied by a younger, much stockier man wearing a suit. I only had my boxer shorts on.

'This is the hotel manager,' the receptionist announced, not nearly as confidently as before. 'Can you come downstairs for a photo with him?'

Catching the door with my left hand I swung it slowly closed. It wasn't a slam; it was far more theatrical than that. And I didn't utter a word, which I hoped spoke volumes. Feeling a combination of anger and guilt about what had just happened, I fell back into bed and instantly back to sleep. So deeply that I woke up when my alarm went off to find the room light was still on.

Day 4: Luxor to Aswan

As rude as I had felt, the hint definitely didn't sink in. At 6 a.m. as I wheeled out of the pink tartan elevator, the same reception-ist, his manager and another few men were waiting for me. I was very keen to get going but didn't want to offend so I lined up patiently for photos. After ten minutes of small talk, I explained that I really had to go and made for the door. The manager took my hand and wrung it enthusiastically.

'You can go on TripAdvisor and leave us a review!' he beamed.

'I can do better than that,' I replied. 'I can write about you in my book!'

Ahead lay a day along the beautiful Nile, before a week of desert sands. The schedule allowed for five days to get through Egypt and day five would be a monster, over 300km from Aswan to Abu Simbel. The first Tour d'Afrique team took this route in 2003, but since then everyone had had to bypass it due to a bor-der dispute between Egypt and Sudan. In August 2014 a trade agreement put those differences to rest and a new land border was built. Keegan Longueira had still opted to miss this section out, getting the boat from Aswan. My opportunity was to set the Cairo to Cape Town once again as an almost unbroken route; taking a ferry for twenty-four hours down the length of Lake Nasser didn't seem in the spirit of cycling the length of Africa. Admittedly I would still need to take a boat to cross the lake at its southern end, and then get on a boat once again to cross the Zambezi river on the Botswana border.

Taking the road from Aswan, which had been a military road for over a decade, also meant I could cross the border any day of the week. The ferry from Aswan left only once a week, around midday on Sunday, and by all accounts was a cramped and uncomfortable affair, a far cry from the idyllic cruise I had first imagined. Keegan ended up losing days here so the land options seemed best, for a multitude of reasons. But organizing a cycle from Aswan to Abu Simbel had taken a lot of time in terms of communication and negotiation. It was all arranged for Tuesday, 14 April, so staying on target for days 1 to 4 was crucial.

Thankfully, Luxor to Aswan was relatively civilized in terms of ambition – only 213km. I couldn't go any further even if I wanted to. I was now in the heart of Upper Egypt – in my mind a confusing name as upper suggests northern, whereas it actually refers to the Upper Nile. In Egypt everything refers back to the Nile.

The Nile is also known as the cradle of civilization, and day 4 boasted one of the greatest juxtapositions in terms of human culture I have ever experienced. At first, life seemed unchanged, as it had been for thousands of years, with subsistence farming, men on donkeys, and families pulling water directly from the river; then there were flashy four-wheel-drives, expensive houses and factories. Sadly there was also the flotsam of humanity, an abundance of produce and people who seemed to have been cast aside by both traditional ways and economic development.

'Hello, hello, hello!'

No one, except the police, had looked twice at me since I left Cairo but now, as I joined the dots along the riverbank, I was starting to cause a stir, to be treated like a foreigner. Strings of villages by the roadside and fields in between were so busy that it was often hard to tell where one finished and the next started. Lots of people stopped and stared as I pedalled through and hundreds of children waved and shouted excitedly. Cairo to Cape Town is a common enough route for there to be regular cyclists, but it seemed my race bike, lycra and speed were slightly different.

While most of the attention seemed friendly enough, one

teenage boy flung a fist-sized rock from the far side of the road. It bounced short but then hit the rim of my front wheel with a thud. On later inspection it had only caused a scratch, but this was worrying at the time and irritating, too. I had been fore-warned about stone-throwing in Ethiopia but had not expected this problem in Egypt. Thankfully it proved to be an isolated incident, and his aim poor.

Less maliciously and more comically, a few hours later I came up behind two younger boys walking in the road. Guiding the bike gingerly over another steep speed bump, I was going at walking speed myself so shouted out 'hello' as I cycled around them to warn them of my presence. Spinning around in fright, the closest boy instinctively flung what he was carrying at me. It turned out to be a large cardboard egg tray, about a foot square, thankfully without any eggs in it. This makeshift frisbee bounced off my head and on to the road behind me. I pedalled on as both boys dissolved into laughter.

The police took no notice of any of this and continued to drive patiently behind me for most of the day, causing a fair number of tailbacks. Vehicles could easily get past me, but not a police pick-up going at my speed, so I spent most of the day with an empty road ahead of me and a queue of irritated locals behind. At checkpoints they would either make me wait until the next group of escorts was ready, or wave me on, giving me ten or twenty minutes of freedom as they had their cuppa and catch-up. Except 30km from Aswan they didn't catch up – and for the first time all day I actually needed them, hoping they could show me the way into another big town. They didn't reappear and I finished the day alone.

It proved to be a much easier day, helped by having an artificially clear road ahead of me and a gentle tailwind behind me. To my right there were occasional stunning glimpses across the Nile with palm trees and fields of sugar cane growing alongside.

The pain in my shoes had subsided since I cut out the toe of the insoles and my main discomfort was now in my shoulders. No amount of training readies the body for long hours in the saddle. I had expected the first week to be tough as my body adapted, but the discomfort wasn't critical and I wanted to avoid painkillers if possible. Conditioning from the cycling position would take time and was far less of a concern than muscular or tendon problems. On that front there was nothing twinging and I felt strong.

For all that there is an abundance of life by the Nile, there are surprisingly few shops or places to eat between Luxor and Aswan. Aish baladi, a local flatbread, and plain rice sufficed for a second breakfast but was harder to order than I'd expected. Tourism and therefore the English language obviously didn't leave the towns. I realized as I reverted to menu charades that learning a few more words of Arabic would have been time well spent.

Throughout the day, at bottlenecks of irrigation, I kept track of the changing landscape on my left as the sands of the desert slowly gave way to the rocks and granite that dominate Aswan. It is this rock that made Aswan the home of the first British Dam in 1902. When British rule ended in 1926 and after the Egyptian Revolution of 1952, extending this and controlling the annual floods of the Nile became a major political and economic focus. President Nasser played a careful game with the US and the Soviets, both of whom craved Egypt's allegiance in the midst of the Cold War, and it was the Soviets who committed their support in order to create the High Dam and therefore Lake Nasser, the world's largest man-made lake.

The day flew by, partly because my senses were constantly entertained. It was also a relatively short day: I entered the busy outskirts of Aswan a few hours before sunset. I finished where I had started, a stone's throw from the river. However, the

St George Hotel, where I had told the police I would stay, was up a small alleyway and hard to find. I stopped at a junction and asked a traffic policeman for directions. He waved me off with a shrug. I tried another policeman who was sitting in his car a short way off. He turned and asked his colleague in the passenger seat, who in turn shrugged. It was not helpful, but I found the hotel in the end.

The St George did not live up to its grand old name but was functional and well kept, with a charming receptionist – a young man who was travelling vicariously by means of his keen interest in and questions to everyone who stayed there. My room was tiny, but with space for the bike if I stepped over the bed. I set about hand-washing clothes in the bathroom sink before hanging them out of the window, a floor above the pedestrians below. I hoped there was still warmth in the sun to dry them for the morning – it had reached the mid-twenties during the day.

Mohammed Abouda called to say that he was in reception. This was the man I was trusting to get me down the old military road and across the Sudan border without delay. We had been in touch for a few months by regular email and his services came highly recommended. A man in his fifties, he wore a dark-grey galabeya – a long, loosely fitting shirt. We ordered tea, and after pleasantries he cut straight to business. Mohammed wanted to know why I hadn't been in touch since leaving Cairo and he wanted to be paid upfront in cash for his services. I apologized, realizing that all communications in recent weeks had been from Una and that I'd assumed he would follow my progress online. I was so focused on each day, and was now leaving planning ahead to others. I learnt afterwards that Una had been trying to update him all week.

Had we got off on a better foot, I would have insisted on paying Mohammed via bank transfer as had already been arranged, to spare the limited cash funds I was carrying. But I didn't feel

I had much negotiating space; his full support was crucial for the next few days. I nipped back to the room and counted out $550.

Money sorted, I started to explain that for a 300km day we would need to start very early, before 6 a.m. 'I have arranged to meet the police at seven,' Mohammed cut in, 'we can't leave earlier.' He had never escorted a cyclist. His usual convoy since the new border opening was overland expeditions by Land Rover, which would take about three hours to get to Abu Simbel. It would take me the entire day. That gave me a target of over 25km/h without factoring in any breaks – not ideal on an utterly desolate stretch of sands.

This was all being done on his terms and there was really no room for negotiation. I pointed out that he could have been in touch to ask about my preferred start time, but didn't make an issue of it. It was clear that there wasn't a chance of leaving earlier.

Once business was out of the way, Mohammed's manner warmed considerably and he offered to show me a great place to eat nearby. By the time we parted after a gentle amble through the market streets of Aswan I had reassessed my first impressions; he was a lovely man, gentle but serious, with a tough past and an interesting life. He spends part of each year in Devon, where his girlfriend lives, and spoke about the hard times for tourism in Egypt, where he had returned to farm and fish. He struck me as a man who understood the value of his network, the complexity of running a tourism business alone but under the watchful eye of the police. I struggled to imagine anywhere further from Aswan than rural Devon.

Mohammed advised against all the riverfront restaurants, the lovely-looking well-lit ones that attracted me like they do every tourist, and instead steered me inland a few streets, through a small entrance to a completely empty restaurant I would never have found – and if I had would certainly not have remained in.

Mohammed met the owner with a handshake and a familiar smile. He then left, and I sat alone, in an empty room. I ordered kushari, because the waiter described it as pasta. A mix of lentils, macaroni, chickpeas and spicy tomato sauce arrived, and the flavour was incredible – I could have eaten the same twice. But curiosity, hunger and an urge for protein drove me to a second main course, this time tagen – skewers of chicken and meat in onion and tomato sauce. Dining alone in foreign lands and discovering wonderful new flavours has to be one of my favourite solo pastimes. I am perfectly happy, absorbed in every mouthful.

I left, and wandered slowly back through the bustling market, stopping to admire an old white Peugeot 504. This antique was European Car of the Year in 1969 and went out of production the year I was born, 1983. Yet here in Egypt they are everywhere. They remained in production in Africa until 2007 and are fondly called the 'King of the African Road'. As I took my phone out for a photo, a man rushed out from a haberdashery store across the street, keen to know if I wanted to buy the car.

I was in the market for cheap transportation as I was still clip-clopping my way around. Six dollars for a pair of flip-flops seemed expensive in the locality, but if they could save my feet from the discomfort of wearing cycling shoes from dawn till bedtime then I would have paid ten times that. Next stop was a food stall and a pile of yoghurt drinks, fig rolls and a stash of my favourite 'Babita', the synthetic choc croissant.

The road to Abu Simbel had rarely been cycled in recent years, but an Egyptian cyclist called Ahmed Mahmoud had been in contact before I left Scotland with information – photographs and distances for every shack, restaurant and medical services – which looked like a lot but in fact didn't amount to much. While I wished to remain unsupported, I took Mohammed's advice to put extra water and food in the car as a contingency plan.

Day 5: Aswan to Abu Simbel

The early-morning light gave me a picture-postcard scene across the Nile to an island where the famous British general Lord Kitchener wintered and where there is now a botanical garden. How that view was going to change!

Mohammed was waiting outside, but there was no rush as the police weren't. In fact he had news: we were to leave town via their station to pick up our escort for the day. At least Mohammed had managed to arrange for a single policeman to join his car rather than another convoy of bored bobbies. Mohammed certainly looked different now in jeans, a shirt and one of those multi-pocketed traveller's waistcoats.

The police station was up a hill on a side street. Mohammed introduced himself at the gatehouse, showed some papers and waited. And waited. Eventually a man about my age greeted Mohammed but did not acknowledge me. His uniform was rumpled, as if he had slept in it, or just woken and dressed in the dark. In any case he looked unenthusiastic and unrushed and lacked authority, as if he had been given the short straw on today's shift. Mohammed immediately gestured for him to sit in the front seat, which surprised me. Mohammed struck me as a man who would always want to be in charge, and certainly not be subservient to a junior officer. But Mohammed was right in that this man could make our lives very difficult and was worth keeping sweet.

Setting off, we rejoined the El Sadat road and started climbing. Aswan was waking up and the traffic building. Within five minutes Mohammed's black car pulled up in front of me and stopped. I could see the policeman on the phone, and after about ten minutes of this I was starting to get pretty worried. Why would we need to stop for him to take a call unless it was about us carrying on? Mohammed sat patiently, and didn't look at me. I held on to the roof of the car, still clipped in. It was nearing 8 a.m. and the day's target was already becoming unrealistic.

After hanging up, the policeman gestured for me to carry on, no explanation given.

The road veered left, away from the river, climbed more steeply for 500 metres, then cut back on itself, and I found myself on Khazan Aswan, the Lower Dam, the road that the British built in 1902. It was a good stretch downstream from the much bigger Soviet Dam, but at the time it was the largest masonry dam in the world. And inevitably there was a police checkpoint.

Once again I was left out of the conversation and sat impatiently on my bike. The body language and tone of voice was not encouraging, I didn't need any Arabic to understand that much. Months of concerted research to enable me to become the first person going for the record since 2003 to complete this stretch lay in the balance.

Finally, Mohammed reassured me that I could carry on, but not across the dam. It was a point of national security and no cycling was allowed. Those two points seemed entirely unconnected to me. Cycling across the dam was hardly a security risk.

'Please tell the police that I will go fast, and stay right behind the escort vehicle – we will be across in minutes.'

Mohammed turned and argued the point. I noticed that our young policeman did not get involved at all in the debate.

Not a chance. It was annoying, but fighting for this kilometre wasn't worth risking the whole day and the crossing into Sudan for. A Toyota pick-up drew alongside. I climbed into the canvas-covered back and sat on the metal floor as my bike was roughly handed up to me. Another two policemen were already sitting there, so had tri-bars and a front wheel thrust in their laps. We immediately sped off, with the tailgate left down and my legs hanging out the back.

After clearing the dam the road started to climb again and I was concerned that the pick-up driver was going to carry on, but after a few hundred metres he pulled quickly to the right and stamped on the brakes. It had been a rough ride, but exciting. After letting me off, the pick-up did a sharp U-turn and sped off, leaving me to check over the bike, then pedal off. The road continued to climb, up and up, on to a plateau that would last all day.

I had left the river and was back in the desert. But this landscape didn't have the ephemeral dry riverbeds and rocky mountains, the scraggy vegetation hanging on for life like further north. Here it was truly deserted: barren, flat and featureless.

The road skirted Aswan airport and then an unexpected outcrop of houses, a village of identical low buildings and neat symmetrical streets. It looked like an unlikely place to call home and I guessed it was built to service either the airport or the military. I was looking for the petrol station which would be the last pit stop for the next 100 miles, as far as I knew.

Set back from the road, it looked very unwelcoming so I free-wheeled slowly past. A smaller building lay off to the right; maybe that was a café. But soldiers were standing on its roof and huge armoured trucks with large-calibre machine-guns were parked on the roadside. Seeing armed soldiers wasn't remarkable, but there was something about their elevated position, guarding a civilian petrol station surrounded by open desert, that was menacing. The Abu Simbel Touristic Road seemed a misnomer.

I was about to pedal on when I spotted a lone attendant. Signalling for Mohammed and the car to wait, I swung the bike into the garage forecourt. The soldiers didn't pay any attention. It turned out the café was open, allowing me a pee stop and the opportunity to buy a bottle of Coke to caffeinate the huge shift that lay ahead.

Day 5 was an absolutely crucial effort, yet there is almost nothing to describe about the journey that day. It was a straight road delineated by power lines stretching to the horizons. All I could see was flat, featureless desert, so parched as to be sterile, void of even a single blade of grass. There was nothing there. Halfway down it I crossed the Tropic of Cancer, but there was no sign.

After 105km I stopped at the first small roadside restaurant and the driver, Mohammed and the policeman took advantage of the break in the monotonous journey to join me for bean stew, cheese and the ubiquitous omelette. The road had been deserted, yet the restaurant was doing solid trade. A couple of old televisions on the walls blared out Egyptian news and a few dozen tables were taken.

At 205km I was delighted to find another small restaurant. Ahmed Mahmoud's notes were not tallying up in terms of distances so I was keen to eat whenever I could, no longer sure of the gaps ahead. This time it was a much smaller shack-like place, set off to the right-hand side of the road. I felt seriously underdressed walking in and taking a seat, my eyes adjusting to the dim light after the glaring desert. Everyone was male, local and wearing long flowing shirts.

It was already gone 3 p.m. and I had absolutely flown, really pushed the speed, helped by a tailwind along perfect speed-bump-free roads. I'd ridden as fast as I could have hoped. But there was still no time to lose. Reaching Abu Simbel by dark was possible, but a stretch.

Five minutes passed and, tired of waiting for the others, I went outside to find the car empty. I couldn't see where the three of them could have gone; the restaurant was surrounded by nothing but desert. There was one toilet, but they weren't there. Walking around the back, I found them kneeling beside each other, in the sand, praying. I slipped quietly back inside and ordered my food.

When Mohammed did come in, just for some black tea, served in a thick glass, I couldn't find a polite way of telling him that he had sand all over his forehead and nose. He suggested I try a local coffee, something to keep me going for the final big push. Mohammed was impressed with my speed, which for a man of few compliments was high praise. But if he hadn't expected this, then I wasn't sure how he had expected me to finish before darkness fell.

The coffee arrived, also in a thick glass, and was dark brown. Infused with ginger and thick with suspended gritty particles, it wasn't what I had expected. I am loath to say that it was horrid, but I couldn't finish it. It might have been perfect sipped slowly over a hookah, but it wasn't the double espresso I was craving.

Back outside, the road shimmered to the horizon as the temperature soared to over 30°C. The contrast with the day before when I hugged the Nile was incredible. I stretched out across the tri-bars, hands resting but not gripping the 'ski bend' that jutted 45° upwards. It was an effortlessly efficient riding position, taking weight off my hands, letting the upper body sit neutral and relaxed. But it put my neck at an acute angle, which was a pain I was expecting and for long hours would be something to get conditioned to. Certainly on these perfect flat desert roads it was the best position. It was exciting, glancing down at the Garmin which read 30km/h, then glancing over my shoulder to the car a hundred metres back. I was flying out of Egypt, covering the no-man's land that few people had cycled for twelve years.

Late in the afternoon I crossed a dry irrigation system, a concrete canal and then a crossroads, the first turning all day. It was left to Abu Simbel and a gentle descent from the desert plateau. What a perfect end after an anxious start – success on such a pivotal day. I was on a complete high as I flew along, bringing the day's average to 26km/h and chatting happily to my camera at arm's length. I had been wary of filming and taking photographs all day because of the security.

Abu Simbel's streetlights and wide boulevard of trees started a few kilometres before the town, suggesting something grander than what actually materialized. It was a small end-of-the-road town. It is reliant on tourists visiting its famous temples, but the journey there requires commitment on their part, even without a decade of military control of the only road. A gentle cruise down Lake Nasser would certainly be an easier way to get there.

Al Humphreys sent a tweet to remind me that in 2002 he had slept in a ditch near Abu Simbel. There were plenty of those, but Lady Egypt had made other arrangements, and I certainly wasn't complaining. We turned left at the only T-junction on to a smaller street and then through an unassuming entrance to Eskaleh Nubian Ecolodge. This was a slice of heaven surrounded by a dustbowl.

Thanking the driver and policeman, both of whom seemed on a complete high despite their eleven hours in the car and the prospect of another three back to Aswan in the dark, I gave each of them a tip, which seemed expected and appropriate. After a quick photo, they left.

A man in a floor-length galabeya and white turban sporting a generous smile greeted Mohammed as an old friend, and then me. A lady came forward with a tray on which were two delicate glasses of red tea made from hibiscus flowers from their garden. As we sipped, the brown clay of the lodge became part of the palate of deep reds from the setting sun. At the end of the patio, across the garden and down the hill, was Lake Nasser, whose waters also reflected the burnt orange and pastel shades of twilight. Birds flew silhouetted and low across the water.

Time could have stopped. There was no sense of urgency here, no world records at stake.

Fikry Cashef, the owner and host of this five-bedroom refuge, welcomed us as if into his own home, which in a way it was. There was no check-in, no formalities, just a request to relax and enjoy the Nubian welcome.

A large archway led through a dark corridor, on whose walls
rugs were hanging, to an immense wooden door. Inside, my room
was traditional and peaceful but also very dark, with walls of
the same tan clay and a tiled floor. Shutters opened on to a small
veranda and an archway led through to a luxurious if rustic
bathroom. A few bulbs cast a faint yellow light. I dug out my
headtorch as soon as I was left alone, in order to unpack and set
about my end-of-day rituals. My watch, cycle computer and
phones needed charging, data had to be transferred and kit
washed.

Fikry had grown up in a village nearby but moved to
Switzerland as a child with his family. The Nubian people of
southern Egypt and northern Sudan have lived for millennia
along the upper Nile, but the building of the Aswan High Dam
flooded much of their ancestral lands. Some continue to work
as sharecroppers, subsistence farmers on resettled farms, but
most inevitably headed north to the urban centres of Cairo and
Alexandria. Fikry came back to Abu Simbel to build this traditional Nubian lodge, a place to preserve his ancestry, albeit with
a generous dollop of luxury.

The eye-watering $211 in cash for Mohammed and me to stay
was a long way off local prices. My daily accommodation budget
was $30, which I knew for most of the ride would allow me to live
like a king. I was carrying a tent, a sleeping bag and a roll – a total
of 1.1kg bundled tightly in the bag under my handlebars – but
I hoped never to need them. Having spent over a year of my life
living in a tent, I wasn't in Africa to prove anything to myself
about living wild. The fastest way down the vast continent relied
on a proper sleep every night and an early start every morning.

Dinner was served outside, and I ate alone. It was a stunning
meal of white fish, straight from the lake that day, served with rice.
As I sat there, I reflected on the fact that my day 5 had taken the
2003 Tour d'Afrique team three whole days, and was described in

Michael Kennedy's blog as 'unimaginable emptiness – well until we got to Sudan'. There had been so much planning put into Egypt that it was wonderful now to relax in such style. From here on, I would be able to go as far as I could manage each day with no authorities to delay me or rules to abide by. But for now I could enjoy not being rushed and acknowledge the passing of the first big milestone in my journey – Egypt.

Part Three

Into Sudan

Day 6: Abu Simbel to Abri

Breakfast at the Ecolodge was a similarly sublime affair, eaten during first light at 5.30 a.m.

There were multiple ferry times for the crossing of Lake Nasser and two providers, one military and the other civilian. Mohammed had arranged for the military one, as it docked on the east bank on to a tar road; the other would have left me with a section of dirt road to negotiate. On the far side it was then a short ride to the Sudanese border. The schedule looked tight to me. The ferry left at 6 a.m. so Mohammed and I had agreed to leave at 5.45.

At 5.50 Mohammed ambled through with a sleepy 'good morning', saying he would have something for breakfast. I was outside, bike packed and ready to roll. Mohammed seemed amused. Gone six, I was wandering aimlessly around as Mohammed finished his tea. 'Don't worry, the ferry won't go without us,' he reassured me. But I was worried. Fully aware that very few things run to time in Egypt, I knew it was a dangerous game to plan your travel around an assumed delay. At 6.20 we left, in no great rush, and retraced our path back to the T-junction, carrying straight on to the port. We were the first there, and Mohammed lit a cigarette with a chuckle.

There was nothing obviously military about the ferry and every other vehicle except Mohammed's car was a truck. Most people stayed in their vehicles; some got out and climbed up to the bridge and small viewing platform. I joined them as we left shore, looking back on the largest of Abu Simbel's temples, four seated pharaohs cut into a hillside. But this isn't where they started out in the thirteenth century. Then, they guarded a wide bend in the Nile river; in the sixties they were dismantled and moved 210 metres back and 61 metres up to escape the rising waters of the lake. It seemed fitting to look back on this wonderful history in a country that also seems to look back more than it looks forward. I had a few miles left of Egypt before the land border, but this felt like a symbolic as well as literal departure.

I found a wooden bench on the open car deck, took off my shoes and lay back for a snooze. The deep throbbing engine and vibrations of the ferry were not sleep-inducing but it was wonderful to lie there and relax. Over an hour during which I couldn't rush anywhere.

The landing ramp and one small hut were tiny compared to the sandy emptiness of the far bank. There was no town, little sign of life. Not many vehicles waiting to cross back either, mainly because the land border wasn't yet open and the first town heading south, Wadi Halfa, was on the Sudan side of the border. Some 55km down the road, it was due to open at 10 a.m., so I was in perfect time.

Wheeling off the ferry ramp first, I had a head start on everyone and started the gradual climb from the lakeside up to the desert plateau. One by one the trucks lumbered past me, then I had an empty road again, until I reached the border and I found them once more, all stacked up, waiting. The wind was picking up from the north and it was promising to be the hottest day yet.

A week before I left for Cairo, Khartoum hit a mind-melting 47°C. I had been in Scotland making final preparations, worried

Left: A family ride with Nicci and Harriet in the chariot near home in Scotland.

Below: Una (aka Mum) at the heart of expedition planning, as she has been since I was twelve years old pedalling across Scotland.

Bottom: Digging deep. Training with Scottish Cycling at the Sir Chris Hoy Velodrome in Glasgow.

Above: Gav and Owen, my bike wizards from Gamma Transport Division, were a massive help before and during Africa Solo.

Right: All about the detail. Going over kit design with Endura.

Below: Survived the flight. Building the KOGA in my Cairo hotel room.

Top and above: At the start line with friend and photographer Jeremy Sutton-Hibbert, and then off, up Cairo's legendary 'hill'.

Right: A ripped sidewall in my tyre was a massive blow after just 100 miles. Next supply package is the other side of the Sahara desert.

#africasolo

Above: On the road and leaving Cairo far behind me.

Right: Can't be too careful. Signs for the slightest kink as the road heads inland from the Red Sea.

Below: Truck stops in the desert. The welcome refuge from the heat and for food and water.

Above: Back on the Nile, with its amazing contrast of greenery and desert.

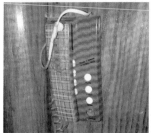

Left: A tartan phone in my Luxor hotel. An amusing reminder of home, but not my favourite abode.

Below: The wonderful luxury of Eskaleh Nubian Ecolodge in Abu Simbel. Fellow round-the-world cyclist Al Humphreys tweeted me to say he slept in a ditch near here!

Above: Crossing Lake Nasser to leave Egypt and its police escorts behind, I was glad to reach the Sudanese border (**right**).

Below: The perfect roads of the Sahara desert, but some wild sandstorms make life uncomfortable.

Above: Meeting world cycling nomad Anselm Nathanael in the middle of Sudan, who, after some scrapes with the Egyptian authorities, was kind enough to supply some of the great images for this book, like the one below.

Below: Bread, eggs and beans was the staple food in Sudan and through much of the African continent. But in Ethiopia I found the local speciality of injera, a sourdough which I was not a fan of (**right**).

Above: Dinner with my fixer Midhat, cameraman Sami and driver Salah, in some rudimentary accommodation (**left**).

Below: The Imperial Hotel in Wad Madani was nothing of the sort, but was palatial compared to most of the accommodation for the next stretch. Certainly better toilets (**below right**)!

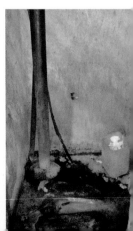

that I was leaving too late. The truth was I couldn't have been ready even a week earlier. The whole project had been pulled together in just over six months. But every other Cairo to Cape Town ride that I'd researched had left between October and March – the summer heat of the Sahara was the biggest barrier.

On the Sudanese side I was being met by Mazar Mahir, the brother of a man called Midhat, known to almost everyone who has cycled through Sudan. Once again there was a link back to the Tour d'Afrique team whom Midhat helped in 2003 to battle the then terrible dirt roads from Wadi Halfa to Khartoum on his trusty old mountain bike. About half a dozen of my lines of enquiry about fixers in Sudan had led back to Midhat so inevitably he got the job. But I was intrigued to meet the man after some difficult communications.

Back in October 2014, with plenty of time in hand, I needed an official letter of invitation from a Sudanese company, which Midhat said he could arrange. But the response took a few weeks to appear and a lot of chasing, until a short email arrived with words to that effect. I knew there was no way any embassy would accept this email so I asked again for something more official.

Every other African visa proved straightforward to arrange, but by February I started to worry about Sudan. Without my visa, the whole ride would have to be delayed by six months. I called for a final time with an ultimatum to send the letter or I would find someone else and Midhat answered his mobile, flustered and apologetic, explaining that he was in hospital in Khartoum for the birth of his daughter. It was a solid excuse, so I wished him well and went back to waiting.

The attached letter that then arrived was on a company letterhead of sorts, but was signed off with a smiley face and had Midhat's contact details as a gmail account. The main text read: 'He visiting the country for sightseeing he will enter Sudan at wadi halfa Border on the 02.April .2015 and .he will visit the sightseeing in the north Sudan cycling'. The team at Visa Express in London who were taking care of my paperwork shared my concerns about this 'official invitation' but, incredibly, it made the grade. I wasn't worried about the specific date Midhat had mentioned: I knew I would arrive in Sudan within a fortnight of the 2nd of April and that I had a visa for a month.

Filming in the Sahara desert was absolutely key to the Africa Solo project. After the start, filmed by Robbie Wright, I wanted crews to join me for about three to four days each in Sudan, Ethiopia, Kenya, Zambia and South Africa, to capture the hugely contrasting landscapes, allowing me to self-film a diary for the rest of the trip. Midhat had told me he would arrange a local cameraman but once again it took too long to get any information across and we ended up finding a different recommendation through Levison Wood and his Walking the Nile expedition. Midhat wasn't altogether happy with my efficiency in finding a different cameraman, but he was still needed to drive. Then it became clear he was arranging a vehicle *and* driver, which made his role redundant. He was coming along anyway.

I had asked for Midhat and the cameraman to meet me a few days north of Khartoum. He had replied saying it was too difficult to cycle the north of Sudan unsupported and that he would meet me at the border instead. I responded clarifying that they were joining me to film part of the journey, not to support me. However, I knew Midhat was originally from Wadi Halfa and his brother Mazar was the fixer meeting me at the border to get me across, so to keep him onside, I agreed. I suspected this was also motivated by getting a few more days' work out of me. Mazar, like his brother, had been difficult to keep in touch with so I was reassured that at least one of them would be there on the other side.

All this added up to my being slightly apprehensive about meeting the elusive yet oddly ubiquitous Mahirs.

ARAB REPUBLIC OF EGYPT MINISTRY OF TRANSPORTATION THE GENERAL AUTHORITY FOR LAND AND DRY PORTS — GOUSOL LAND PORT. It was an impressive title emblazoned in blue above the new but old-looking gates, which were firmly shut. It was only 9.50 so they would open any minute now.

At 10.35 a guard walked out, leaving the gate ajar. The nearest huddle of chatting truck drivers looked over but made no move to return to their cabs. Mohammed spoke to someone behind the gate and a few minutes later we were beckoned through. The gate was closed behind me. Ahead lay a few hundred metres of no-man's land between the Egyptian authorities' border post and the Sudanese one beyond it, with more closed gates.

I was told to wait for another ten minutes by my bike before being taken around the far side of a building for a passport check. Mohammed took my passport from me and asked for 200 Egyptian pounds, the equivalent of £20. A young officer met us and gestured for my passport, opened it, found the note, pocketed it with a knowing smile and beckoned us to follow him into a small room, where a more senior officer checked my documents.

My bike had been left out of my view for fifteen minutes while this was going on, which made me nervous. But it was untouched, and Mohammed ushered me over to the customs house and a small room with a bag-scanning machine. The senior officer here gestured for the bike to be lifted on to the conveyor belt. It was a ridiculous suggestion – anyone could see it wouldn't fit – so after a long pause I lifted it on to its side to illustrate the point. The guard walked over, opened the top zip of the smallest bag, peered inside, lost interest and waved me on.

I was officially out of Egypt, and walked down the road with Mohammed as far as he could go, tipping and thanking

him for his support. He assured me that he had been in touch
with Mazar on the Sudanese side and everything was set up.
'Good luck, Mark, stay safe in Sudan as the people are not as
friendly and for your bike their roads are not as good – lots of
loose stones.'

Mazar spotted me before I knew who he was. Breaking from
a group of men, he walked towards me with a broad grin and an
extended hand. He asked for my passport and told me to go and
wait in the shade of a brick building on the right. I wasn't completely comfortable watching this stranger walk off with my
passport but had little option. I sat on some steps and waited. It
was a while before anyone appeared, by which time I had dug
out the new map of Sudan and was considering the options for
that afternoon, and reflecting on the fact I had lost quite a few
hours' ride time. By now trucks were rolling past and the borders were fully open. It was gone eleven. There wasn't much to
look at in the many miles ahead of me, but it was all tar now,
unlike a decade ago when the next 400 miles would have been
little better than mountain-bike tracks. So Mohammed's warning about poor roads surprised me.

Another man came out of a door at the top of some steps,
walked down them and over to me until he was standing right by
me, then chatted to another man standing out in the sun by his
vehicle for about ten minutes. It was slightly odd to be sat so
close under him, but I didn't move and went back to my map.
The conversation ended, and the man above me broke into
English: 'Let's go and get your passport now.'

Surprised, I stood up, grabbed my bike and caught up with
him as he strode off. This was Midhat. No hello, no introduction. He wasn't being rude; I would soon find out that he was
just being Midhat. Tall, maybe in his late forties, with lighter
skin than most Nubian men and a trim moustache, Midhat
looked like the older brother.

Sure enough his brother had had my passport cleared and Midhat took me into a very large hall filled with people unpacking suitcases. The floor was strewn with clothes and officers walked around, looking on. I weaved my bike between the crowds of people enduring their lengthy custom checks. The senior officer was slumped in a chair near the far wall, settling into a long shift. He wanted me to unpack as well, which I really wanted to avoid. I particularly didn't want to explain my tracking device, a bright yellow matchbox-sized box of electronics. Anything to do with satellites was best hidden. I hoped my trick would work.

Unclipping the two fasteners on my Apidura saddle bag, I unrolled the ends rather theatrically, taking longer than necessary. Reaching inside, I pulled out the first item, a pair of Speedo pants, and held them towards the officer.

'OK, carry on,' he said, obviously not wanting to see anything else.

He then took a permanent marker pen and flippantly put a dash across the headset on my carbon frame. He had no way of knowing the bike's value and wouldn't have cared anyway. It was my baby and had taken five months to build, so to watch a customs officer who was too lazy to stand up brand it like he would a cardboard box riled me. Caring so much made little sense when I was battering it across nearly 7,000 miles of Africa, yet still I treated it with kid gloves. 'Who cares, no damage done,' I reminded myself.

Emerging back into the baking sun, I wheeled my bike into Sudan. A grey Toyota Land Cruiser was parked off into the sand, an old steel mountain bike tied to its roof. In the front seat an older man was asleep, and in the back a young lad with a baseball cap was also stretched out. They had driven 900km overnight to reach the border.

Midhat jumped up and started untying the bike. We hadn't

said much yet, but he paused, took another look at my bike, and announced, 'I can join you later.' I breathed a sigh of relief. I did not wish to offend my new friend, but slowing down was not an option, especially with the intimidating gaps between supplies on the road through Sudan. I knew that Midhat was a keen cyclist, but it hadn't crossed my mind that he planned to cycle with me.

Midhat was famed for cycling in trousers, a shirt and sandals, and for being fast and fit across the dirt roads. But that was a very different style of riding to mine. No one could keep up with a road bike on an old mountain bike, especially on perfect flat roads with a tailwind.

'Give me your bags and we can go,' he said.

'No,' I replied, 'I carry all my kit. The vehicle is just here to film from.'

Midhat looked taken aback. 'I supported Keegan from here, all the way to Ethiopia.'

'Thank you, I'll carry my bags,' I repeated. 'Let's go.' And with that I pushed the bike off the sand, back on to the road.

I'd had no idea from Keegan Longueira's blogs that he was supported through Sudan – every photo showed a heavily laden touring bike. It obviously makes a massive difference if you can ride an unladen bike.

The wind really was bellowing from the north. Away from the buildings where it picked up, showers of sand tinkled on the carbon frame and stung my legs. I only discovered its strength when I made a 90° turn off the highway 35km later, heading into the town of Wadi Halfa. Reduced to jogging pace, I battled with the final kilometre. It was like cycling with brakes on.

Wadi Halfa was a collection of mud houses scattered in apparent randomness across the desert. In 1997 they had thirty minutes of rain which destroyed over two hundred houses. Rain and mud houses don't mix. This must have been one of the most remote parts of the Sahara in the times of only one dirt road and a closed border to the north. But even now the highway misses it out. The trucks thunder straight past and you need a reason to visit.

I had one: I had no Sudanese money or phone. Plus it was lunchtime. I knew that Sudan, like Iran, had limited international financial links. However, hopeful that the new border had changed this, I stopped on the outskirts and asked Midhat if there were any ATMs.

'Haha!' He was genuinely amused. 'Your next ATM is in Khartoum!'

I seriously hoped that he was wrong, as this was a worrying thought. There is no more isolating feeling than running out of cash in a foreign country. Especially one as cut off as Sudan. I was carrying a wad of US dollars but, unlike most touring cyclists who can live on a shoestring, I needed that to pay for fixers and film crews, which took my costs per country from hundreds of dollars to thousands of dollars. It was far from ideal to be cycling along hiding stacks of notes.

Gav and Owen at Gamma, my mechanics in Edinburgh, had devised a lightweight metal bung for inside my seatpost that could only be undone using an Allen key. So you needed a 6mm key to undo the seatpost and then a 5mm key to undo the bung. Inside, neatly wrapped in clingfilm, were copies of all my visas and $1,000. This was the emergency stash, which made this seatpost the most valuable I had ever owned.

Midhat knew everyone in Wadi Halfa – this was where he grew up – and we stopped at a poor-looking bric-a-brac shop where three older men were sitting, whiling the day away. This turned out to be the local money exchange, although you would never have known it until one of the men pulled a massive brick of Sudanese bills from his pocket. It turned out to be an issue that I was carrying twenties, which I had done on purpose because so often it is hard to get change for large bills. But here it was the opposite: smaller bills were worth less so I got a lower exchange rate for not having fifties and hundreds. It was only because it was Midhat that they took twenties at all. I received 8.8 Sudanese pounds to the dollar, and my 4,400 Sudanese pounds was also an offensive wad of cash.

Across the street I was keen to find a Sudanese SIM card. The mobile shop was the only modern-looking establishment I could see; everywhere else resembled market stalls. I stepped inside to find a few staff in white office shirts surrounded by wall displays marketing the latest deals. There was nothing remarkable about this, it could have been almost anywhere in the world, but it did seem very out of place in Wadi Halfa.

I had picked up a cheap smartphone in Cairo, a Microsoft handset I could put local sims into en route. Midhat took it from me, commenting critically, 'Was this made by Egyptians?' It wasn't the first out-of-context remark telling of a deep distrust and dislike for his northern neighbours. Remembering some of Mohammed's comments, I realized the feeling was obviously mutual.

Further down the street the Land Cruiser pulled up outside a market-style restaurant, all the dishes already cooked and laid out. This made me nervous about the potential for stomach upsets, but there were no alternatives. We had already lost another hour in the town sorting the money and the phone and I seriously wanted to push on, to make that day's miles count. The driver, Salah, and the young lad, Sami, the photographer, did not join me, opting to doze in the car while Midhat raced off to run errands.

As I left, he called over some kids who were playing in the street and handed them three plastic footballs out of the back of the Land Cruiser. This was his community and I could see it was still his home, except he lived in the big city, 1,026km away.

Next to the restaurant were four stone steps up to a very old and elaborate-looking doorway engraved with Nubian patterns, some that looked like the sun, a few birds that looked hieroglyphic and an Islamic crescent. At the top was a very faded sign saying MASHAN SHARTI FOR SERVICE. The same name and a facsimile of that doorway had adorned the top of Midhat's letter of invitation.

'That is my office here,' he explained. 'I plan to rebuild.'

It looked ruined. The door was broken and piles of bricks and rubble covered the ground.

The roads of Wadi Halfa were partly tarred but mainly dirt. I didn't need to backtrack the way I had come, but it had still been a detour, and the road was strewn with sand so that the edges merged seamlessly into the desert. Streetlights gave more structure to the town than the mostly pale-green buildings, which were all set back from the road, with the odd tree clinging on for dear life. Everything else was sand coloured, apart from lots of old, mainly blue Bedford trucks which I would soon realize are the backbone of Sudanese transport, and the odd tuk-tuk with canopies pulled right down to keep out the blowing sands.

In 2003, Michael Kennedy wrote: 'There are no real roads. Some graded tracks have been cut through the desert and almost always they become horrible, corrugated or sandy, making the going painful on the wrists and bum. The first day we only did 50km but in the sun and with the soft sand I thought I would never make it. You learn to read the sand, avoid the rocks and bumps as best you can, but you really need to concentrate. Rough trails and numerous tracks can be disconcerting as you are never quite sure you are going the right way. I just used my watch compass and headed south! One horrendous day, which took ten hours of toil, we covered only 77km and I had to carry or push my bike for half of that through thick sand; riding was impossible.'

I knew the roads had been tarmacked since the days of the first Tour d'Afrique, but didn't fully appreciate that these would now be the best roads in Africa, if not the best roads I have ever cycled on. The Chinese have laid a ribbon of the smoothest tar imaginable all the way to Khartoum and a cracking northerly pushed me along at a staggering pace.

Midhat had his mind set on reaching the town of Abri, which was just over 100 miles south-west, which I thought was very ambitious, but then again there wasn't much else to aim for. Akasha, Ferka and Kosha, all shown on my map, were not places we could stay, Midhat assured me. And all these towns were off the road, down on the Nile which the road followed, but mainly out of sight.

For the rest of the afternoon only sands surrounded me as I barrelled along. It was stunning riding, only spoilt by having a vehicle shadowing me. But I didn't mind the reassurance of their presence as I headed into the unknown depths of a new land.

Sudan is on the US list of countries that reportedly provide support for acts of terrorism; it has imposed on it strict unilateral sanctions and much of what you read about the country is negative. There are only three nations on this state-sponsor-of-terrorism list so, as was the case when I entered Iran on my world cycle, there was understandable trepidation. Still, over 99.9 per cent of Brits have never visited Sudan, and if travelling has taught me anything, it's this: only take advice from people who have actually been to the place. I also had the perspective of knowing that Iran stands out as one of the favourite countries I have visited, and many cyclists who have pedalled through Sudan had given similar rave reviews. So I hoped for the best.

The sun set in a stunning lava flow of colours to my right, and I was left in the fading light pushing really hard to reach Abri. The road cut almost due west for the final 25km and climbed a bit. I was now very near the river, but couldn't see it in the low light. Without a vehicle with me I would have been reluctant to carry on for that final hour. Then again, what options did I have? Camping out in the sands with limited food supplies and almost no water? I was determined to carry on riding as unsupported as possible. But it was impossible to know my mindset and the decisions I would have made without an escort behind me.

Distances at night are always misleading; lights from towns 'just over there' prove to be an hour or more away, especially in the still desert air, and this final push took ages, even though I was sitting at over 30km/h. I stubbornly didn't dig out my bike lights, thinking for over an hour that I had less than ten minutes to go. And so it got darker and darker until I was left in the faint pool of my headtorch, with no tail-lights. But that part didn't matter – the road was deserted.

Abri was once again a few kilometres off the road and I followed the Land Cruiser gradually down and then right again – so I was going back on myself – through the first low brick buildings. My skinny wheels squirmed in the soft sand. I gingerly picked out a route on the most packed path but under the patchy shadows cast by the streetlights this was hard to judge, so I kept dropping a foot for balance, and to scoot along with. The village looked asleep already.

We arrived at a dead-end street and the Magzoub Nubian Traditional Guest House, a nondescript white building with a very small sign. This wasn't a tourist guesthouse that you would stumble across. And it was locked. Midhat called the number on the door and got through to a man in Khartoum, who owned it, but whose brother lived locally. I had a fifteen-minute wait, during which I ate a bunch of bananas and some bread. I was seriously hungry. It had been nearly fourteen hours since leaving the luxury of Fikry Cashef's open home and it was now definitely night-time.

The brother came, a tall Nubian man in traditional garb.

He didn't seem particularly happy to be receiving guests. Then, as I continued to eat, sitting on the tailgate of the Land Cruiser, Midhat started negotiating. He seemed aghast at the price for the four of us to stay at the guesthouse, although they were speaking in Arabic so I could only go off intonation and the fact that we were still stuck outside.

This sort of deal-making was above the brother's responsibility, so his brother in Khartoum was brought back on to the phone for a heated debate. It was 250 Sudanese pounds, the equivalent of $28; Midhat wouldn't pay any more than 200, a saving of $5. After the relief of making it into Sudan and putting in decent miles, I couldn't have cared less about $5. It was a tenth of the price of last night's bed. But I wasn't about to stop Midhat mid-rampage.

Day 7: Abri to Al-Goled

The Magzoub Nubian Traditional Guest House had a dozen rooms, each of them bare whitewashed concrete, with a metal-framed bed and chair. It was very basic, rustic, but all we needed. Waking at 6.30 a.m., I saw that my room opened straight on to a small outdoor courtyard, and I padded out, appreciating the cool stone under bare, sore feet. I had never suffered from sore feet before. The acute pressure had passed since cutting my insoles, but they still felt bruised.

At first light forty minutes later I wheeled out of the guesthouse. On my right down a small bank, to my utter astonishment, was the Nile. Just 15 metres away, completely silent and vast, it flowed serenely. Having arrived at night I'd had no idea it was right there, although that did explain the mosquito nets over the beds.

It was a few kilometres over the sandy but packed tracks from Abri back to the road. They were easier to navigate by day and I was relieved to find a small stall open at which I could stock up on supplies.

Turning right back on to the highway was like slipping from a gentle tributary into the fast-flowing main stream. I was soon once again barrelling along the perfect pavement at 45km/h, feeling the constant downwind assistance. The barren golden nothingness of sand and rocks passed in fast-forward, a conveyor belt of indistinguishable features.

Fast miles are like fast money: the more you get, the more your greed grows and the more you need, desperate to cover miles before luck runs out. By 10 a.m. I had happily covered half a day's miles, but rather than being contented, my mind obsessed on the miles I could go on to bank. In the heat, the road's end wasn't a vanishing point but a watery blur of pastel shades. People can lose their minds in the desert, parched, cooked, dreaming of a moment's shade and heavenly liquid, tormented by a horizon that looks like it could quench the thirst of a thousand armies yet is as baked and arid as the ground beneath you.

A ramshackle restaurant punctuated the sameness, and as I drew closer a figure appeared next to the roadside, crouched on his heels, taking photos. I wasn't planning on stopping, my mind set on bridging the big gaps ahead. But the man straightened up and greeted me warmly.

'Hi Mark, how are you?'

Braking fast, dropping off the slick tar on to the soft sand, my tyres sank in and I stopped.

The man had even madder hair than mine, sand-blasted vertically, and wore sandals, rather short but baggy shorts, a dirty brown long-sleeved jersey and a similarly coloured neckerchief, with a pair of sunglasses suited more for fashion than sport tucked into his collar. As I should have clocked by his camera-readiness, Anselm Nathanael was also a cyclist and had been waiting a while for me. Except it took me a minute to figure out what he was doing here at all as his heavily laden touring bike was sitting in the deep shadows under the building.

Anselm was obviously delighted to see me. And I was delighted and surprised to meet another cyclist. But I also felt incredibly agitated. What would a few moments mean? These are the chance encounters that make travel so memorable. Yet one moment I was utterly in the zone, making miles, making sums about miles, and now I was stopped, making small talk but still thinking about making miles. I felt antisocial and couldn't snap out of it. When you are in a rush, and going in the opposite direction to someone, it is always hard to know what to say, whether that crossing point is in the local supermarket aisle or the Sahara desert. Where do you start?

Pete Gostelow, the well-known English cyclist who has so far clocked up over sixty countries and 50,000 miles cycling around the world, had been through some of Malawi, Tanzania and Burundi with Anselm. I haven't met Pete, but we have kept track of each other's adventures and he had shared my plans with Anselm, who therefore knew he would meet me on the only paved road through this part of the Sahara.

Anselm was in high spirits in spite of what he had been battling. Getting off this southbound travelator was bad enough, I couldn't imagine trying to beat it north. He had been worn down to walking pace on his weighed-down steed, sometimes taking roads east and west off the tar and on to dirt as the lesser of two evils so as to tack his way north. Soul-destroying stuff, certainly bad for your hairdo, but Anselm was in no rush.

His bike was sand-blasted and dirty, bits of wire holding parts on and a small foam globe as ornamentation on the front rack. With a fuel bottle, lots of water bottles, six bags, a mirror, bell and a music system he had got in Cambodia, this battered but well-loved machine was a shire horse next to my thoroughbred.

Anselm was celebrating 19,000km in Africa already and knew parts of my route ahead intimately, which I was keen to ask about. He was also in need of some information. Not helped by the unrelenting headwind, he had outstayed his visa – not something I would be very comfortable with in any country, let alone one as isolated from international diplomacy as Sudan. But it didn't seem to faze this happy-go-lucky wanderer. We stood on the roadside rather than go inside as I didn't really want to stop. Neither did I want Midhat to fly by.

Anselm had broken a cleat, which made pedalling even harder. This was something I could help with and I quickly reached into my framebag for my spare set. They weren't there. I looked inside, then emptied that compartment. At that moment the Land Cruiser pulled up.

'Why are you stopped?' called Midhat, assuming something was wrong and striding over.

'This is Anselm,' I said, introducing the young German. 'He's cycling north and his visa has run out. Can you or Mazar help with the Egypt crossing?'

'And this is Midhat,' I added to Anselm, 'a man who knows everything about cycling in Sudan.'

'Why didn't you contact me before?' Midhat barked without a word of greeting, and paying no attention to my flattery. 'I help *all* cyclists travelling Sudan,' and he leant on the word *all*. 'I cycled from . . .'

I zoned out as I unpacked my entire bike looking for those tiny blasted cleats wrapped in clingfilm, as Midhat gave Anselm a history of his life on two wheels and why he really should have contacted him before setting out.

Half an hour had now passed, I hadn't found the cleats, and Anselm insisted I lose no more time. A quick photo and I was on my way, but not before he gave me a SIM card from Ethiopia, something you can't get without a lot of difficulty. It seemed a rather unsatisfactory meeting, without sitting down, food or water, and without much help at all from me aside from some thoughts about his road ahead, and the introduction to Midhat. If I had been Anselm, on a meandering journey up the continent, meeting me, impatient and in racing mode, would have seemed a complete whirlwind, and the antithesis of his travels. Here was a man in high spirits, loving exploring Africa despite having contracted malaria three times already!

In spite of having to face an overbearing Midhat, the meeting proved very useful for Anselm who received a one-month extension to his visa without charge from brother Mazar, as well as getting to stay in his family home in Wadi Halfa. However, Wadi Halfa takes a day not a month to explore, so Anselm soon crossed into Egypt and retraced my route north, where his luck ran out, I later heard.

One hundred metres from Asia, on the banks of the Suez Canal, he made the mistake of taking a photo. Within seconds he was kicked off his bike, pinned to the dirt and searched, before being thrown in prison. The German Embassy managed to secure his release after three days, but he never got all his possessions back. The Israelis then wouldn't allow him entry because of the Sudanese stamp in his passport, and some months later, at nearly 5,000 metres on the Pamir Highway in Tibet, he crashed, breaking his foot and buckling his bike. Undeterred, at time of writing Anselm has been on the road for just over two years and clocked up over 18,000 miles. His photographs of people and landscapes capture moments in a way I never could, not least because of the speed of my journey. In return for sharing some of his images for this book, Anselm simply asked for a new tent, since his old one was stolen – a fitting barter.

By two in the afternoon it was 42°C – not quite the 47°C I had feared but an unrelenting dry heat nonetheless. Pedalling along created a gentle breeze for myself. But when I stopped, the northerly blast felt like the draught from an open oven door. Covered in sleeves and a cap to keep the sun off as much as possible, I started to notice salt deposits building up on my lycra. I wasn't wet, at no point was I visibly sweating, and the dry heat and wind was wicking away any moisture, but I was certainly getting slowly cooked.

The Nile kept me company, sometimes dropping out of view as the road cut out a bend in the river. Although I rarely saw the water, the trail of life – palm trees and vegetation – cut a sharp line of contrast through the never-ending-ness of sand and rock. A few bus stops equipped with huge clay urns of water for travellers were the only roadside attractions. A few small villages slipped by, all a few kilometres off to the right-hand side, each built around the tower of a white mosque. Some villages signposted lokadas, small hotels, or tourist attractions, ancient sights including the temples of Sulb and Sesibi.

The area I was coming into is home to around 255 pyramids, which Midhat was quick to point out was a lot more than Egypt had. For significant parts of history, until just over a hundred years ago in fact, this was all part of Egypt and these pyramids were built after those of modern-day Egypt, so there is an intertwined history that makes it hard to justify these incredible relics of yesteryear as strictly Sudanese creations.

Eventually the road cut west, crossing the Nile and moving back into farmland for a while. Dongola is the capital of the northern state of Sudan, and boasts a university, but is home to less than fifteen thousand people so is really a smallish town. I was through it before I realized, skirting the edges. It was mid-afternoon, and this was where I had aimed to reach today, but it seemed crazy to stop short while the going was so good.

Midhat was also very excited about my speed and progress.

He kept saying that he had never seen anyone cross the desert so fast, having never seen the efficiency of the aero position. For hours they had been having a lot of fun trying to film me at certain points racing across the desert alongside at 50km/h. Driving fast on the sand looked exhilarating, but it was pretty bumpy for camerawork. His praise was certainly flattering and a good boost, but his enthusiasm needed tempering.

'It is only another 160km to Al Dabbah,' he informed me. 'We can make it there and I know a man, a good place to stay.'

I had already covered 250km, over 150 miles, and it would be dark within a few hours, and Midhat still thought I could pedal on for another 100 miles.

The driver, Salah, who was a very quiet man, suggested that he had a friend midway, in a place called Al-Goled, whom he could call. Another 50 miles would make the day's total just over 200 miles so even that was a stretch by dark. His friend was not answering, so I saddled up assuming a plan would fall into place.

Those last few hours I really pushed it; glancing down at my power and heart-rate readings, I knew this was unsustainable and a tad foolhardy. But it was exhilarating. I rode for exactly twelve hours that day, and by the time we reached Al-Goled I was feeling under-fuelled and light-headed. I stopped on the roadside and stood swaying against the bike, leaning heavily on the bars. A seriously big day in the hottest conditions yet. Midhat mentioned again that I could push on another 70km or so and reach Al Dabbah. I did not even entertain the idea.

A bashed-up old white pick-up eventually bounced its way across the sand towards us – the first dirt walls of the village were set a hundred metres back from the road, and tracks in the sand were the only delineation of the desert. There were fairly lengthy welcoming pleasantries until I jumped on my bike, as politely as I could, saying we had to go. It was nearly dark and I was about to keel over with hunger and exhaustion. Sami, the young cameraman, seemed to understand better than Midhat, Salah and our host, who all looked put out at being rushed along.

Following the two vehicles through the sand was nearly impossible. I jumped off and pushed the bike, the sand beneath quite deep in sections. It turned out that our host, whose name I never got, had a house that was empty. Apart from a few stray dogs and a donkey and cart there was very little to see – wide sandy streets, houses behind high walls.

Turning past some metal gates, we were shown to a large room with a dozen army-style wire lattice beds. There was nothing else, except bare bulbs and electricity (two of the plug sockets were distorted where the plastic had melted). The toilet was a long-drop in an outhouse about 10 metres from the house.

My left calf started to cramp, not seriously, but that intermittent deep tightening that has its own category of discomfort. I was also caked in salt, which was part of the same problem. I was keen for a wash, but also needed food quickly. While I ate what biscuits I had left, Midhat said that the host would bring a bucket of hot water for me to wash in.

The bucket was placed in the outhouse and I threw on my briefs (the aforementioned Speedos) to dash across in. There were only men around, yet as I stepped outside Midhat caught sight of me.

'What are you wearing?'

'Pants. I'm going for a wash.'

He looked around, visibly concerned. 'Go quickly. Watch for women seeing you.'

I guess I did look a bit exposed wearing only pants, sandals and a headtorch. But the only other clothes I carried were shorts, a T-shirt, a rain smock and a thin fleece, and I wasn't planning to get them wet.

I dashed over, locked the door behind me, wedged the

headtorch in a gap in the bricks and used a metal cup to ladle lukewarm water over sore limbs. It was blissful, and I emerged feeling much better, smiling contentedly at the thought of 321km – a massive success. It had been the first day when I could really go big, unhampered by the Egyptian authorities and border delays. And at this first opportunity I had smashed 200 miles.

The town centre was close by, a square with restaurants and a few food shops with goods stacked up to the ceiling so only the owner would know where everything was. While the streets were empty, this small town centre had hundreds of men sitting in it, eating and talking. For the few hours that we were there I didn't see a single woman.

Food was prepared in huge open pans like woks, some with boiling oil, others for dry-frying. Midhat recommended the liver, which I am guessing was cow or goat, and beans, along with the obligatory omelette. While this was being cooked I explored with Sami and stopped at one of the stalls for drinking yoghurt. I was looking for crisps or salted nuts to replace the salt I'd lost, but there wasn't anything that familiar – except for the ubiquitous Coca-Cola.

I asked Sami why women seemed to have been pushed to the back of public life in Sudan. He was young and worldly, smart enough to put his own culture into some context, and he was also married. His response was quite resigned: this was the way women preferred life; they didn't wish to be seen or heard. He couldn't see a time when this would change, and there were no issues with the way things were. I didn't want to raise this with Midhat, who was older, but over dinner I did continue the conversation on the subject of family life, congratulating him on his newborn. It was our first opportunity to chat properly. Every conversation since the previous morning had been focused on the race, the mission.

It was Midhat's first child and he proudly showed us pictures of his daughter on his phone. I reciprocated, showing Harriet aged one and a half, and her picture got quite a response, in part because of her bright-red hair.

'She is at that fun age,' I explained, 'saying her first words and really starting to interact.'

'That's really late,' Midhat protested. 'In Sudan, children can speak when they are nine or ten months.'

I caught Sami's amused glance. Having been in the car for the last two days with Midhat he was obviously very used to this one-upmanship.

The market centre got busier as we ate, and I was the only non-local among hundreds, certainly the only European. I had on a pair of long grey shorts, mountain-bike baggies with the chamois taken out, and a white T-shirt. These and a very thin fleece and rain jacket were the only non-lycra kit I carried, and at moments like these I was glad not to be in cycling gear. The town seemed very conservative; it was friendly, but everyone noticed me, and I could tell that conversations were being conducted about me. If I hadn't been with Midhat I probably wouldn't have ended up here at all. There didn't seem to be any hotel or guesthouse.

I was glad for the gentle walk afterwards, down dark sandy streets with dim, widely spaced streetlights. My legs were the tightest they had been, and my left calf retained that tense discomfort from the earlier cramp. I didn't dare stretch, too worried about causing an injury – far better just to sleep.

Someone was snoring loudly within minutes so I lay there awake for a good while, mainly thinking of Nicci, Harriet and home.

Day 8: Al-Goled to Khartoum State Line

Midhat shook me awake before my alarm and was on full-systems-go. A middle-aged man with a childish enthusiasm, he was immensely likeable, despite often being irritating. He was

quick to sulk if anyone disagreed with him and on a real mission
to prove his worth, but any annoyance of mine quickly disappeared because of his unreserved willingness to help.

I was pretty sore and slow to get up. Wrapping the thick rug
under which I'd slept around my shoulders, I sat cross-legged on
the bed as I worked my way through some biscuits and yoghurts.
My dirty kit was not pleasant to pull back on and I rubbed paw-
paw cream into my skin to counter the irritation from the salt.

By 7 a.m. it had been light for half an hour and the sun was
about to show up. After wheeling the bike through the gate we
were about to leave when three older men came out of the house
alongside – our hosts, whom I hadn't met. They were obviously
expecting us to go and join them for breakfast, but with Midhat
translating I thanked them, apologized, and told them I was in
a rush. I wasn't sure how much of an offence it was to leave without accepting their hospitality. One man rushed off and soon
reappeared with a tray of coffee. What a stunning send-off. It
was a wonderful ten minutes of calm, time just to appreciate
where I was. As I straddled my bike, sipping strong black coffee
from a delicate cup, Midhat and our hosts chatted away. It was
interesting to see that Sami, much younger, hung back and was
neither invited nor tried to get involved.

'Shokran,' I said, shaking their hands with heartfelt thanks.
They had after all hosted us for nothing.

'Rihlah muwaffaqah,' they replied, wishing me a successful
journey, watching as Midhat and I pedalled off.

It was the first time Midhat had got the bike off the roof and
he had a point to prove. He flew off over the sand, helped by his
wide mountain-bike tyres, but he was undoubtedly skilful as
well. I foundered with my skinny road tyres and he was at the
main road long before me. Turning left, we rode for about 5km
shoulder to shoulder and it was wonderful to have company. My
legs were seriously tight and I was happy to start cautiously.

Midhat was wearing leather shoes, long white trousers and a striped rollneck jumper, his glasses perched on his head. He had good strength to keep up on a mountain bike.

The main road was gradually turning eastwards, and the wind was from the north-east. Overnight this had built to the point that Midhat was warning of a haboob, a sandstorm, by late morning. For the first 50km I was thankfully guarded from the worst of this as my route turned in a more southerly direction. This was time to ease in the legs, along with my aching shoulders and cricked neck.

Nearing Al Dabbah, the road kinked left. What had been helping me for days was now turning on me. Or, more accurately, I was turning into it. The effect on my speed was devastating. My map told me that the Nile wasn't far away, but there was now no break in the moonscape to prove it. The rocky dirt had given way to golden sand, the Sahara of our imaginations. To complete the vision I came alongside fifty or so camels, and while I braced myself against the whipping sand, these ships of the desert nonchalantly ambled along, flanked by their handlers, herding them as they had since biblical times.

The menace on these straight roads was coaches. Some were more like the classic old American school bus, which didn't cause too much trouble, but most were more modern coaches, the type with bug-ear mirrors. Many had Arabic slogans printed across their back windows and most were brightly coloured. Careering along, they brought with them a wall of wind and sand. Those heading south had to swerve around me – their biggest bend in hundreds of miles. This made them wallow alarmingly on their suspension, looking top heavy. It must have been a rollercoaster for the passengers whenever the driver met a cyclist, donkey and cart or other snail-paced road user. Slowing down certainly didn't seem to be an option.

The coaches coming the other way were worse, and the sand

seriously stung me – I would get alongside and close my eyes for a second while this hit. Opening them again a little, I'd still be in the swirling sand. On a few occasions coaches were tailing each other, I assume to cut down on their fuel. Whenever I saw a convoy coming I had to stop, turn away and let the much bigger wall of sand hit and pass by.

At a place called Multaga, the road cut south again. My spirits were pretty low having struggled for over 50 miles – the toughest miles yet. It is amazing what a difference a few degrees make in terms of wind and speed, and now the sand no longer stung as much; it was still coming in from the left, but behind me just enough to be a help. Between coaches it was utterly quiet now that the wind was generally with me, and I grew mesmerized by the gentle tinkling of sand hitting my carbon frame. One minute it was hitting my feet and wheels only, then it would come up over my head. My helmet was off, hanging beneath the tri-bars from its straps, and my hair was thick with sand, as were my ears. The road carried waves of sand, pretty patterns drifting across it, that made the surface appear to move, as if it were liquid. Stopping in the small village of Tam Tam for lunch I found a tissue and blew a lot of sand out of my nose. It had got everywhere.

Options were very few for places to stay. Camping out in this wind and sand was not appealing at all. It didn't matter too much sand getting everywhere while I was cycling, but opening bags, trying to eat and pitching a tent would be a nightmare. Late in the afternoon Midhat drew alongside; he hadn't been with me all day as I'd wanted Sami to film more of the desert and village life rather than just me riding my bike. He thought there was a truck stop in the desert, maybe 50km ahead. I had passed the last village on my map, Abu Dolooa, and there was nowhere obvious to stay. From there it was 180km to Khartoum and there was no way I could make the capital by dark.

Committed to a final big push, I knew I wasn't carrying enough food if I ended up short. With the vehicle I obviously wouldn't be left in a difficult situation, but I was still fighting Midhat's offers for it to become a support vehicle. He found being kept away frustrating and thought it was crazy to have a car near me and not use it. I had conceded only that he refill water bottles on a few occasions, which he did with brilliant enthusiasm, obviously hoping to be asked more often. With Sami filming and Salah driving, Midhat's role was fairly redundant, as I said, but he was obviously loving the road trip anyway.

At 7.30 the daylight had almost completely gone, and my bike lights were on. For the final few hours the haboob cleared and conditions were calm and clear; it was superb riding as I pushed for another huge day. After a second 200-mile day my thoughts were full of dreams about a sub-forty-day finish. But it was naive to think this would continue and I knew for a fact the good flat roads would soon end, along with the tailwinds. Still, caught up in the moment, I got lost in the fantasy.

The truck stop turned out to be 68km away, just far enough past Midhat's guess that I was starting to doubt it existed. But there it was, a cluster of makeshift shacks, temporary-looking but decades old. Una had reassured me that there were some buildings visible on Google Earth, but no community was shown on my paper maps. Interior lights run off diesel generators glowed out into the desert but there were no streetlights, only a few spotlights at a gated checkpoint. These had been ten to a day in Egypt and I hadn't missed them, but this was the first in Sudan. It didn't look like I would be allowed past in the dark. This was the outer reach of Khartoum State, Sudan's smallest but by far most populated state not just because of the capital itself but its neighbouring, more populated city of Omdurman too.

I was tired and sore after 225 miles, but also feeling fantastic. Midhat made a beeline for one of the half-dozen roadside stalls.

I have no idea why the one he chose was the right one; maybe he had stayed there before.

The roadside was lined with trucks, one set of wheels on the tar, the other on the sand. More arrived as the night drew in, and the makeshift stalls slowly filled. Some of the trucks had wicker-weaved bedframes strapped on to their backs or tops, allowing the drivers to bed down anywhere in the desert. A row of these was also lined up outside the shacks, like sunbeds round a pool. Behind these was a low metal rail with small urns – water for travellers to wash their hands and feet. It was all very charming, but I still couldn't see where we would sleep.

'We will eat here,' Midhat confirmed.

'And sleeping?'

'There.' Midhat seemed surprised by my questions, as if it was obvious we would sleep under the stars, lined up at the roadside.

'OK,' I said, surveying the scene.

I knew there was no way I would sleep well with my bike and supplies lying unlocked next to me in the sand so I walked inside the shack itself. There was an open space about 5 metres square at the back, a whitewashed room with no windows, partly taken up with plastic tables and chairs. I dragged one of the wicker beds to the furthest corner so that I was right next to the open kitchen, a drape of fabric between me and it. That would have to do.

Waiting until no one was walking by, I stripped and threw on my baggy shorts and T-shirt. My face was streaked with grime, and I attempted to scrub it clean with a few baby wipes, and a few more for my backside to stave off the dreaded saddle sores. Mine was definitely feeling like a skelped arse after the best part of 500 miles in forty-eight hours, but the skin hadn't broken, which was the important bit.

By the roadside, a few half carcasses – the hind legs and lower backs of goats – hung from hooks under the canopy. This looked like dinner. Next to them was a huge bladder of hide which Midhat explained was the skin of the goat, cleaned and sewn up, then filled with water. These were then tied on to the grilles of trucks: as the trucks move through the desert, the water is cooled by the airflow, giving the driver a supply of chilled water even on the hottest day.

The podgy young chef, the first overweight man I had seen in Sudan, offered me some of this water. He had a jolly, happy-go-lucky manner and was immediately likeable even though we didn't have a word in common. Tempting as it was, I opted for the safer option of bottled water. The bank of fridge-freezers, brimming with Mountain Dew, Pepsi and ice creams, looked very out of place. They were the only nod to modernity I had noticed in most roadside shacks in Sudan. Cooking was still done over an open fire and the food was just as traditional. While tea was the customary drink, it seemed normal to wash food down with a fizzy drink – a global tragedy. Somewhat hypocritically I gulped down a few bottles, desperate to make up for lost calories before dinner was ready.

Sitting in the gloom, using my headtorch to identify each mouthful I took, we dug in with our fingers – community eating at its best and most rustic. There were freshly cooked flatbreads, like the Turkish pide, delicious and useful for spooning and soaking up beans and meat stew, with a few slices of raw onion thrown in and a green spicy sauce. Each part of the meal came on its own metal plate, which reminded me of the cat bowls we used to use on the farm I grew up on, and the whole lot was served on a table-sized round metal tray.

Eating together was sociable but competitive, and I had to order more as there wasn't nearly enough by the time four of us had grabbed and eaten what we could. My second course – omelette and beans – arrived but I turned down more meat. The guys helped me finish that as well. I asked the jolly chef for some more bread, making a point of not putting that on the table, instead wandering around eating. Anything put on the table was fair game for sharing and I needed a mountain of food, having burnt over 7,000kcal that day.

It was a broken night's sleep. Truck drivers sat around eating till late and my bed was just a few metres from the nearest table. Once this area had been cleared there were still people coming and going all night. My corner was in the dark but I was obviously the topic of conversation. I woke on a few occasions with a torch shining in my direction, newcomers obviously keen to see me with their own eyes. My bike was wedged down the wall side of the bed so I wasn't worried about security. The bed itself was a bit broken, with a foot-long hole in the webbing material along one edge by the frame. It wasn't sitting flat on the sands either so I woke up a few times wedged in the hole, the thick rug covering me having fallen on to the sand.

Day 9: Khartoum State Line to Wad Madani

At 5.50 a.m. my mobile rang – it was before my alarm call. 'Hello Mark, this is Jonathan,' said a fast-speaking Irishman. 'Where exactly are you? I think I must be pretty close by.'

As well as joining me to cycle through Khartoum as quickly as possible, this man was here to save the day as I had a bit of an issue. Una, back at base camp in Scotland, had engineered a solution to a problem I should have foreseen.

I needed US$3,200 to pay Sami and Midhat for their services. I didn't have that on me. I had assumed there was some way of paying from business to business, an international transfer to Midhat that he could then use to pay Sami. I had found it odd that he hadn't asked for any payment for my letter of invitation, and I knew there was no high-street banking between British and Sudanese banks, so an alarm should have gone off, but still I assumed I'd be able to pay somehow over the web.

Assumption, the mother of all . . .

Midhat, who had slept outside on one of the wicker beds and thin foam mattresses, seemed relaxed, as always, making it clear that a lack of payment wouldn't prevent my progress – it was a nuisance that he dealt with regularly, being involved with tourism – and that there was no issue with trust. But I didn't know if El Tayeb, Sami's boss at the production company, would be so understanding and would just let me leave without paying, plus I didn't wish to take such a liberty.

The British Embassy in Sudan had introduced us to a man called Jonathan who was neither British nor a diplomat but part of the expat community in Khartoum, and known as a mad keen cyclist. Jonathan, after conversations with Una, had volunteered to cycle with me, and had then received a further call from Mum asking if there was any way he could also lend me $3,200. It was supremely kind and trusting of him to be handing over to me this impressive wad of cash. Jonathan had bank accounts outside Sudan which we could simply transfer funds into.

I was just up, packed and ordering some food by the time Jonathan arrived. He was a slight man in his late forties, but looked younger. It transpired that a career on the track meant he was a pretty serious athlete, though he was now working in finance for a major Sudanese farming business. He arrived with his driver, bounded out, fixed the wheels on to his bike and was ready to go, all the time chatting at speed. Jonathan was a man who needed no caffeine.

I did. I asked the jolly chef, who didn't seem as jolly this morning for some reason, and was duly served a very creamy-looking glass. As this cooled a skin formed across the surface, so I assumed it had been made from straight unpasteurized goat's or camel's milk. It tasted OK, but it wasn't what I had hoped for. Jonathan and I huddled in a dark corner to complete our transaction. I tore a page out of my notebook and scribbled a receipt. Stuffing the money into my bike frame, I looked around with a guilty conscience about what I was hiding. There was no reason for people to take any more notice than before; the bike was perfectly conspicuous and nickable as it was.

I was ready to leave and doing my customary final check when I noticed my phone was missing. I dug back through my bags but just couldn't find it anywhere. Taking my headtorch, I went back into the shack and scoured the sand and my bedding: the wake-up call from Jonathan was the last time I had used it. Back outside, I looked through the bags again. There weren't many places it could be, and losing it would inevitably cause a huge amount of hassle.

'Where did those two Egyptians go?' Midhat piped up.

I hadn't been aware of anyone hanging around, and this was the first mention of Egyptians. I wondered how Midhat knew anyone was Egyptian.

'Is this it?' Jonathan was standing by the bed. The phone had got wedged down the side of the mattress. I gave him a massive hug, which he seemed a tad taken aback by. And we set off.

Jonathan had been watching the tracker over the last few days and was seriously impressed with my speed, to the point that he was worried about keeping up. We set off at a cracking pace, not the usual slow start to get sore legs warmed up. But I was quickly distracted from the discomfort as it was simply great to have company on the road. Jonathan was not a hugely experienced cyclist but obviously an all-round athlete and we chatted about his athletics, work, travels and our families. Jonathan had married late and his Russian wife was a good bit younger. He was full of apologies that he would have to leave me in Khartoum as he had an 11 a.m. appointment at the hospital, a pregnancy scan.

I was the first person he had told outside the family. We spoke about this for a while before I added, 'Nicci is ten weeks.' I am not sure if I told him in order to show support, understanding for his situation, or because it was the biggest thing on my mind that I wasn't telling anyone.

Nicci had found out at the end of February. The exciting announcement came at a time when life was already in overdrive. A brother or sister for Harriet was wonderful news, but as the weeks went by it was horrid to see Nicci struggling with morning sickness while I was busy getting ready to leave. I would be away for the twelve-week scan, which is one of those moments in life you never forget, the first time you see this little living being kicking and swimming around. I felt sorry not to be at home with Nicci and sad to be missing the scan.

Running a boarding house, looking after Harriet and being pregnant without me there was a lot to ask. Ever practical, I'd suggested we get a nanny, someone to live in and help for the two months I was away. Nicci was not a fan of having a stranger living at home with her so she contacted her bridesmaid from America. Abbie and Nicci had met on Camp America as teenagers and been best friends ever since. Nicci simply asked if Abbie fancied a career break, a few months off to come and live in Scotland. Her boss said no, but the next thing we knew Abbie had quit her job and booked her flights. I felt slightly responsible for this drastic action, but was also delighted that Nicci would have a friend with her while I was away. I don't suppose I can expect Nicci's friends to quit their jobs every time I go on expedition, but this certainly worked out very neatly.

I had imagined we would speak every day while I was on the road, but the reality was trickier. Nine days in we had spoken a handful of times, and each was only a brief summary of our lives since the last call. I was on a mission and I could tell that my mind was both exhausted but also blinkered by the task. It was very hard to relax into a meaningful conversation. And yet alone on the bike I spent long hours thinking of home, thinking of the pregnancy, excited about another baby, daydreaming of the adventures we would have together. I was soon using these daydreams as something to focus on, realizing that this race down Africa would one day become important to the life of my unborn baby: it would be the world record that Daddy did the year they were born.

Neither Jonathan nor I were prone to wearing our hearts on our sleeves, I could tell that much about him already, but there was an excited nervousness about his scan and a vulnerability about his sharing the news that I could relate to.

We reached Omdurman, a huge city I had never heard of, in great time. It occupies the west bank of the Nile, while Khartoum is on the east. This is where the Blue and White Niles meet, better described as the brown and muddy Nile and the slightly clearer and less silty Nile. The Blue comes in from the south-east and is the smaller tributary. Nearly seven million people live here, in the middle of the desert, over double the population from when the Tour d'Afrique first pedalled through in 2003.

It was my first major city since leaving Cairo and I was keen to get through without any delay. Inevitably there were choices to be made, not least about which bridge to cross. Jonathan had arranged to meet three other cyclists at the Old White Nile Bridge, so they could carry on with me once he turned back. We were now in the hustle of traffic, lots going on all around; life on the pavements spilt on to the roads and junctions were an impressive flow of committed drivers. The only rule seemed to be never to stop, and everyone seemed to possess a remarkable spatial awareness.

Midhat turned off on to a smaller street and kept going. We hadn't stopped all day but had discussed the fact that we were going to the Old Bridge to meet the other cyclists. Midhat had suggested that the Shambat Bridge was better. Jonathan was willing to concede, saying it was six of one and half a dozen of the other, but hadn't managed to get hold of the other cyclists by mobile, so we had pulled alongside the vehicle before reaching Omdurman to update and confirm that we were sticking to the plan. So where was Midhat off to now?

Jonathan managed to race ahead, catch the car and get it to come back; I wasn't about to sprint off after them, expending unnecessary energy and risking injury. Midhat wasn't at all happy about being upstaged; guiding was his job and he was insisting we go his way. I cut him short. While I didn't know the city, I did know that there were cyclists meeting us so we had no option. I left Jonathan and Midhat to discuss the details while I bought a drink from a local stall, hoping Midhat would get his head straight.

As we approached the Nile, the streets quietened and became leafier. It seemed a sleepy place, not a business district of glass and concrete but instead promenades and palaces. Tarred with the awful term 'rump state', Sudan has been left considerably poorer since South Sudan seceded in 2011. The opulence at the heart of its capital seemed at complete odds with the poverty and lack of infrastructure in the rest of the country, the obvious exception to that being the best road in the world which I had enjoyed for the past three days, thanks to the Chinese.

The cyclists were where they had agreed to be, and we carried on. The roads were now quiet enough to allow some chat, but the two local riders who spoke little English hung back. The youngster was meant to be a promising racer and the older rider was the club coach, but conversation was difficult. The third was an interesting-looking man, an Englishman called Nick who had long ago converted to Islam and taken the name Achmed Raman. AR, as he was introduced to me, may have been a similar age to Jonathan, but without the athletic shape, and he had a massive beard – a lihyah – that made him look every part a Muslim, although with sandy-coloured hair.

Nile Street led to Manshia Bridge and across the Blue Nile. On the outskirts of the city we all stopped. A safari-themed restaurant that only served meat was all we could find, but it's just as well we did stop to refuel as the road ahead was pretty empty. It was time to say goodbye to Midhat, Sami and Salah. The local cyclists turned back, as did Jonathan. But he promised to come after he had been to the hospital and meet me further down the road, as well as to pick AR up.

El Tayeb turned up. He was meant to have come straight from DHL with new tyres which had been sent out after the rip on day 1. They had arrived but were being held in customs. This was a blow. I knew the roads in Ethiopia were going to be much tougher and I had no spare.

Despite the recent strop, I was sorry to see Midhat go. He had been a huge help and had been with me for longer than I had originally planned. He had certainly loved the speed of this race, had been happy to do anything to help me and was rightly very proud of his country. Sami had been committed to the filming but fairly quiet, overshadowed by the gregarious Midhat, so while he had also been on the road with me for three days, I hardly knew him. The driver, Salah, even less so.

The road ran directly south-east to Wad Madani, 110 miles ahead. There were no turn-offs, no way to get lost. But Jonathan was keen to look after me and had asked Nick, aka AR, to stay with me for the next stretch. It was well meant, but I would have been better off alone. AR was undoubtedly a keen amateur but he wasn't very fit and nor was he a good bike rider. Rather than smooth constant pedalling he had that novice tendency to pedal for twenty to thirty seconds, then rest for a few seconds and repeat. This makes it very difficult to ride together. He wanted to go ahead, take the wind and help me along, which was kind, but he just didn't have the strength to keep the speed up. After 10 miles I nearly rode away from him, making my excuses that I had to go faster, but decided that despite the frustrating pace I could still make Wad Madani by nightfall, and I couldn't go further than that without having to camp.

So we pottered along for the next three hours, AR telling me about converting to Islam and the challenges he had faced because of his choices. It had taken a long time to be accepted by his wife's family in Sudan, but he now had a good life for himself. However, he eventually wanted to return to England. The problem he faced was being a white Englishman converted to Islam. His view was that it was much harder for a converted Muslim because any discrimination couldn't be put down to racism. AR had moved to Sudan long before 9/11 and he saw the changed global attitudes since then as essentially locking him out from working in his country of birth.

In just over 50 miles AR went through four bottles of water compared to my half a bottle. The plastic bottles that were stuffed into his back jersey pockets were finished one after another and thrown into the verge. This unconscious show of disrespect for his adopted country seemed at odds with the moral values he was advocating.

Jonathan raced past us in his 4×4 and pulled in to the side of the road. He'd brought with him a cool box filled with deli sandwiches and cakes. This was my first taste of home-style food in Africa and I relished every mouthful – such simple pleasures. AR didn't know about the scan so nothing was said on that subject, but Jonathan seemed in great form, which I took as good news. There were more chocolate macaroons than I could manage, so, hanging my helmet underneath the tri-bars, they became a basket of treats for the road ahead.

It was sizzling nicely around 42°C, the hottest day yet, but I was just relieved to be past Khartoum and out of the Sahara without having had to face the extreme temperatures I'd been worried about. Khartoum was my second big milestone. The roadside had changed from endless sands to patches of irrigated farmland or scrubby wasteland. And the road surface was considerably worse – not terrible on the scale of bad roads, but worn and used compared to the velodrome of smooth riding north of the capital.

It was wonderful to be alone and I sped up considerably, back up to the rate at which I had started the day with Jonathan. Shortly before Wad Madani the road turned to dirt, a section of a few hundred metres before a T-junction. It was my first glimpse of untarred roads and I rolled the bike gingerly around a queue of traffic. It was unclear which way to go. Pulling in front of a row of stalls, I asked a teenager if there were any hotels nearby. Beaming with pride in front of his friends, he jumped on his moped and shouted for me to follow him. We turned right, the opposite way from the road towards the Ethiopian border, back across a wide bridge over the Blue Nile and down a dirt track to the Imperial Hotel. All the while the young man rode alongside me, waving at a few bystanders, gleaning the most recognition possible from this important job. After I shook his hand with thanks, he pulled the throttle, skidded the back tyre around, and sped off. His juvenile exuberance and hospitality made me smile as I made my way inside.

The Imperial was very basic but roomy and functional. It even had wifi in reception. Its name suggested empire, but this concrete block definitely post-dated the British departure in 1956, even if it hadn't been updated much since. I had a busy evening of sorting ahead of me. Firstly, though, there was my first shower in Sudan, which was cold but welcome. The drainage barely worked so I had to shower in stages so that the flooded floor didn't overflow into the bedroom. Once the water had slowly seeped away I started again. I removed an amazing amount of sand from my hair.

When fixing my ripped tyre on day 1, I hadn't pulled off the two connector sleeves for the dynamo hub properly before taking the wheel off. This had caused one to break off, so I had no way to recharge batteries while riding. For nine days I had been reliant on using a small external battery pack to recharge the Garmin while riding. It was a system that worked so I was starting to doubt the need for the dynamo batteries and all the wiring that went with it. This battery system worked as long as I could get to a charge point every few days. The truck stop was the first night without any electricity. Apart from food, water and good rest, the fact that everything needed charging was another strong reason not to be stuck out in my tent. I had ambitions to get this small metal sleeve replaced, but not surprisingly there aren't many electrical or DIY stores in the Sahara . . .

Dinner was served in the hotel's huge empty restaurant. I seemed to be the only guest. I caught up online, sharing the stories since Abu Simbel. There was certainly growing media coverage of my race down Africa. The cycling press in the UK seemed to have been waiting for some evidence before promoting my ambitions. Nearing a quarter of the way down Africa, I was half a day up on my 150-mile-a-day target, and a long way ahead of Keegan Longueira's progress. I had only managed to put 25 extra miles into the bank that day, compared to the 75 miles extra each day over the preceding few days, but considering that I'd had to get through a capital city, and taking into account a few other delays, it was still great momentum.

Wandering into the centre of town, I found a supermarket packed with everything I could possibly need, an Aladdin's cave of choice after the roadside shacks of the north. I headed back to the Imperial while gorging on ice cream and a slab of chocolate, and then called Scotland.

Una had managed to get DHL to release the package and Midhat was back involved: he planned to pick it up and drive out and meet me on the road to Gedaref, the largest town before the Ethiopian border. It wasn't that simple, though, as Jonathan needed to be brought back into the loop to lend more money to pay for all this. It seemed a ridiculous expense and runaround for a couple of tyres, and I nearly cancelled the whole plan. I hadn't needed any spares since day 1. But the next possible pick-up point was in northern Kenya. After a bit of debate, caution trumped bravado.

Day 10: Wad Madani to Gedaref

The road to Gedaref ran almost due east, which meant I would be battling a headwind all day. The first 45 miles gave me some time to warm up tired legs as the road went south-east before facing the easterly tack. I was also climbing all day – nothing steep, but diverging from my friend the Nile, whom I had been with for a week. It would also prove to be the hottest day yet, which came as a surprise as I had assumed the heat would subside quickly as I left the desert and started to climb.

My main concern was water. By 8 a.m. the temperature was in the mid-thirties, and by ten it was well over 40°C. While I hadn't used it much, I no longer had the comfort of a filming vehicle nearby. To be safe, I stuffed extra bottles in my back pockets for only the second time on the ride. The rest of the Sahara I had managed with 1.5 litres of water on the bike, drinking lots when I could find it then rationing carefully between stops. It was camel-style riding, sitting on the bike, telling myself I could have a sip of water each half hour, and counting this down. This also gave me something to focus on. But as temperatures climbed over 40°C the discomfort intensified quickly. The roads just radiated heat. I would drink over 10 litres of water on day 10, well over three times the normal intake.

Heading away from the Nile, I was briefly back into desert for a number of hours, but this time the horizon was broken by rolling hills. On the bike, things tend to change gradually, but now, like a flipbook, the end of the desert crept up on me and then suddenly it was gone.

Bushes and stunted trees grew thickly along the roadside and for tens of miles I watched men, women and children working to cut them down. These scrubby trees looked parched and primed for a big wildfire. Maybe this was why they were being felled: this clearance looked too large-scale to be subsistence gathering for firewood. Quite a few men were working in balaclavas, which seemed insane in the soaring temperatures. Children, some looking younger than ten, balanced long branches on their heads, transporting the wood to massive piles. Women did this too but with bigger trunks and bundles; they also wielded axes and helped in the felling. I watched in awe, putting my own definition of a tough day's work into perspective.

The roads were much worse now, without any hard shoulder, so the coaches that had been a menace in the desert were now a serious risk. There were also a lot more of them. Twenty-two-wheeler lorries were also deserving of my utmost respect, but didn't match the coaches for speed and aggression.

As I reached the first hills and the road rose between them, I passed a village of roundhouses with thatched roofs. These earthen huts were of a very different build to the desert dwellings of the north, and the first of what I was expecting to find in Ethiopia. The scenery now had a rare and raw beauty. Rolling hills embraced boulder-strewn valley floors. As the day wore on, deep shadows moved across them. The sun had been so high and the world so flat, I hadn't seen many shadows in Sudan before now.

Supplies were more readily available than I had feared: every 50km or so there was something, a roadside stall or a garage. Omelette, rice, beans and bread sufficed at 66km and then again at 143km, topped up with biscuits. I hadn't realized how much I had been relying on Midhat to order food when we stopped, so it proved a challenge asking for what I wanted. Pots hanging over open fires – this was back to very rural life with poor infrastructure. There were some decent cars on the road, and a few expensive-looking buildings, normally brightly painted behind security walls, but life for the average person making a living from travellers by the roadside was very basic indeed. I liked their food, enjoyed watching it being cooked outside and in front of me. The simplicity of it and the wonderful flavours, mixing in a bit of spice with each mouthful, made these roadside meals the highlight of my day.

Twenty-five miles from Gedaref, I both smelt and saw an enormous camel market. There didn't seem to be much infrastructure here either – no ring, no buildings, just hundreds of animals in a well-trampled clearing in the trees. Others were being pushed along tracks on the roadside.

I then reached a massive sesame factory which gave off its own incredible but much sweeter aroma. It also gave me false hope that I was on the edge of town. But there was another gap between set-tlements and the wind was pretty fierce in the late afternoon, so I stretched myself over the tri-bars, tucking into the wind, and ground on. The turn-off to Gallabat and the Ethiopian border came before the town of Gedaref itself and a cheery traffic police-man, dressed all in white, assured me that there was nowhere along that road to stay. I had only covered 140 miles, but with nowhere to stay and no sign of Midhat yet, there was no sense in carrying on. Pedalling into the town instead of on my route south, I asked another policeman for directions to the El Motwakil Hotel, the only place Una could find online that had recommendations.

Midhat didn't arrive until 8.30 p.m., and despite my offer to stay was keen to turn around and do the five-hour drive back to Khartoum. He arrived just after I had finished a call-in with Radio Khartoum, a surprisingly liberal station. It was in English, so it was the station most expats listened to. The presenter had obviously spent his formative years watching American sitcoms: he was overenthusiastic in the very best way, an extrovert who had been given the airwaves in order to talk gibberish and amuse himself and others. He also had a sidekick, who was there to fill any pauses with similar excitement, so there was very little space left for meaningful answers. I spoke genuinely about what a wonderful welcome and experience I had had in Sudan, and of my wish to come back with more time to explore.

'You must do that, Mark, you will always be welcome as our guest,' the presenter enthused. 'Now before you go, we always try and bring the latest sounds to our listeners, the freshest music and new influences. Tell us what hip-hop you are listening to.'

'Ummm . . .'

Coincidentally Jonathan was listening to this interview back in Khartoum and he called me as soon as it was over, highly amused by my grappling for an answer to this off-the-wall question. He also confirmed that all was squared with Midhat, and wished me a safe onward journey. What a gent.

It was a late night after changing tyres, servicing the bike, charging and repacking. I had taken an hour before the radio interview to walk into town and get dinner. My hotel was near to the Animal Resources Bank, which I thought was an original name for a financial institution, and I headed over a railway line into some bustling market streets. I don't think I have ever seen so much livestock in the middle of a town, in particular donkeys, which seemed oblivious to the rest of the human, motorbike and vehicle traffic. Walking down the street was an obstacle course of moving things. It was alive and exciting, a reminder of the traveller's experience I was partially missing by cycling through places.

With two countries all but done, I sat over a plate of very spicy chicken studying the map of country number three, Ethiopia. After the meal and the interview I needed my torch to get back to the hotel, even though everyone else seemed to be doing fine without one.

Day 11: Gedaref to Maganan

Gedaref can also be spelt Al Qadarif, which is derived from the Arabic phrase Alli qada-Ye-rif, meaning 'He who has finished buying or selling should leave'. I only wish Scottish town names meant something so forceful. Just imagine if Glasgow meant 'Pick up your litter or flee!' Gedaref is surrounded by hills on three sides and still has a daily market, famous for its sesame seeds auction. It is now also a university city but best known as a trading post, the last stop-off or first port of call in Ethiopia.

It was 6km to backtrack to the road heading south and before leaving town I made sure I was well stocked up for the desolate stretch ahead. At 6.30 a.m. there wasn't much choice, but a small corner shop was just opening its doors and I bought some slightly stale pastries and drinking yoghurt for breakfast, which I enjoyed sitting on the dirt pavement surrounded by cats.

The road was narrower, without markings, and it was a gradual climb for most of the day. The road mix was a lot of stones and not much tar, with looser gravel embedded on top, so it was seriously rough going. Road surfaces make a massive difference to mean speeds. After being used to 30 to 40km/h averages throughout most of Sudan, I was struggling to make 20km/h now – slower than the day before, and I wasn't fighting a head-wind. It was also stiflingly hot without the familiar breeze.

After an hour I came across a big white V6 Toyota Prado parked right across the road, its rear wheel off, its axle resting on boulders. There was no one for miles around. It was a very strange sight, not because of the missing wheel, but because it had been left in the middle of the road. It hadn't been in a crash.

This was the first sign of the different world I was about to enter. A world with far less order.

The views were fairly uninspiring as I crossed small khors – tiny dry valley creeks – and passed dead-looking trees surrounded by tinder-dry bushes. In some patches the branches right up to the treetops were peppered with plastic bags and other rubbish, telling of windier days and more fly-tipping. But as the day wore on – and it was a slow mover – the trees got greener and the soil earthier, less sandy. It wasn't any cooler, but I was nearing the Ethiopian Highlands and this watershed was evident.

Some 20km before the border town of Gallabat, the road became perfect again, the fresh tar giving me a brilliant last impression of Sudan. I had entered the country with trepidation. As I often find, preconceptions can be wrong. Like Iran, Sudan for me stands out as one of those hidden worlds, distrusted and misunderstood yet with an exceptional tradition of friendship to travellers. Outside Khartoum people live a harsh life and this has bred a need to help each other. Granted, Sudan has dubious political credentials and, although covering 1.8 million square kilometres, is graced with few natural beauties unless you are into rocks and sand, but in my experience its people are wonderful. The tradition of hospitality is so ingrained, yet I didn't feel crowded, like in Egypt. Most of all I felt perfectly safe.

Just before 2 p.m. I came over a brow and descended fast into Gallabat, little more than a village, a few hundred metres of buildings before a very makeshift-looking border. There was a metal gate, but it was no more than you might find at a farm entrance, and the fence on either side of it was a wide lattice of uneven timbers. This was on a very different scale to the border in the north. The gate was lying open and at that moment a donkey was walking into Sudan pulling a cart that had car wheels with a cargo of an oil drum and a man sitting on the top. He looked a bit like an adult riding a kid's toy.

I needed lunch before going across so found the nearest restaurant and wheeled the bike inside. Land borders always make me nervous: they attract opportunists in greater numbers than anywhere else. Plastic chairs and tables on the dirt floor, a man standing by a selection of blackened pots in the corner. I tried to ask him for whatever he had but he walked off, coming back a minute later with his daughter, who was in her late teens. She looked very shy, but used to her role as translator. The only issue was that she barely spoke any English. I didn't want to spoil her father's illusion, so I persevered.

In the meantime a young man walked in, sat down opposite me and introduced himself in good English. This sorted lunch quickly, but I had already guessed the reason for his appearance. He assured me there was no bureau de change and he was the best option for exchanging money. I wasn't overly worried about this as I hoped to find a bank on the Ethiopian side, but it would have been daft to carry on with no money. While I ate, he sat and chatted away, giving me a bit of time to suss him out. I suspected that once I walked to the border I would meet ten of him and be trying to figure out the best plan at the side of the road. So I preferred the option of being seated inside before pulling cash out.

A quick call back to Scotland to check the exchange rates confirmed that he was offering a very good US rate but an absolutely lousy Sudanese one. The real rate was nearly 3.5 to 1 and he was offering 2 to 1. There was no budging on this, but I didn't want to be left with Sudanese money that I couldn't change outside the country so gave him all of it, but only a small amount of

US dollars. This is what he really wanted, but because he wouldn't give me a better Sudanese rate, I wouldn't give him more dollars. It was an enjoyable haggle.

Crossing the Sudanese side of the border was a three-part process, in separate buildings, but all very straightforward and quick. It was very useful to have the local to show me in which order and where these offices were. There was a 450 Sudanese pounds registration fee to pay, which was an odd thing to be doing on my departure. But I was lucky, as a few years earlier this would have had to be done within days of entering the country, meaning a trip to a government office and undoubtedly a delay. As I walked up to each building my money fixer held back, not wanting to be noticed. Approaching the border itself, I saw the gate was now shut and the young man once again hung back. For his help I gave him a $5 tip.

There were two men standing guarding the gate, except they had no uniform and no guns. I wouldn't have known they were officials at all if they hadn't beckoned me over. Even then I was sceptical that they might just be more self-appointed fixers and moneymen. The first explained in very broken English that I needed to take the bike up to another hut for a full unpack and kit check. Again, I really wanted to avoid this, and had my Speedos and dirty socks packed on the outside at the ready. But then the other butted in and started debating something. He broke into English for a few sentences to explain that he thought the rule for a full kit check was only for motorbikes, not bicycles. They continued their debate and I was left standing there, watching lots of pedestrians pass through the gate without any checks at all. After a few minutes they simply waved me through and I pushed the bike over the short strip of no-man's land into Ethiopia.

Parking the bike across the open doorway of the Ethiopian passport office, I stepped inside to be met with frowns of disapproval. A lady was sitting behind a desk, but a man was perched on a desk opposite with his shirt rolled up over his large, bare belly in an effort to cool down. It was very hot and an overhead electric fan was making a noise but spinning too slowly actually to create airflow.

'You can't put your cycle there,' he barked at me. 'Move your bicycle outside, this is a government office.'

'There are no thieves here,' he added as an afterthought.

You mean no one would steal from you – that was the obvious response, but I kept quiet and went back outside with the bike. It was out of my sight now so I kept returning to check it every few minutes, which I could tell was irritating the officials. There were too many people hanging around for my liking. Maybe this behaviour made me seem twitchy, untrustworthy, because they then had a lot of questions for me.

'Why is there no exit stamp from Egypt?' the woman asked a few times.

'I don't know.' I had no idea why, as the man had checked it in that dark office with Mohammed, shortly after the younger official had pocketed the cash. Why would Ethiopia care anyway?

'Where are you staying in Ethiopia?'

'I am cycling to Moyale' – I traced my finger across the map – 'and staying at towns along the way.'

'An address?'

'OK, use the address of a hotel in Maganan,' I suggested. 'I will stay there tonight.'

'What is the address?'

'I don't know, use any hotel in Maganan. I will be staying there.'

'No, I need an address.'

This went on for a few more minutes.

'I don't know any addresses in Ethiopia except a friend in Addis,' I tried. 'I can give you his address.'

'Are you staying there?'

'Yes,' I fibbed.

'Where is your guide book?'

I thought this was a strange question. 'I don't have one,' I replied. 'I'm racing through as quickly as possible. I'm going for the world record from Cairo to Cape Town.'

'What is your profession?'

'I am an athlete.'

'Professional?'

I paused. I didn't like where this was going. If I said yes and they started questioning my tourist visa, I could be in a tricky situation. 'No, amateur. This is my holiday.'

'But you don't have a guide book, a tourist book?'

'No, I don't.'

We were going in circles. I was fairly sure that a bloody guide book wasn't an entry requirement alongside a valid passport and visa.

She eventually took my fingerprints – an amazing bit of technology to find in this crumby office. All the time the man watched on, airing his tummy. There was a very odd dynamic between the two of them. They needed me to know I wasn't going anywhere before they said so, which is the same for any passport office, but this was more of a personal power play than a professional line of questioning. More fool me for placing my bike across their door.

After a non-existent customs check, I finally pedalled into Ethiopia. As with Sudan, first impressions were fantastic: perfect roads that gently undulated for the first 35km to Maganan. Arriving there at 5.30 p.m., I whooped in celebration at the sight of an ATM; the cash rationing and juggling in Sudan had left me very nervous. If Midhat's projections were right and there were no ATMs before Addis Ababa then I would soon be undoing my seatpost for the emergency supplies. I took out 1,000 bir,

and enjoyed that lovely moment of relief when the machine
started whirring. Being the biggest option on the screen, I
assumed a thousand was enough to get started. Further down
the road I did the conversion – £31. Back I went.

The next town where I could rely on a place to stay was Aykel,
over 100 hilly kilometres away. I pored over the map, my elation
of fast miles, a new country and securing finances quickly being
replaced with the frustration that I couldn't carry on. There was
nowhere to aim for by nightfall, and I wasn't going to attempt
camping. For another 20km gain it wasn't worth getting stuck
out in the open. Judging by the first 35km of Ethiopia there were
people every few metres. After the sparsely populated spaces of
Sudan, this now seemed like one big village.

The shotgun-wielding bank guard in Maganan suggested the
guesthouse next door, where I was given a room for the equivalent of £12 with dinner added on for a fiver. The guesthouse was
built around a small courtyard and seemed to be run by four or
five girls in their late teens or early twenties, a few of them with
toddlers running around. There were no men. It was so nice to
see and speak to women after not one in the whole of Sudan.
These girls were laughing, joking and utterly relaxed around me.

They served up a plate of meat that was beautifully spiced,
which took me back to my travels around the Commonwealth,
when Ethiopian Airlines had the best in-flight food on the continent. This was very promising; I was looking forward to a
break from omelette, rice and beans, if possible. I ordered a
second plate of meat. This dish was served with a thick crêpe
made from a sourdough grain. It was pretty odd in texture and
taste, something I would need to get used to. The girls mentioned there was an internet café across the street and I was
impressed again. The coffee turned out to be revolting and the
wifi wasn't working.

However, I returned to my room to hand-wash kit feeling

positive and excited about the road ahead. It had been by far my poorest mileage day yet, only 122 miles, which felt pitiful after the recent 225-mile days. But I was still well up on target and ahead lay the biggest mileage country of the entire route. The next week was crucial to get right, to keep up the momentum.

Part Four

Hard Miles

Day 12: Maganan to Addis Zemen

'YOU, YOU, where you go?'

The question was repeated thousands of times. I'd first heard it within metres of crossing the border, but hadn't taken much notice. Those first miles to Maganan were the honeymoon after my arrival, where nothing could spoil my excitement to be in Ethiopia, a country I had long wanted to explore.

'Hello, hello, what's your name?' was a common phrase from the roadside in Egypt and Sudan, especially from teenagers. But most people and all adults pretty much ignored me as I pedalled past. In Ethiopia, however, I was a star attraction; everyone stopped and stared. Many men and almost every child shouted at me: 'YOU, YOU, where you go?' It became louder and louder, repeated again and again if you didn't answer. How does an entire country learn just one phrase? Why ask a question you aren't going to understand the answer to? Why the explosion of interest, which often seemed to border on aggression? The question started to jar in my ears.

That first full day in Ethiopia was the toughest yet, by a long way.

The Gonder rise, a quaint name for the biggest climb on my route, started the moment I left Maganan and climbed over the

next 150km to an altitude of over 2,000 metres at Azezo by the
turn-off to the city of Gonder itself. The scenery was stunning,
and it just got better the further I climbed. But it was seriously
slow going, which made the torrent of shouting harder to bear,
and by the end of the day I was numb from it. Leaving Maganan
at first light, I had actually tried to answer the first shouts with
a cheery 'Addis Ababa!' but soon gave up.

In the first hour stones were thrown at me twice. I started to
dread the villages – it was cycling the gauntlet. The kids stared at
me as I approached, shouted at me as I drew close, then reached
for stones once I was past them; they weren't bold enough to
throw stones as I approached. It was a game, one they had
obviously played many times before.

I managed 17km in an hour, a distance that would have taken
twenty-five minutes in parts of Sudan, before reaching a small
village and going on the hunt for breakfast. A group of about
fifteen teenagers were on the road and inevitably shouted at me
as I passed. I kept my head down and ignored them, but also
spotted lots of people eating on the roadside. Stopping a hundred metres down the road, I considered if it was worth going
back. One of the teenagers ran towards me excitedly and I asked
him for the best place to eat. As soon as I engaged with the
group, they were friendly and welcoming. Their manner couldn't
have been more different. It wasn't practical to stop all the time,
but it was a relief to find that when I did stop, the aggression was
a show.

The chef was a slightly older man, with a huge wooden chop-
ping board and large curved knife, like a machete in reverse.
There was a deep indent in the middle of the board from countless strikes and he worked incredibly quickly, while chatting and
looking around. Each plate of breakfast was being prepared
individually, starting with a few cloves of garlic, mixed in with a
large pinch of spice that sat in a plastic dish beside him, then

beans. Another option was eggs, which were scrambled with a mix of spices as well. I was served quickly, as their special guest, and it tasted absolutely superb, so I went back for more. This second portion took longer, as there was quite a crowd now sitting or standing around waiting.

At the edge of the building was an overhang under which was a small pool table. The youngsters were playing a game in which they had to roll a pool ball by hand, first bouncing it off the side of the table. I couldn't figure out the objective, but the first guy who had run after me was keen that I get involved. I made my apologies, saying that I had to get back on the bike.

'You give me some money!' He held out his hand.

'Why?'

'Because I look after you.'

He hadn't made my breakfast. I had paid the man for that.

'No, but thanks for your help.'

'You give me sunglasses?' He held out his hand again as I went to collect my bike, which was leaning against the wall of the building. I wasn't sure if he wanted to try them on or to have them, although I strongly suspected the latter.

'Why do you want them?'

'Because I have a problem with my eyes.' At that he screwed up his face to demonstrate.

'These are the only ones I have, sorry, I can't give them away.'

It was funny, and it had been an enjoyable stop despite the initial trepidation. But this experience soon became very familiar. It is amazing what a border can do to attitudes. In Sudan I had left good-natured, hospitable people who often didn't want paying at all, but here in Ethiopia I very quickly realized that white people are associated with handouts, perhaps because of half a century of international aid and meddling in their affairs breeding a culture of expectancy. There was nothing malicious about it, but it entirely changed the way I could interact with people, because I was always wondering what they were after, and what they would take given the chance.

I could taste my breakfast for hours, and the mega dose of garlic made me thirsty. Climbing was hot work anyway, but the countryside remained stunningly beautiful. The trees and the buildings crowded the road; everything felt very close. The exception was the occasional dizzy view when the road clung to the mountainside, trees as far as the eye could see to a jagged horizon. Still winding upwards, I cycled under huge columns of rock and cliffs where the road had been cut into the mountain.

I had no idea that I was near the top when I decided to stop again, this time at a small shack. There was nothing else around. The front was partially open to the road, and inside there was only room for about a dozen people. A bus pulled up alongside as I left my bike on the verge, and an interesting group tried to get on it. There was one man with an entire dried animal hide hanging across his back, maybe a goatskin, which was baked hard rather than being supple. A few other men had hunting rifles slung across their backs. Four of the women had white chalk on their cheeks and noses painted in thick stripes.

'Could I have some food?'

There was silence. The two ladies who seemed to be serving looked at me blankly, and some men sitting around eating also stared at me. I resorted to charades. A man by the door, who was eating, eventually spoke up.

'No food,' he said.

I considered the scene. I needed food. I didn't want to leave my bike out of sight, but I needed to sort this. There was a door into the kitchen at the back, where it was very dark. I walked in to see what I could find. The older lady followed me, obviously uncomfortable with my being there. There were two big pots of food being kept hot on an open fire. I pointed at them, pointed at my tummy, and walked back out. Beans and sourdough crêpe appeared quickly. It was hard to eat because it was seriously untasty, but I was seriously hungry and had every bit of it.

It was a thrill to leave. I was ready to keep climbing for ages more but within fifteen minutes found myself on a sweeping, fast descent. Coming round one corner I encountered a massive herd of donkeys being driven down the road. I jammed on the brakes to pass them.

As the day wore on I got better at spotting water stops. In Egypt and Sudan they were obvious as most shops had open fronts. But here in the mountains, where it actually rained some-times, the wooden roadside shops were poorly advertised. I guessed they only really served locals who knew where they were. I must have had about eight bottles of fizzy drink – not at all good, but they were all I could find.

There were about half a dozen stone-throwing incidents that day, but only one serious attack when a man came out in front of me wielding a stick. I ducked around him faster than he could swipe, but I had to fight the urge not to turn round and confront him. Surrounded by a group of young men, he was just out to impress.

Other things had changed since the border too. Ethiopian fea-tures are quite different from the Sudanese, often tending to the willowy shape of the middle-distance runner. There were no more Arabic-style clothes either; most people I saw wore T-shirts and trousers, except up in the Highlands where I came across a few religious groups at the roadside dressed in white cassocks. Home-made bunting decorated their altars and they rang bells as people passed. Quite a few of the women had crosses tattooed on their foreheads. I took their bell-ringing as encouragement for the climb, like on the mountain stages of the Tour de France, and gave them a cheery wave as I passed, dripping with sweat. I was deriving a deep pleasure from getting stuck into a huge ascent after nearly a fortnight of flatlands.

After the Gonder turn-off the road relented slightly and started to loop south around Lake Tana. The source of the Blue Nile and the largest lake in Ethiopia, Tana sits pretty high at 1,800 metres – half a kilometre above the summit of Ben Nevis. The lake is littered with islands boasting exquisite monasteries and painted chapels as well as flamingoes – all pretty hard to imagine when you have witnessed the absolute poverty and hardship along the road around it.

To show just how far I had come that day, as I pulled into Addis Zemen it started to rain lightly. Rain! I couldn't believe it and stopped to look up and appreciate it, feeling the refreshing drizzle hit my face. I was very sore and tired, my legs felt tight, and even my upper body was weary from hauling itself out of the saddle. It had been a very hard-fought 140 miles with 3,500 metres' climbing, not much food and less than ideal hydration. But I felt all the better for winning that fight, especially standing at the edge of the road enjoying the rain.

The word 'hotel' can be misleading. It suggests a minimum standard, something more than a bed and a place to eat. Out the back of a restaurant – a name that once again suggests more than this place was – was a small courtyard of about six small rooms, each with sheet metal doors. The middle of the courtyard was junk and mud. Wheeling my bike in, I looked into the open doorway of one room and it seemed like people were actually living there. Mine had a bed, a wooden chair, cream walls discoloured with grime, a loose socket and a bare concrete floor. The toilet was at the end of the courtyard where there were no lights. The squat bowl was alive with maggots and reeked of shit. I have a pretty high tolerance for disgusting stuff, but this was very nearly too much. Going to the toilet by the light of my headtorch nearly made me sick. There was no sink or tap.

Sitting near the door on to the street, I ordered a bowl of meat and two bread rolls. Then the same again. I assumed it was goat and it tasted pretty good, but I was glad it was piping hot because health inspectors had never been to this dive. I enjoyed this time to stop, eat and write my diary. So much was happening so fast; each day was so full. Sometimes it felt like another day when I sat there scribbling about that morning. I noticed that the palms of my hands were red and bruised from the handlebars, but overall I felt strong, considering the accumulative mileage and time on the bike: over 130 hours' riding in the past twelve days.

Afterwards I stood on the street but under a canopy, enjoying the rainfall. Some men sitting at a table outside offered me a beer and a smoke, but I declined. Across the road in the dark was a bunch of trucks parked nose to tail. I watched three ladies approach and chat to a group of drivers, and realized they were probably working.

I fell asleep to the sound of rain on the tin roof above me. At 10 p.m. I woke to a knock on the door, a pause for a few minutes, some voices outside, and then another knock. I lay there, looking at the deadbolt lock on the inside, and said nothing, did nothing. The next thing I heard was my phone alarm at 5.30 a.m.

Day 13: Addis Zemen to Finote Selam

It ached to get started; my legs were seriously tight and I felt generally bruised and stiff. But there was also a deep pleasure in all that – the satisfaction of paying for a massive day's ride. At 6.26, as I started the Garmin and freewheeled out of Addis Zemen, I couldn't think about the next twelve hours in the saddle, but I could focus on finding breakfast – that was far enough.

It was further than I'd hoped, but thankfully a rolling and fast 30km to a very similar set-up to the day before. I sat on the street drinking very sweet black tea and eating eggs and spiced beans. This time I didn't cycle past the group of teenagers so they didn't have time to start shouting. Besides, the chap whom I asked for recommendations and who came with me spoke reasonable English. He was wearing two-striped Adibas tracksuit trousers and a Piere Carrot top – amusing rip-offs of the original brands. I bought him breakfast by way of thanks, but he didn't ask for anything and just chatted away to me or his friends. As a result I didn't feel such a goldfish in a bowl, which became the trend of the day. Breakfast for the two of us cost 20 bir – about a dollar.

As the countryside opened up, more arable than forested mountains, the houses were set back further from the road so there were fewer children and people around. I wondered if there was better school attendance as I got closer to central Ethiopia, and more employment. There were only a few flying stones, and I was going much faster today so I was a harder target.

Managing to get the Ethiopian SIM card from Anselm cut to size in the next village and topped up with credit for $2 made communications suddenly easier. Una was busy planning my meeting with Colin Cosier, an Australian cameraman based out of Addis Ababa.

The scenery of the Ethiopian Highlands was like nowhere else on my route to Cape Town, the least like the Africa of our imaginations, so I wanted to film this stretch properly. When it came to my own filming, I was struggling. The diary-style pieces to camera and self-filming of places and people had always been a big part of my journeys right back to the world cycle. But this time, while I had a Canon Legria Mini X and a GoPro Hero4, two tiny camcorders, to capture the story, I didn't have the time or energy to film – I'd taken only a few hours' footage in nearly two weeks. This made me worried about the documentary; but I kept reminding myself that there was to be no compromise, no forfeiting any miles for filming. I was not to leave myself looking back and regretting the fact that I could have gone faster. This mission was all about recording my absolute best.

The most important times to film are when the ride is toughest, but thinking back to the day before on the massive climbs and being tormented by kids, the last thing on my mind then was stopping and pulling out the camcorder. This showed what a completely different mindset I was in from the world or Americas cycles, where the filming had been as important as my progress across continents, sometimes more important.

The roadside views were changing quickly, not just with the more open, cultivated land but the settlements too. Buildings still featured mainly corrugated tin roofs and vertically stacked tree trunks for walls, like the jerry-built homes I had seen in the north, but here the houses were much bigger, more expensive-looking. There wasn't much grass growing on the arid soils so the Boran cattle – the breed with a hump on its shoulders and a wattle of loose skin below its neck – looked miniature from poor nutrition compared to their cousins in other countries. Huge stacks of hay lay beside some smallholdings for them to graze on, and hens seemed to be the other valuable commodity. There were very few fences, almost nothing to divide the land up. Pack donkeys, hauling huge hessian sacks strapped to their backs with thick rope that must have cut into their bellies, were herded along the road by men wearing plastic sandals, shorts and often colourful chequered shawls. Stalls selling local craftware started to appear, hundreds of them, mile after mile of the same products – animal-hair dusters, footstools made from cow's hide, and wicker baskets.

Arriving in Bahir Dar, the capital of the Amhara region, for lunch, I found a modern city with boulevards of palm trees along perfect roads, manicured and well-irrigated public gardens and monuments. Shanty houses hemmed in modern high-rise office blocks; expensive four-wheel-drives overtook donkeys and carts. The juxtaposition was amazing to witness. I found a restaurant – and this one really was recognizable as a restaurant – and sat down to a plate of spaghetti bolognese. Ethiopia is proud to be the only country in Africa never to have been officially colonized, but it was occupied by the Italians for a few years during World War Two, hence their cycling heritage and love of pasta. It was a wonderful break from beans and goat, and I ordered a second plate of heavenly carbs then sat out in the courtyard enjoying my first proper Ethiopian coffee, one that lived up to its great reputation.

At 6 p.m. I reached a cracking descent, a fast open road where I could actually let the brakes go, not worried about potholes or meeting unseen donkeys or people. Then I reached an unexpected T-junction. I had arrived in the town of Bure, my target for the night, a good half hour before I'd expected to. But the road to Addis Ababa went left, and the town was signposted right. I pushed the bike over to two policemen, who were standing doing nothing. They spoke no English at all and weren't willing to help.

Just as I was digging the map out to check my options, a young man dressed in a salmon-pink blazer walked over. His hair was gelled and he wore shiny leather shoes with pointy toes. An aspiring urbanite in the sticks, he was certainly making a style statement. He was very keen to help, and a crowd of about twenty was soon standing around me. 'There is a hotel twenty-five kilometres ahead,' he said in pretty good English, pointing left. Another man jumped in and told me there was one here in Bure, just a kilometre away. I asked which was better; it was going to be dark within the hour. 'Finote Selam,' the young man said, pointing the same way. This brought a chorus of disapproval from the spectators, and comments that I couldn't understand. I sensed that he was being chastised for his disloyalty to his own town. But I also sensed he was telling the truth, so I carried on, hoping for more descents, otherwise I would be riding into the night.

The road kept fairly level, gently descending in parts, and despite clocking over 150 miles it had felt like a recovery ride after yesterday's climbing so I put a bit more effort into this last 25km, keen to beat the falling darkness. The wind picked up and brought with it spots of rain, which were once again very welcome.

After a few small inclines I thought my luck was up when two teenage boys joined me from the dirt at the roadside on their bikes, and the road started descending again. I was freewheeling away from them when the closest yelled, 'Where you go?' This time I did answer, being in a much better mood and having not been shouted at with the same intensity since Bahir Dar.

'Finote Selam,' I shouted, pulling on my brakes. 'Do you know a good hotel there?'

'Yes, Damot,' one of them yelled as he caught up.

'How far is it?'

'Nine kilometres.'

I was impressed with both his knowledge and English. I kept feathering the brakes while he pedalled like billy-o to keep up.

'Are you going to Finote Selam?' I asked.

'Yes.'

I stayed alongside him for a bit, thinking it would be fun to cruise into town with him. Then his friend, who was a few metres behind, started yelling: 'Money, money, money! You, you, MONEY!' So I released my brakes to fading shouts of 'YOU, YOU' and freewheeled the final 7km into town.

The recommendation was useful as the Damot was certainly not the first hotel I came across. But it did seem in another league and cost a relatively pricey $20. This quality meant I could revel in having soap, a towel and a toilet seat. The only downside was a power cut that lasted most of the evening. The restaurant was full of NGO and charity workers. I sat there wearing my headtorch, surrounded by diners using their mobile phones for light, and considered my choices. Normal Firfir, Quanta Firfir, Meat Firfir, Special Shiro, Tegabeno and Shiro Bozena. None of this meant anything to me but I opted for the Special Shiro, which turned out to be a floury chickpea stodge but beautifully flavoured with chilli and tomatoes. It was served with the dreaded sourdough crêpe, which I now discovered was called injera.

I told the staff that I would be away before breakfast started so they gave me four hardboiled eggs and some bread to take to my room. There was even patchy wifi, so I stayed up later than I should have, trying to upload data. This was proving a real difficulty. The plan was to upload daily stats for people to follow and for Guinness World Records, but the reality was that I had managed this just twice, and only from my watch, not my main cycle computer. It was incredibly frustrating trying to get the data to upload and failing time and time again. I eventually gave up at 11 p.m. and went to bed, cheered by the news that Nicci had been for a check-up. I felt a million miles from home, but Nicci seemed to be getting through the unpleasant first trimester of pregnancy well.

Day 14: Finote Selam to Gohatsion

I woke with the glands in my throat very swollen and a cracking headache – a bit of dehydration judging from my pee. I was drinking as much fizz as water, which was disgusting but often the only liquid available. Four eggs later and I was on the road at 6.30 a.m.

Around each corner I was expecting to meet Colin Cosier, but he didn't appear until much later. I first spotted him filming me from a tripod positioned on the verge, so he must have driven past, spotted me, and gone up the road. I pulled up and shook hands with him and his Ethiopian driver, Antenna (I checked I had heard that right). Colin was my age, clean-shaven, with short brown hair and an athletic build. To be honest I was a bit annoyed as I was paying by the day and he was late. The original plan had been to meet the evening before.

Colin had a pretty good reason to be late.

On 19 April, while I was in Sudan, a video had emerged of twenty-eight Ethiopians and Eritrean Christians being shot and beheaded by people claiming to be a part of Islamic State in Libya. Three days later a massive demonstration took place in Addis Ababa against ISIS. Colin and his partner Kay had spent the morning at Meskel Square reporting on the rally, which at that stage was peaceful. After he left, it escalated into rock-throwing by the public and the firing of tear gas by the Federal Police.

He left the protest with a few other journalists and they were walking towards the Radisson Hotel when they noticed a group of women passionately chanting in Amharic. A couple of Federal Police were standing in the road and the chanting women were approaching them. Colin took his iPhone out and recorded twenty seconds of the event, alongside a couple of other bystanders.

Suddenly a Federal Officer grabbed him and started pulling him towards a park in the middle of an intersection, where a large group of police was gathered. He called out in English and Amharic that he was a journalist and tried to show his green press badge, but they took no notice. Three or four of them kicked him to the ground and beat him with their fists, feet and batons. One of the officers told him he was going to kill him. Scared and badly hurt, Colin lay there until one of the police ordered him to get in a car. He was then driven to the police station.

Later that day, the Commanding Officer agreed to let Colin

go, but not before he erased the video. Colin deleted it in front of him and then was told he was free to go, and also never again to show these things happening in Ethiopia. Luckily Colin's fellow reporters had seen him being detained and beaten so had been able to alert higher authorities to get him released. Antenna, the driver, had picked Colin up from the police station, stopped at his home to allow Colin to pick up some camera equipment, then driven north to find me.

The Blue Nile Gorge was now looming, where I would leave Amhara and enter Oromia, the largest of the country's nine regions by size and population and one in which I would stay, with the exception of a few miles, until the Kenyan border. To the east, the vast Somali region bordered both Somalia and Kenya. Beyond that lay the Horn of Africa.

The Blue Nile Gorge was also where I would leave the Abay Wenz, as the Blue Nile is called in Ethiopia, for the final time. It is the climb of Africa, the one that every cyclist had told me about, the one written about on blogs in reverential tones. I pushed hard all day in order to reach it, realizing I would be finishing the day with a plunge to the river, and then a climb back up the other side.

Over much of its length the Blue Nile Gorge is more than 1,500 metres deep, just as deep as the Grand Canyon of the Colorado river in Arizona. Like the Grand Canyon, the Blue Nile Gorge exposes sandstone, limestone, granite and old lava flows laid down over hundreds of millions of years. However, in many ways the Ethiopian gorge is the more intimidating. The river enters it near Lake Tana and then does not leave it for 250 miles, creating a vast obstacle to travel and communication from the northern half of Ethiopia to its southern half. And while many people have enjoyed rafting down the Colorado through the Grand Canyon, no one has ever floated down the Blue Nile and lived to brag about it.

Unlike the northern Highlands, there was no constant climbing, no prelude to the main event. Most of the day was spent riding through open, fairly parched farmland and through the town of Debre Markos before, without any warning, the earth opened up. Looking straight across the gorge, the land seemed to continue at the same level – a fairly flat horizon. But in between the road became gradually steeper until it disappeared into the abyss, a serpentine descent for nearly 14 miles.

The temperature steadily increased as I dropped into the vast canyon, which was in parts lushly vegetated, in others a muddy brown. It lacked the impact of the red Grand Canyon but had a similar grandeur. I had the GoPro on my helmet to capture the descent, which wasn't the fast, sweeping alpine one I had hoped. The tarmac was deeply folded and rutted, caused by trucks slowly labouring their way down in the heat. I passed quite a few of these trucks when there was a clear stretch. It must be a terrifying drive, using engines to save brakes from overheating, often clinging to the edge of the narrow road with its sheer drop and no chance of a safe run-off. The ruts could be ridden along, avoided with care, but the folds in the road – just lumps of tar barring the way – were a real menace. I flew over a lot of these, jumping the bike as best I could if I spotted them late; but the bike was not built for this cyclo-cross course. When I did pick up a bit of speed, certain it was a smoother section, I came around a blind corner and straight into two donkeys. They didn't even flinch as I swerved past them. Colin and Antenna were trying to keep up in the Land Cruiser, and they saw the close miss, which we laughed about at the bottom.

The main canyon was a myriad of intersecting box canyons and tributaries so it wasn't straightforward; the road picked an elaborate route of least resistance. It was a half-hour, hair-raising descent. My arms were sore from the bumpy ride and constant braking, but it was wonderful. Just before the bottom I let the

Land Cruiser past so Colin could film from a bridge. Halfway across the span of this huge concrete structure sat a soldier, right on the edge, dangling his feet over the giddy drop to the river.

The road cut left as soon as it hit the far bank and started climbing. I stopped alongside the vehicle where half a dozen soldiers were sheltering from the sun in a small wooden shelter. They were going through Colin's paperwork, and for a man who had been so mistreated by the authorities he was wonderfully cheery. I realized they could make our lives very difficult for filming the bridge.

From 2,440 metres I had descended a kilometre and a half – nearly a mile – and the southern side of the gorge rose back up to 2,550 metres. This took me just over two hours' constant climbing – the third fastest ascent on Strava (see Appendix 1), and I would like to think the fastest while carrying kit. As I climbed, the sun started to sink and the colours of the world turned autumnal, until I could look back down to where the river snaked into the distance as if it were a flow of molten lava.

The air was still and baking as I sat deep in my saddle, pouring with sweat, spinning my lightest gear. When it steepened and my legs started screaming I rose out of the saddle for a few minutes, gently rocking the bike. Halfway up was a small town where I stopped briefly to get water, and the road flattened slightly for a few kilometres after that – a blissful break. There was also the odd small cluster of houses, and inevitably groups of children on the roadside. What an unbelievable place to live. Unlike elsewhere, they seemed to have some respect for the challenge and remained silent. A few even cheered me on sportingly. On occasion I looked up and could see sections of my road far above, so it was best not to look up. Nearing the top, I could turn and see ribbons of tar a very long way below me.

The Land Cruiser, which had struggled to keep up with me on the descent, now kept jumping ahead as I didn't want to be sitting in its exhaust fumes. Colin took to sitting on the roof rack, filming down on the gorge and me. Energy-sapping and seriously tough, it was one of the hardest roads I have ever climbed. The broken tar, the unrelenting gradient and the heat, the sweat making my eyes sting – it was glorious.

191km was only 119 miles and my slowest day yet at an average of a pitiful 10mph, but I didn't mind. It was such a massive milestone to get past the Blue Nile Gorge. Besides, I had loved it and was on a complete high. Colin was also thoroughly enjoying the adventure and was delighted with the footage he'd got.

Just over the brow of the gorge we reached the town of Gohatsion, and found a small hotel for the night. By this time it was getting dark. A teenage boy was sent to carry two buckets of water up to my room for me to wash, which Colin thought would be funny to film. I had to leave my cycling shorts on for this television event, but it was still blissfully refreshing after such a slog.

Sitting outside with a plate of k'it k'it, a broth made with bones and meat, and some bread, Colin and I had a chance to meet properly. That was when I heard the full ordeal of his last forty-eight hours. I watched him enjoying a cold beer, and despite every intention not to drink until Cape Town I couldn't resist the celebration – two weeks on the road, and now the mighty Blue Nile Gorge. It tasted absolutely stunning.

I woke a few hours later and rushed to the toilet to be sick. My stomach was rejecting absolutely everything it had in it. I managed to fall back asleep, feeling better, but woke twice more to be ill again and lay awake for quite a while.

Day 15: Gohatsion to Bishoftu

At 5.30 a.m., when my phone went off, I felt seriously rough and brushed my teeth to try to get rid of the taste of sick. I then sat on the bed and forced down a packet of biscuits. Half an hour later when I stepped out it was first light and surprisingly chilly, thanks to the altitude. I carried the bike downstairs and out on to the pavement. Colin appeared, and one look told me that he had been ill as well.

We were a subdued party to start with. Riding was grim, mainly because I felt so weak, but also because of the continuing discomfort in my stomach and the need to keep stopping. Mentally it was the lowest I had been, even though I knew this was just the hangover from a massive day and being ill. I really struggled to focus on the bike as I worked towards Addis Ababa. More hills, more parched farmland, and the day got busier and more developed as I neared the capital.

In Chancho we stopped to get some lunch. I had no appetite but really needed to eat. Antenna, being local, was asked to order but was told that they weren't serving, and to look elsewhere. We were already sitting inside, opposite a bar where a television was showing the news. This was not a mountain shack where they might only be looking after locals. Antenna accepted their word and suggested we go. I stood up, took the young waiter by the elbow with a smile, and firmly walked him through the back to the kitchen. It was very dark and in the corner food was being prepared in huge black pots.

A few minutes later a plate of tibs – cubed, spiced mutton meat – and some injera arrived, much to Colin's amusement. It was clear now that they just couldn't be bothered to serve foreigners or white people. I brushed over the previous setback and thanked the waiter profusely, making a fuss over his efforts. It turned out to be very good food.

Colin, to my surprise, turned out to be a big fan of injera and spent some time telling me how this miracle food was high in iron, calcium and protein, while being gluten-free. It's made from the world's smallest grain, called tef, a hardy grass that has become a staple of Ethiopia and Eritrea. I needed over 6,000kcal so forced it down, but it was food for fuel not for pleasure. The tibs on the other hand was delicious, but I thought there was a good chance that I would just be sick again. I certainly couldn't finish the plate.

I felt better as the afternoon wore on for having some new fuel in the system. But I spent the day producing the most revolting eggy burps – proof that my gut was rotten and struggling to cope with whatever had turned it.

The road was very hilly, but nothing steep, just long gradients across burnt yellow landscapes. Small enterprises dotted the roadside for many miles, the first suggestions of a major city ahead. Among the fabricators and vendors were odd pockets of tourism like the Paarki Haniimuun Honeymoon Park, which was advertised on a sign donated by Pepsi-Cola. A light-pink painted wall surrounded by rubble was the welcome for newly-weds (or possibly newly-mets) to this low breeze block hotel.

I had been warned about a serious climb before Addis and then a nosebleed-inducing drop into the city. The first, thank-fully, proved an overstatement. However, what didn't help the climb was my derailleur not working. The rear mech moved over without issue, but the front wouldn't move. At first I worried that this was a serious break as I couldn't possibly have worn the battery flat in fifteen days; the Di2 is meant to do ten thousand shifts. But as I climbed, I reassured myself that with the extreme heat and constant use the battery was probably to blame. I didn't check till past the top so had about an hour of quiet concern.

As the road ascended it came into a thick forest, a wall of nature on the hills above Addis to hem in the pollution. It was the first managed forest I had seen in Africa and I could imme-diately have been on another continent; it reminded me of roads on the Continental Divide in the US. Long before the top I reached traffic, which was nose to tail. I enjoyed pedalling past cars and lorries that had passed me miles before. Colin and

Antenna were caught in this jam. Near the top I came to the reason for it: a military checkpoint where some vehicles were being waved through, others stopped and searched. They waved me through, but I waited and waited while the Land Cruiser was stopped and everything was unloaded and searched. Colin had all the correct paperwork, but with professional cameras he was inevitably made a fuss over.

The long delay gave me time to completely unpack my seat bag and find the gear-charging unit – something I had hidden well as I thought I would never need it. In fact I'd even entertained the notion of not bringing it at all. Running this by USB from the external battery pack, my gears immediately started working again. What an incredible relief.

Shortly after the checkpoint, the trees cleared to reveal a smoggy vista across Addis Ababa to my south, endless buildings to a hazy horizon. We had two choices to get past the city: straight through downtown or the ring road. The latter option was further and Colin wasn't sure whether bicycles were allowed on it. Downtown would be more direct, but during Friday rush hour could be one long line of traffic. While it would be ideal to film the city, I would likely slip through much quicker than the vehicle; the chances of being able to stick together were slim. Considering the lax laws on road use in most of the African continent, I decided to risk the ring road. The attitude of 'do it anyway and act surprised if you get stopped' can get you a long way. And a small amount of baksheesh can smooth over most minor misdemeanours. Ethiopia is not somewhere you can get fined for jaywalking.

Traffic or not, the Land Cruiser still struggled to keep up with me. The initial descent was indeed frantic and fast, and then I turned right on to the ring road and after a kilometre of following the contour around the hillside it bore left and back downhill. The next half hour was an absolute blur and pretty dangerous, but a huge amount of fun. The dual carriageway kept dropping into the ground, allowing the roads into the city to bridge over-head. High walls on each side bounced around the noise and pollution from countless trucks and cars. I sat at over 50km/h, swinging wide into the middle lane and overtaking truck after truck. The air was thick with fumes. I was almost certain that bikes were not meant to be on this road, but it was certainly a fast way of bypassing the capital. The skyscrapers of downtown and the concrete office blocks and flats closer by kept coming in and out of view whenever the road surfaced and wherever I could glance away from the road ahead. It was like being in a real-life Mario Kart.

By the time I rejoined the main road through Addis I was south of the city and back into an industrial and retail area. But even from here I could see the juxtaposition of skyscrapers, boulevards and also huge swathes of slums. Addis Ababa is a modern city with an ancient heart, built around Addis Mercato, the largest open-air market in Africa, but has many of the con-tinent's social challenges.

The road out of the city was much flatter. Somehow, incred-ibly, Antenna had kept up. Colin reported that he had been driving like a lunatic to keep me within sight. The road remained rough, with long sections of roadworks and parts where the dirt verge became another lane. The congestion was intensified by the ubiquitous belching Chinese trucks.

Antenna knew of a decent hotel only a few hundred metres from the mayhem of this artery road, perched on the edge of a volcanic lake about 15 miles south-east of Addis Ababa. After 240km – exactly my 150-mile target – we pulled in. Given my weakness that day, and the fact that I'd made my way across another major city, this total was a resounding success. I felt a combination of ecstasy and queasiness. I was also absolutely caked in pollution, my face as if it had been smeared in dirt. It didn't bear thinking about what I had been breathing in.

It was an idyllic place. The balcony of my room and that of
the restaurant overlooked the huge crater, which was lush with
trees and vegetation. The smoggy city was out of view and immediately out of mind. However, there was only one room left, so
Colin and I were sharing. I felt sorry for him considering I was
still not well. Then again, he wasn't much better. Whatever we
had shared had not been fit for human consumption.

I managed a small amount of dinner, but was sick again afterwards. In normal circumstances this would have been the right
time to stop, recover, probably take a day off. But there was little
time to unwind. Colin was leaving in the morning and there was
work to be done backing up all the footage and, just as importantly, the Garmin GPS data. This, as I said, had been planned
as a daily system of uploading over telecoms, but everything had
so far failed, and trying to use flakey wifi to get all the data away
was both time-wasting and frustrating. I also discovered that
both devices, the bike unit and watches, were nearly full. Within
a week I would have no means to collect new data. This was a
surprise and an issue, so I had to back up and clear the memory,
which sounds like a ten-minute task but kept me up until midnight. I was shattered as I crashed out, setting the alarm for 5.30.

Day 16: Bishoftu to Leku

Inevitably I felt pretty rough and sleep-deprived in the morning.
My backside and hands were painful, and my guts were really
struggling. I had diarrhoea and I felt exhausted. But there was
much to look forward to. I was now south of the Highlands, past
Addis, and with a big three days planned to get to the Kenyan
border. That schedule was more important than ever as I was
meeting a security escort at Moyale to see me through the
dangerous northern region of that country.

After just 15km I punctured, on the back wheel. It should have been a ten-minute fix, but in my tired, rushed state I unpacked, took the wheel off and then put the same inner tube back in. For ages I couldn't figure out what the issue was. On any normal day on the bike I would have had the cognitive skills to realize my stupidity and laugh about it. But I got more and more irritated by the crowd of silent onlookers, and my inability to fix a simple puncture. 'Thanks for all your help,' I jibed at my onlookers who by then had been standing over me for the best part of an hour. I had lost my sense of humour altogether as I packed everything up and got going.

Back on the road my left knee was twinging – nothing serious, but enough for me to try to protect it, ride carefully. After an hour the capital city was but a distant memory and Colin was able to film me cycling through a very different landscape. Known as the Lake District of Ethiopia, the scenery south of Addis Ababa was progressively more verdant, almost tropical. We stopped for breakfast at a decent-looking hotel and I managed to keep down an omelette and a pile of toast. Grateful that my appetite was returning, I quickly began to feel better. In fact, I had literally got back my Mojo – bizarrely, this was the name of the place!

Surrounded by middle-class families from Addis with immaculate waiters in shirts and ties, I was also acutely aware of how disgusting I now looked. My lycra was stained with grime, and given that I could smell myself, I imagined I smelt far worse to them. Apart from my returning appetite, I also celebrated the first decent wifi in Ethiopia and managed at last to upload all my data. Jason Waghorn, my tech guru back at home, was taking care of all this, but he needed me to send it all across. This may seem like an odd obsession, but I was worried about world record verification and needed to prove my progress. I was about to head into another barren stretch for communications so this would likely be my last update for over a week.

After Mojo, and the turn off to Kenya, the road continued to drop steadily south and into the Rift Valley, a flat plain broken only by occasional hills on the horizon. It was effortless riding, the perfect recovery spin after illness and hills. After a while, Colin and Antenna turned back and I carried on, spirits soaring, my energy returning. The first 170km of the day were downhill and I happily cruised along at 30km/h. Still, for all this descending, it was gradual and I was still at 1,600 metres.

A few miles outside the town of Shashamane I saw a sign with Bob Marley's face on it. Colin had told me all about this community, and while determined to push to make at least 150 miles, I planned to stop and see for myself.

In reggae mythology, Africa and in particular Ethiopia is the Promised Land. In 1948 Emperor Haile Selassie I made a substantial land grant to accommodate, for free, any Caribbean of African descent who wanted to 'come home to Zion'. 'We're leaving Babylon, we're going to our fathers' land,' Marley sang. A wave of resettlers in the sixties and early seventies created the town of Shashamane. Bob even visited, albeit briefly, in 1978.

But language and religion were just some of the barriers stopping this new community from integrating into Ethiopia. Haile Selassie and the monarchy were violently overthrown in a coup in 1973. The Derg, the communist regime, then fell to rebels in 1991 and a new federal republic was declared in 1994. During this period anything connected to Selassie fell out of favour and the Rastafarians of Shashamane were persecuted, much of their land reclaimed. Despite enduring these tough decades, no repatriates have ever been granted citizenship or even an identity card. So despite all the prophetizing and singing about the 'movement of Jah people', this probably amounted to a peak of a few thousand people, many of whom didn't stay. This little island of Rastas was a community at odds with the rest of Ethiopia but all the same very peaceful and spiritual.

The main road through town seemed like any other in Ethiopia, with lots of rickety wooden stalls, except these were far more colourful, painted in the red, yellow and green Rasta colours. The scooter taxis were also painted psychedelically, Bob Marley adorning many of their plastic back windows.

'Hey, wa gwaan!'

This was just about understandable as a greeting of 'What's up?' The youngster was exactly as you would expect: sunken cheeks, a lock of dreads halfway down his back, and wearing a T-shirt made for a man twice his size. I could make sense of most of what he was saying, but it was a strain. It was listening to a version of English but only understanding half the words.

'Good, I am good, thanks. How are you doing?' I shook his hand.

'Mi nuh have nutten fi complain bout, mi life irie,' he replied, or words to that effect (I jotted down the gist of our conversation afterwards).

After a few more pleasantries I asked him where he was from, interested after my journey around the Commonwealth and through the Caribbean nations.

'Mi baan inna yah,' he replied. Of course he was born here; it must have been his parents who came from the Americas.

He asked where I was going and I explained from Cairo to Cape Town, for the world record, so far at 250km a day.

'Wah!' he exclaimed. It was a succinct and heartfelt response.

Ours was a difficult conversation, and while I wanted to ask more, I needed to find some food.

'Sum high class?' he said, pulling a small bag of grass out of his trouser pocket and holding it at his side rather than towards me, not wanting to make the offer too public. This wasn't some cheap resin but a bag of buds, enough for a big pile of spliffs.

'No thank you,' I laughed, 'that won't make me ride faster. But it could help with the pain!'

He laughed at this, sensing a possible sale.

'No, I am good, enjoy,' I added, drawing a line under the conversation and pushing into the road.

'Me a go,' he shouted, which I thought was odd, considering he wasn't going anywhere.

'Thanks, goodbye,' I yelled back, enthused and amused by our brief chat.

I did find some lunch, but no one else as chatty, so I never got to delve any deeper into the life of a Rasta in Ethiopia. While a weed-peddling youth wasn't the best ambassador for their community, I enjoyed the honesty of our chat. Weed is illegal in Ethiopia, although I guess the authorities have bigger issues to worry about.

Shashamane was a fun town to ride through; I admired the graffiti, the Rasta symbology and the obviously laid-back way of life. Nobody yelled at me here. No stone-throwing either. It's not a place where I imagine much happens except music and love and smoking. How odd it must have been to return to their motherland, only to build their own enclave, to be shunned from society and to live a world apart.

By the time I reached the lakeside town of Awassa the fast afternoon miles had drawn me into an optimistic mindset. Colin had said this was where the moneyed middle classes of Addis holidayed and that it would be the perfect target for the day. Except it was only 5 p.m. and I had covered 140 miles. I wheeled slowly past quite a few entrances to some very luxurious hotels and manicured driveways to properties on the shores of Lake Awassa. But I couldn't make myself stop. At the pace I'd been going I could just about close the gap ahead and reach the town of Dilla, 50 miles on. It was ambitious, considering my churning gut, but by projecting the same speeds from the day so far I knew I could make it by dark.

A few miles south of Awassa the road ran out. A track dropped on to the dirt on the right-hand side and ran parallel to it; huge piles of earth and tar were piled on the main road where they were rebuilding right from the foundations. I picked my way along the track at 10mph. It was jarring, a construction road instead of a well-graded dirt road, with lots of rocks.

Tttttssssss. Puncture. My front tyre rolled flaccidly over the stones, which is a horrid feeling: you fear the rim getting damaged. I was still in buoyant spirits, though, and set about changing this quickly. Bike propped against a dirt-coloured house, within minutes I had a crowd of children and youngsters watching, not coming close but standing back and shouting 'Where you go? Where you go?' As I worked away, bent over, pumping up the new inner tube, a few stones came clattering across the dirt. They were poor throws but all the same I was a sitting duck and I lost my cool. Dropping the wheel, I scooped up a handful of gravel and flung it at the group. They ran off shrieking in excitement, into doorways and behind buildings. But within seconds they were creeping back, and then the shouting started again. I regretted fuelling this aggression and this time stuck to the task, ignoring the next few stones that came my way.

Soon after starting off again, ignoring the parting taunts of the teenagers, it started to rain. Steadily to begin with, but gradually with more intent, until the fine dirt across the track was turned to a greasy layer of mud. The 45km to the next town was now impossible. It was gone 6 p.m. and a look at the map, which was soggy and starting to disintegrate at the folds, told me there wasn't anything promising. I regretted not having stopped in Awassa. I could have been in the lap of luxury right now instead of crawling along a dirt road in the rain and gathering dusk.

The dirt road eventually bumped back up on to the tar and I could speed up. While there wasn't anything on the map, I was constantly passing houses on the roadside, and there were people everywhere. As the drizzle continued and I pushed on as fast as I could, feeling a growing nervousness about where I would end up, two motorbikes started following me. Each of them carried three people, the driver and two passengers, so the little 125cc frames sat heavily. Each driver wore a jacket back to front to shield himself from the rain and all six youths looked too young to be driving. They buzzed around and behind me for a while, then came alongside, very close. They didn't shout, didn't look for my attention, but all of them, especially the four passengers, stared at me, talking to each other.

After fifteen minutes of this I was getting worried. It would soon be dark and this unsmiling bunch had latched on to me for some reason. None of them was wearing a helmet so I could see their expressions clearly. I was thinking about stopping and confronting them on my terms, in a friendly but firm manner, rather than being followed into the darkness. But before I had found an open public place in which to do this, they opened their throttles and buzzed off. I was left wondering what it had all been about. A minute of ogling from youths on motorbikes is common enough when you are pedalling your bicycle across the planet, but these guys had been with me for a good while. Still, they were gone, so I got back to worrying about finding a bed.

Reaching a small village, I spotted three policemen in the road and stopped to ask about options. The youngest of them spoke surprisingly good English and explained that I could go 3km off to one side for one hotel or 24km ahead for another. A few hundred metres ahead I could see the road once again turning into a construction site.

'How far do these roadworks carry on for?' I asked, expecting an answer in kilometres.

'Until the border, until Kenya.'

My heart sank. That was nearly 500km. It was the start of the rainy season and the Ethiopians had decided to redo this entire trunk road in one go. None of my research had flagged this because even Keegan Longueira, a few months earlier, had had

Above and left: After the perfect empty desert roads of Sudan, my first impressions of Ethiopia were of greenery, mountains and crowds of people. Then there was the surprise of finding terrible construction roads.

Below: Sharing dirt roads with the locals and their donkeys. Wonderful scenes of everyday life as I pedal furiously south.

Above and left: One of the many stunning Ethiopian mountain views before a hair-raising 1,500-metre, 14-mile descent into the Blue Nile Gorge.

Below: Plastered in diesel fumes after pedalling through Addis Ababa.

Above: Colin Cosier was great company and a superb cameraman, but we both suffered from food poisoning.

Above: I wish I could have stayed longer in the Rastafarian town of Shashamane, but my overall impressions of the crowded, congested, partly built Ethiopian roads were unfortunately not the best (**right**). Seriously hard miles.

Above: Battling through the torrential afternoon downpours and nursing the bike over the muddy, broken roads of northern Kenya (**right**).

Below: The company of local Kenyan police and Saladin security, a necessary precaution in these troubled parts.

Right and below: Multiple punctures every day and a bike that struggled to cope in the clay-like mud were made worse by my getting ill from the dirt-caked water bottles.

Right: The equator at Nanyuki was an important mid-way milestone and a busy tourist trap.

Below: A typical lunch stop, this time at the 'Modern Hotel', with a goat wandering around my bike whilst I tucked into goat stew and rice inside.

Above: New chain and repairs after managing to get supplies through the customs red tape.

Above: The roads in Tanzania were progressively better, but I didn't want to take this dirt one to Dodoma, thanks to the sound advice from Joshua Malanda, who then became a very welcome domestique (**right**)!

Above and below: The African roads are littered with constant reminders of the risks, with the aftermath of accidents, as seen here in Ethiopia, Tanzania and Zambia.

Left: My first plate of chips! A welcome change of cuisine in Tanzania.

Below: Chapattis made to order for breakfast. People in roadside communities were incredibly welcoming and kind.

Below: Unidentified goat offal and offcuts served up in Zambia, as well as the Scottish-inspired EET-SUM-MORs.

tarmac roads. The dirt wasn't meant to start until Moyale on the Kenyan border.

Focusing on the pressing matter at hand, I couldn't cover another 24km, which would take nearly two hours at my current speed (it would have been forty-five minutes at this morning's pace!). So as much as it pained me to do so, I turned off and did 3km in the wrong direction to find a bed. The road soon dropped into a valley for a cracking descent, every second of which I was thinking I would have to climb back up it in the morning, so I didn't enjoy the proper thrill.

The out-of-the-way village of Leku is not used to foreign travellers. As soon as I stopped on the dirt road on the only main street, a crowd of maybe thirty people surrounded me. I asked everyone where there was a hotel, and there was unanimous silence; they just stared at me. I wheeled my bike through the crowd and they shuffled after me. At that moment a tall, well-dressed man around my own age stepped forward and asked what I wanted. He introduced himself as Ayele Lanokomo.

'Come on, I will show you, you must be careful around here,' he said, leading me towards a large metal gate which an elderly guard was sitting behind. He slid this open and I was shown into a bare concrete courtyard with six simple rooms along one side. The first had no electricity and the second had no light; I agreed to pay for them both so I could charge things. They cost less than $5.

As I was wheeling the bike in, three policemen turned up. My arrival had obviously been heralded. They wanted to check my bags and take away my passport. 'No, you can't,' I told them. 'You can look at my passport here if you want.' I was losing my patience with all the unwanted attention. I stood with a stern look on my face in the doorway, making it clear they couldn't see the bike and kit. They obviously weren't used to being refused and weren't sure what to do. It didn't help that they didn't speak any English and were relying on Ayele to translate. He clearly wasn't enjoying being the middleman, being friendly to me but trying to be respectful to the police. I handed over my passport and they spent a few minutes thumbing through it, obviously with no idea what they were looking for. I took it back off them and found the Ethiopian visa page to show them. They looked at it, took no notes, talked some more, wasted some time. I eventually lifted it out of their hands, without snatching, thanked them, shook their hands firmly and said goodbye – before they could make any response. They stood there, looking unsure, then shuffled off.

Ayele said the only place to eat was right next door and invited me to join him. I agreed to do so after washing. There was no shower but I poured water out of an oil drum into a bucket and used a plastic jug to rinse my legs and arms, which were caked in mud. The toilet area had no lights and was stinking, so I washed quickly under my headtorch.

Ayele was sitting with a friend by a very dark table. I would have used my headtorch again, but they seemed perfectly happy without light. He explained that he was a government official, in charge of marketing for the region. His friend, an older man, spoke no English, so stayed silent for the meal.

Inevitably the conversation soon turned to families, and Ayele explained that he had a daughter the same age as Harriet, and that his brother now lived in Seattle. He showed me pictures of him on his phone.

'The US have a programme where they accept fifty thousand people a year from Africa,' he told me. 'You can apply and are given permanent citizenship after some years. You are set up with a new home, a job and a new life. He has been there for seven years now.'

'Have you been to America?' I asked. 'Would you like to take your family there?'

'No, I have never been, I will never be able to afford.'

'And have you seen your brother?'

'No. I hope one day his family will come back to visit, God willing.'

He carried on: 'Why does your country not do this as well? You are from a rich country?'

'I honestly don't know what my country does like this,' I explained, feeling as if I was being held to account for the UK's immigration policy. I moved the conversation back to his job and family. The church was at the heart of his life and as it was Sunday the next day, he invited me to join them.

Ayele hadn't asked for anything from me and had given me a warm welcome, so I bought dinner for the three of us. Afterwards he took me to a few local shops where I could buy a new plug and some food for breakfast. Then he walked me back to the guarded gate and advised me not to go out again that night. I had no intention of doing so, not least because I was in need of as much sleep as possible.

Day 17: Leku to Gedeb

Day 17 started with breakfast in bed, as usual: four packets of biscuits, a Red Bull to wake up and some painkillers. This excerpt from my diary gives a concise and accurate summary of the rest of the day:

142km in 12 hours and 2229m of climbing. Nightmare day. Back up at 2550m! Tons of climbing, which I hadn't expected. They are digging up the entire road to the border. Made 70km by lunch – crawling along and worried about bike and tyres. Had 2 pinch punctures – after half an hour and one before lunch. Put spare (old back) on front as more tread. Bought pile of raw meat for lunch, which I sent back. At 4pm heavens opened – huge thunderstorm. Children and youths a real pain today – worst yet, or maybe I am just going slow enough for them to terrorize more. Some kids nicked my arm sleeves and cap off the back of my bike. Got a stick on back of my head, which bled. Quite a lot of stone-throwing. Crowds when I had a puncture and stopped. Some boys quite aggressive. Made it to Gedeb at just gone 6pm. Just before here I ended up walking with the bike across a number of fields, carrying the bike to find road (so much mud and construction chaos). Helpful kids showed me the way but then wanted to be paid. Bike caked in mud.

Despite it being a serious effort over twelve hours, 88 miles was a disaster, my average speed just 12km/h (7.5mph). Some people could run this distance quicker.

With the first puncture I found a house on the other side of the track which had a small overhang, enough room in the dry to work away. It wasn't raining any more, but the overnight downpour meant the roads were still muddy. This time only five children joined me, along with what might have been one of their mothers. But they didn't keep their distance, they joined me under the canopy, and one very confident boy started picking up and examining bits of kit. They stood and stared at me silently the whole time, no more than a few feet away. I felt like a zoo attraction.

Being Sunday, very few shops were open so I carried as much food as I could. But the only portable food was dried biscuits – a dozen packets for the day, which equates to about two biscuits for every mile covered. I can't imagine the biscuits were helpful to my digestion, and I was still ill, though thankfully not vomiting. Cycling with a revolting gut isn't pleasant at any time, let alone in countryside where there are people everywhere. Spotting a few gaps during the morning, I had to race to the roadside and hide in the trees to be ill. Despite this my energy levels felt good and I remained determined to keep going, no matter how slowly.

There were a few paved sections, but most of the day was spent in the dirt. In stages the mud built up between my front forks, then the tyre clogged up entirely and I would grind to a stop. The only way to restart was to drop the wheel out and use a tyre lever to clear out the mud.

My prop for the second puncture was a bulldozer. The workers here were standing around, waiting for I am not sure what. They were better company than the kids, though, and I could use the bulldozer to rest all my bags on so they weren't in the mud. After no issues since day 1, I could now see the vulnerability of these tyres when off-road. They were tough on the tar, but with a thin sidewall, making them much lighter, they were near useless on this surface. And I had a long way to go.

The road was never flat, constantly steep and hilly, and added to the poor surfaces, this made my first day in the north of Ethiopia look like a breeze in comparison. It was also tougher mentally because I hadn't seen it coming. It was my own fault for overlooking this terrain. My course notes made it look like the Ethiopian Highlands were where the tough mountains were and after Addis it was a downhill journey into Kenya. False expectations of a fast ride until Moyale, which is where the dirt road was meant to start, made slow progress harder to stay positive about.

By the end of the day I was still 340km from Moyale, where I was due the following evening to meet Ed from a company called Saladin – my security escort through north Kenya. At this rate it could take three days, and that was a serious worry.

During the afternoon the skies had darkened and I was expecting more rain. On these steep tracks, when the heavens opened streams immediately started to flow down the middle. It wasn't so muddy at this altitude, more rutted and rocky. Sure enough the downpour came, and it quickly became torrential, angry rain hammering down as I pushed the bike uphill. Riding was nearly impossible and no quicker than walking the bike.

Up a very steep bank on the right I spotted some small houses and I could see one with a canopy outside. It was the first potential shelter for miles, and I went for it. A dirt footpath zig-zagged for about 30 metres up to it, and as I pushed the bike above me, a man dashed out from the house in his flip-flops. Sure-footed and agile, he took the bike from me and dragged it up the hill. I slipped up the path after him, struggling even without the bike. Ducking underneath the canopy, I was met by the interested gaze of about a dozen children and two men. The men, one of whom had helped with the bike, immediately invited me inside and gave me a seat. The children were told to go away, to stop staring, but they had nowhere to go: the weather was filthy.

The room had no lights, just some old posters on the wall, a couple for beer and one of a white girl in a bikini. There were a few crates of soft drinks and a battered old fridge in the corner. The table took up most of the room, with benches down each side. Everything was a deep earthen colour – the floor, the walls, the ceiling – making it very dark indeed. Through a small doorway was the cooking area.

I accepted a Mirinda, an orange-flavoured soft drink, and was then offered a coffee. I was in the heart of coffee country, the lush tropical part of Ethiopia with hot springs and fertile soils. There was no conversation as we didn't have a word in common, but the men were doing their best to be good hosts and I was very grateful for their hospitality. I was dripping wet. I dug out the soggy road map, which showed that I had a fair way to go until the next town. So if the rains didn't stop or if I didn't get back out in them, then this could be my stop for the night. The children were fascinated by the map, even more so by my camera, which I handed to them, turning the screen around so they could see themselves. I pressed record and let them hand it around.

My coffee arrived, black in a small black cup – a very welcome pick-me-up. I took a sip. It was salty! If everyone hadn't been watching I would have spat it out. Truly disgusting. Salt water is a great emetic. Salted coffee, in my opinion, is even harder to keep down. The English and the Scots have long argued over salt or sugar in their porridge, but I can't imagine there are many coffee lovers who prefer two spoonfuls of salt. So as not to be rude, I finished the cup, grateful that it was no more than a double espresso.

The rain stopped as quickly as it had begun and I thanked my hosts warmly. Both men and a few boys took my bike down the steep path. After paying them for the drinks, I carried on. The rain had washed away sections of the road, so I walked most of the next few miles. With a hardcore trekking bike or mountain bike it would have been passable, but on my carbon race bike it was impossible. Certainly with my level of off-road skills.

In Gedeb, the main dirt road was thick mud and loads of people milled around, mainly wearing sandals, carrying on with life as normal, in spite of the quagmire. I spotted lots of young people with a tissue stuffed up one nostril. It was too common for nosebleeds to be the reason, and I suspected something more troubling. But I never discovered the reason. It was pretty much dark by the time I tracked down anywhere to stay.

This flat-roofed, single-storey breeze-block building behind a solid metal gate down a slippy muddy slope had half a dozen rooms with doors that opened on to a junkyard of old cars. It was not an advertised guesthouse and the place seemed deserted. I was about to leave, but word of mouth must have alerted the owner, who came through the gate. He was wearing black leather shoes, walking in the exaggerated manner of someone trying to keep their feet dry.

For the sum of £3 I was given a room with a concrete floor and bed. A few other people had now turned up and a group of prying teenage boys were shooed back out of the gates, which were then closed. A young lady set about covering the doorstep of my room with wood shavings. I have no idea why. Was it to absorb the wetness or keep out some insects? Inevitably these shavings ended up muddy and strewn across the floor. A young man was ordered to pull water out of an open well shaft in the ground and put a bucket in my room for me to wash.

The bike was absolutely caked so I asked for some more well water and set about cleaning the frame as best I could with my hands. Seeing what I was doing, the owner instructed two of the youngsters to do this for me. They gave it a go but weren't making progress so I took over, thanking them and insisting I would do it. In the light flooding out from my open doorway, my bike propped up on the bumper of an old truck, I freed the bike of the day's mud. There was no toilet so I had to wait until everyone had left before going behind one of the scrap cars. All in all it was a wet, dirty and pretty disgusting pit. But at least I was out of the rain, which had started again. Using my tent around here would have been far, far worse.

There were no shops open, but a shack next door was serving food. The rain was dripping through the roof, making the dirt floor muddy. There was a small bar where half a dozen young people were standing around, drinking in the near darkness. I sat down on a red plastic Coca-Cola chair, once again using my headtorch, the only person who apparently couldn't see in the dim light. There didn't seem a clear line between staff and customers, and the group ignored me entirely, which was actually a welcome change. An omelette, meat stew and more injera was all they had, which I wolfed down, despite my continuing dislike for the sourdough crêpe. I remembered Colin's love of the stuff, but still could not see the appeal. This really was food for fuel, without any of the pleasure.

Back in my room, the tin roof amplified the battering rain as I set about patching three of the inner tubes. I had climbed nearly a mile and a half that day, and all my kit was wet with no chance of drying out, but I was in a pretty good place mentally. There was no point in worrying about how long Ed would be waiting on the Kenyan border, or my plummeting daily average mileage; I had a roof over my head and my stomach was settling down. Tomorrow was a new day, and I reassured myself that the long-term average mileage would take care of itself if I put in the same effort each day. I had certainly put in the time and effort on day 17, it was just a bit of a shocker that I had progressed less than 90 miles.

Day 18: Gedeb to Camo

At just gone 6 a.m., at first light, I set off, determined to make better miles. The rain had stopped in the night and standing water had partially drained away, leaving the mud denser, but it was a long way from drying up. The atmosphere was muggy and damp so pulling on my wet kit had been very unpleasant, but preferable to packing it away and putting on dry kit that would quickly get wet. Only one small stall was open, as far as I could see, just before the road climbed out of town, and there I stocked up on biscuits for the road ahead. The cappuccino-flavoured ones were proving to be my favourites in Ethiopia, followed by chocolate, but they were the very cheap sandwich type: dry, tasteless packages designed to last unchanged for years. Still, it was pretty much the only food I could find for long stretches and I ate ten packets that day.

It proved to be an amazing day of contrasts, starting in thick jungle, descending through forests, and ending in arid terrain. In mid-morning I was passing families of baboons playing on the roadside, and by lunchtime had reached a camel market. The contrasts and hurdles along the way made it feel a very long

day, and certainly I eked out every mile possible before nightfall.
That still made for a fairly unimpressive total of 121 miles,
but considering the total had been 50 miles by 1 p.m., it felt like
a triumph.

The first two hours were the slowest, again including stretches
where I had to walk, at one point carrying the bike over unrideable rocky construction sites. There were very few vehicles on the
road, but a constant stream of people. Endless kids shrieked at
me, and if not answered they would repeat 'YOU, YOU, where
you go?' an octave higher. There was a new call as well: 'China,
China, CHINA, CHINA!' I guessed the Chinese who built these
roads were the only outsiders some of these teenagers had seen a
lot of, so perhaps they thought of all foreigners as Chinese.

One group of boys saw me coming on a slow rocky uphill
section and with more confidence than most came into the road
from the verge, shouting at me before I had reached them. Then,
as I got within a few metres, one stepped forward and pulled his
fist back. It may have been an act of bravado in front of mates,
but I was at the end of my patience and hammered my pedals
forward, accelerating straight at him, shoving my open palm
into his face. It was undoubtedly the best hand-off of my life,
which isn't saying much given my woeful schoolboy rugby career. The teenager stumbled back and his mates exploded in
jeering, but no one ran after me. If they had wanted to catch me,
I couldn't go that fast. It was a stupid thing to have done. But
I didn't feel at all bad afterwards. I remembered with fondness
the empty desert.

Breakfast made up for it. Good food lifts the spirit like
nothing else. Once again the main road of this town was a construction site, but a small strip of shops off to the right had their
own concrete pavement and were the most civilized establishments I had seen since Shashamane, which felt like a week ago.
I parked my bike outside a café – and I would happily give it this

title without qualification – and sat outside, as I couldn't risk leaving it.

A chap around my age came out and introduced himself. It was hard to define what set him apart from many of the locals I was coming across. He wasn't dressed any smarter, but he certainly held himself differently, relaxed and confident. The fact that he introduced himself, didn't seem surprised at seeing me, and didn't act like I had dropped in from outer space, showed this. He also spoke reasonable English.

A big group, maybe forty kids, was gathering on the road, staring at me. Without warning he yelled at them, really bellowed, then bent down to pick up a stone. At this they bolted, but only momentarily, gradually creeping forward again. I just ignored them. It was unkind that I liked the café owner more for his aggression towards them, but it was just so welcome to have someone in my corner after running the solo gauntlet on the road.

He served two big portions of scrambled eggs, runny and perfectly done, with two big rolls of soft white bread. Best of all he brought three mugs, one after the other, of very sweet coffee. I was in heaven and didn't care about the horde of kids watching me. I paid the man for this feast and also paid him for a spoon whose handle I thought would be useful to clear between my bike's forks so I didn't have to keep dropping the wheel out of the quick release when the mud built up.

Soon after that I reached my first decent descent, picked up speed over the rocky terrain – and bang, the front tyre blew out. The sidewall had a slit big enough to put my finger in. I clattered to a stop and set about changing this again, but I was plunged once more into worry. I now needed to reach the Kenyan border: Ed would have new supplies for me, but until then I had no more spare tyres, no more spare unpatched inners. The bike was seriously struggling with the conditions. I snapped a tyre lever trying to fix the puncture and managed to cake the inside of the spare, very worn tyre that I was putting back on with mud, so it all took a while, inevitably under the watchful, silent gaze of a dozen people. In the middle of nowhere in Ethiopia, people just appeared. India is the only other place where I have experienced rural populations like this.

At 55 miles I sat down to two huge plates of tibs – protein overkill, but my appetite was fully back again and I mopped up both plates with sweet white bread. The butcher was in a hut right next door, with a few carcasses hanging in full view, in the open air. It was very fresh meat, but maybe not the most hygienic. I made sure mine was piping hot when it arrived.

The restaurant was branded with St George lager. The emblem for this Addis Ababa-brewed beer is a rearing white stallion with a knight in full metal armour spearing a dragon, which looks a bit like a crocodile. England and Ethiopia share St George as their patron saint along with other unlikely places such as Palestine and Serbia. Next to me four men sat at a table full of empty bottles. They had enough lager-fuelled English to get by.

'You bicycle South Africa?!' one translated to the others, to a ripple of exclamations. 'Drink beer!' He offered over a bottle.

'Thank you.' I laughed amicably. 'Next time.'

'You Americans are always crazy, I see the films. Hollywood.'

'I am Scottish,' I corrected, 'and you are not the first person to call me crazy. Talking about crazy, you have some crazy roads here in Ethiopia. When does the asphalt start again?' I knew this word would be better understood than tarmac.

'This way is bad, very bad,' the man replied, pointing northwards. 'This way is perfect,' he added, gesturing towards Kenya.

I couldn't trust a half-drunk man, but his words gave me reason to be slightly optimistic.

An hour later I front-punctured again, just as I found a paved road. Inevitably the road was not perfect, but it had flattened out a lot, which meant it was a better grade, not as broken by crawling trucks and streams of water. After patching the tyre I stopped at a small shack. As I asked the vendor for a pile of biscuits, someone joined me.

'Where are you going?' he asked in perfect if heavily accented English.

'Moyale. Do you know the road?'

He explained that he was an optometrist at the hospital, gesturing across the road. He went on to explain that the worst was behind me and there was mainly new road all the way to Moyale, except the final 100km. I could have given him a hug. With that news I might just have clawed back a day, having been resigned to the fact that it would take another two days to reach Kenya on the dirt roads.

The road wasn't completely new – it kept dropping off the edge on to short sections of dirt where new viaducts were being laid – but on the whole it was much faster, and definitely flatter. For the next hour, as the skies darkened, I raced along, trying to keep ahead of the rain. Buoyed by huge horizons compared to those in the jungle and mountains that morning, I was capitalizing on being back on tar, on a high with this unexpected good fortune. The villages had also started to become far more spaced out, with fewer people on the rural roadsides as well. Looking back to the north of Ethiopia there seemed a correlation between mountainous terrain and population density. It was also getting cooler, so I barely touched my water.

At 3.30 I rolled into a small town with quite a few places to stay and it was painfully tempting to stop. But 65km ahead there was another hotel symbol on my map. I stopped at a tea-room on the roadside with a few tables and chairs in the dirt, all under a canvas canopy. Now I was out of the mountains, once again people didn't seem to be reacting to me in the same way. The local youths who were sitting around barely took notice of me.

I approached one to ask about the road ahead. With a combination of gestures and individual English words he explained
clearly that it was all tarmac and all downhill. But he advised me
to stop here and gestured towards the rain clouds, which were
now very close. I so nearly gave in to this. As I quickly repacked
to make sure everything was thoroughly waterproof, the guy
had a laugh with me and his friends about how wet I was about
to get.

Getting up to speed quickly, I found myself effortlessly at
35km/h – an unbelievable speed in comparison to the morning,
when at times I was carrying the bike. Then the first drop of rain
splattered on to the road. After that, someone really turned the
tap on. It was an incredibly fierce deluge but I pedalled along
with my sunglasses on, singing at the top of my voice, triumphantly and defiantly. I have rarely seen or cycled in such
conditions and had the road surface been dirt, it would have
been impossible. As things were the road was perfect so the only
challenge was focusing with the amount of water streaming
down my face. The first ten minutes were thrilling, but after
about forty minutes I fell silent, then the final hour was a pretty
miserable slog, as the rain did not relent even a tiny bit.

But the going remained fast and this final 65km took just over
two hours. I arrived at 5.45 p.m., although with the rains it was
already getting dark an hour before sunset. I nearly rode out the
other end of the one-street town before stopping at a place that
looked like it might have rooms. A young guy stood under a canopy with a young woman in the doorway behind him. I asked
him if this was a hotel and they both laughed. I realized I may
have misjudged it in the torrential rain; possibly they only rented
rooms by the hour. Another guy walked out and, holding his
jacket above his head, told me to follow him. A hundred metres
back up the road he showed me a sign for 'pensions'. These are
what I had been in the last few nights, what I now understood to

be places to stay with no restaurant. For another 100 bir (£3) I had a tiny room just bigger than the bed. I tried my utmost not to make everything soaking wet.

Having taken some time to sort myself out I was now shivering uncontrollably as I cooled down. It was hard to get my lycra off, my hands were shrivelled up and white around the edges, and my backside felt even more saddle-sore than usual from having been in a damp chamois all day. It was the first time I had felt properly cold in Africa, and the shivering carried on for a while. My tired body was simply trying to cope.

I ran across the road and ate more double portions of tibs and bread for dinner in a dimly lit bar with lots of neon lights, a TV playing Champions League football and a barman who wanted me to drink some tequila. The volume was up loud to compete with the rain cascading off the tin roof. The barman seemed to be friends with the other five customers, who were all in for beers and to watch the football.

By 7.30 p.m. I was back in my room. It was still bucketing down outside. With nothing else to do, and still feeling chilly, I went to bed. I was in good spirits, though, celebrating the fact that I had started that morning expecting dirt roads and more massive hills but ended up on perfect roads and descending into flatlands. My daily average speed was only 17km/h, so considering the final hours were so fast, that showed how painfully slow the start had been. It was a day of extremes, and I just hoped I was now past the worst of it.

Day 19: Camo to Sololo

At 5 a.m. the rain stopped. I know because I kept waking with the noise. At six I was about to wheel out when I spotted the front tyre was soft. It wasn't flat, so I pumped it up and hoped for the best. It was cold in my wet kit and I just wanted to start. I was on the road by 6.40.

It was about 100 miles to the border and I could not wait to get out of Ethiopia. Bike, body and mind had taken a battering in this troubled land where I felt aid had promoted dependency, not given relief. I could find little room for optimism about Ethiopia, which is a terrible thing to admit. Every country has its juvenile delinquents – almost always male teenagers – but in Ethiopia they seemed to be more numerous and malicious. In their defence, lack of education and work breeds ignorance and idleness. I am sure that I saw only one side of Ethiopia's story; I am sure it has a great many stories to be proud of; but what I did see was very real, at the grassroots, in the remote parts of the country where fewer westerners venture.

The first 30 miles were plain sailing, with a tailwind that slowly dried my kit out . . . and then the dirt roads restarted, as promised. Now, in the flatlands, the earth was no longer a dark soil but a reddish clay. This made for the most gloopy progress yet. My lower legs were caked, as was the bike, which kept grinding to a halt. It was like cycling with the brakes on, which made for leg-sapping miles. My left knee was twinging again, a cause for concern, but as long as it didn't worsen I was sure it would ease off given a few days of good roads.

In late morning, the sun broke through the clouds and very quickly the roads dried out. In fact they baked, the clay forming a corrugated obstacle course through which I gingerly steered the bike. Another puncture hardly registered a reaction from me, they were now so routine. I was nursing the bike to the border, willing every kilometre to pass without further punctures or, worse, a broken spoke. I was so impressed with the abuse the bike had taken. I'd only been let down by the tyres – and to be fair, they weren't designed for this. The Ethiopian roads made Egypt and Sudan seem like a distant, happy memory, a gentle warm-up before Africa really started.

The final 10km to Moyale were tarmac once again and I was in buoyant mood. I had persevered and made it a day before I thought I would, especially given that ripped tyre. I knew that a new road was being constructed from the border and I would have more long stretches of bad surfaces, but this would be a proper graded dirt road, not a temporary construction road, and it wouldn't be in the mountains. Whatever Kenya had in store, I was sure there was no way it could trump Ethiopia. I smiled from ear to ear and laughed out loud as the border gate came into view.

The guard on the gate turned me around and sent me into a complex of whitewashed buildings. A security guard sitting underneath the shade of a tree gestured for me to leave my bike, but I wheeled on. There were far too many people milling around to let it out of eyesight. Outside a concrete office was a row of maybe twenty seats along the walkway. They were all taken, and there were quite a few people standing too. Everyone was Muslim, based on their clothing, which came as something of a change as I hadn't seen many people in Ethiopia dressed in galabeyas, the floor-length gown with shirt buttons, or women with hijab scarves. Nothing was happening quickly; a number of men were passing the time playing with their prayer beads, or in conversation.

Inside the open door of the office were two desks with a lot of paperwork lying around. Travellers were being called forward one at a time. It was clearly a very lengthy process. My visa was in order; all I needed was a quick passport check, and I really didn't have a few hours to sit in line. Ed from Saladin would be waiting a few hundred metres away on the Kenyan side.

As I walked up to the door I suddenly felt underdressed so I went back to my bike to put on my baggy shorts. No one in the queue protested as I walked straight back to the office door, although I was chancing it. I was signalled to leave by one of the men behind the desks, a lazy wave of the back of his hand. I remained by the door, leaning on the frame, not making a fuss but making it clear I wasn't about to leave. I stood there for forty minutes. The man at the left-hand desk departed and another replaced him, a changeover which meant it took ages before the next person was seen. The passport officer on the right kept leaning back in his seat and yawning. From what I saw each person took about ten minutes to process. It was a painfully slow procedure, mainly because the officers made it slow. They were in charge, and seemed to be very bored by the whole thing.

I waved my passport every time the yawning officer looked up. Eventually this tactic wore him down and he gestured me over, told me to sit down. The stamping and form filling took less than two minutes: he definitely wanted me out of there so that he could get back to his usual routine.

I wheeled the bike back to the gate and walked through without any customs checks to be met by a square-jawed, military-looking Englishman. It turned out he wasn't ex-military at all, but Ed had that expat ruggedness about him, together with the khaki shirt and trousers, the boots and a smiling efficiency. It took less than five minutes to clear Kenyan passport control; they were waiting for me and were a smiling bunch. Jackie Brown and the team at the British High Commission in Nairobi, along with Ed, had helped smooth the way.

There wasn't much of a town on the Kenyan side. I should have stopped for food on the Ethiopian side but had been in such a rush to get through. Now under armed escort, I was keen to get going without delay and make as many miles as possible. Ed had an old green safari-style Land Cruiser with canvas sides. In the back were two Kenyan policemen.

The conversations about security for Africa Solo had started back in the autumn of 2014 when I employed Ship Security

International (SSI) to do an intelligence sweep of the entire route and come up with a report on relevant incidents and security concerns in recent years. Rather than just going off news headlines, which tend to designate areas as either dangerous or safe, this was a more thorough report, talking about the likelihood and nature of issues and the probable severity of consequences. Ethiopia had a very high likelihood of petty crime and low-level unrest, especially considering the population levels, whereas northern Kenya is very sparsely populated and mainly separated on tribal lines so the chance of opportunist crime was much lower.

However, the incidents that had happened in Kenya in the recent past were very serious: murder and revenge attacks supposedly in the name of religion. The Garissa University attack by Al Shabab that left 147 dead had occurred over 300 miles to the south but less than a month beforehand, on 3 April. Closer to my route, but still nearer the Somali border, was the bus attack by Al Shabab in November 2014. Gunmen separated Muslims from non-Muslims by asking passengers to read from the Koran. Those who failed were shot in the head. Twenty-eight dead. These sorts of attacks were incredibly unlikely, though; the chances of a road-traffic accident or contracting malaria en route were higher. Dan Martin, a fellow Brit, had happily cycled through northern Kenya alone and unsupported only a month earlier.

But – and this was a £1,500-a-day 'but' – after the Atlantic experience and with Harriet in the world I was no longer willing to put myself in a situation knowing it could have terminal consequences, no matter how unlikely. Security bought peace of mind for me, Nicci and everyone back home. Was it absolutely necessary? I certainly hoped not. I probably would have ridden without security a few years earlier, but it's hard to know for sure. I simply didn't see any benefit, except a healthier budget, in taking any risks.

Employing SSI actually to provide the on-the-ground

security as well as the intel report would have meant flying out a team from the UK and hiring vehicles, and much higher costs. So I got in touch with Saladin Security, who had an office in Nairobi. They knew some of the route and knew how to get the local police onboard. Ed had explained in the run-up to the start that it would take some diplomacy, in the form of meetings, tea-drinking and using their network, to get the police onside. And then they would need to be paid, although this wouldn't be much – about $20 a day. Having Ed, who seemed utterly rational about the risks, with me was just what I needed.

My plan had been also to have a cameraman for this northern stretch, as I thought it would be remote, tough and in stark contrast to anywhere else on my route. But this quickly fell through. Kenya was in a general state of shock after the recent attacks. One of the Nairobi-based cameramen, who I got as far as a signed contract with, emailed mentioning the need for twelve armed guards to come to Moyale! This clearly wasn't possible, affordable or practical. I would be making myself more of a target by drawing so much attention to myself.

This may have been bandit country, a spillover from rebel problems in neighbouring Somalia, but the people I saw as I left Moyale were smiling, and a few waved enthusiastically. I could hardly believe it. I hadn't seen such normal warm behaviour for over a week. The road bumped its way downhill. It was very rutted and I was feeling a bit pressurized by the vehicle, causing me to push much harder than I had on the Ethiopian side. Just a few miles into Kenya, the road cut sharp right and ran parallel to the Ethiopian border for a while, still descending, with lots of evidence of earthworks – foundations for tarmacking this entire road. But I was reassured by the fact that Ed was carrying a big box of new supplies for me.

Bang. That was inevitable. I fixed the puncture quickly, this time with a new inner tube, and carried on.

My first night in this new country was looming. 'Saladin Security will not support night-time cycling due to security concerns' was one line from our agreement. But the reality in north Kenya is that there are big gaps between places where you can stay. Our options were to camp out in the bush or pedal on well into the night. Ed seemed keen to do the latter, as was I, especially as I had been growing queasy again since the border. I didn't want to be stuck out in the middle of nowhere being ill.

In the final hours of the day I reached tar again and made much faster miles, pushing as hard as I dared. I felt very sick, but my legs were strong, and there was absolutely no one about, very few vehicles passing, so I didn't feel in any danger. At least it was dry for the first evening in four days. The world around me was now semi-arid with scrubby bushes and burnt grasses. The skies darkened until I was left in the pool from my Exposure light, oblivious to anything around me. The Land Cruiser sat behind me, casting a bit more light.

The rudimentary hotel where we stayed for the night was the first building we came to, set back off the road. Ed went in to arrange rooms as Martin, the driver, and the two policemen bundled out. They seemed pretty excited about the adventure, impressed with my speed. It was good to see they were onboard, as the border had been so rushed I had not had time to make proper introductions.

Ed and I were shown a bare room with no windows and two metal-framed beds. There were no lights, but a lady returned with a few candles to place on the floor. After leaving our kit in there I was walking out when I saw Ed place a pistol under his pillow. I had thought he wasn't going to be armed, but was quietly reassured that he was. I didn't mention it and didn't see it again.

I figured out that the mud that was covering my water bottles must have turned my stomach again. It was certainly the most likely culprit. I went for a wash using my headtorch and a big bucket of warm water that was brought to a stone outhouse around the side. I felt pretty weak and nauseous, but wasn't sick.

I joined Ed for dinner. A big pile of meat stew and rice was placed on the table, and I really needed it after a seriously long day. I had clocked up 140 miles, amazing considering the broken roads and delays at the border. But I hardly ate a thing, feeling bloated.

There was no airflow in the room. It was a sweatbox, and it was noisy outside. After a few hours of fitful sleep I had to get outside. Ed woke as I slowly pulled the door open, but I assured him I just needed some air. Ten metres from our room, a group of locals were crowded around a TV, watching a game of football with the volume turned up. Both policemen were still awake, maybe on guard, but I wasn't sure. They jumped up as I appeared. Putting them at their ease, I grabbed a plastic chair, walked away from the cars and sat there for twenty minutes, in the dark.

I felt ill, but apart from that it was a lovely moment, feeling the cool air on my bare chest, looking up at the vast starry night sky, wriggling my toes into the cool dirt. A new country – that was always exciting. It was my first chance to be properly still and to think in days. At every other moment I was on a mission, even when finding meals or cleaning my bike or trying to get some sleep. It wouldn't be too long before I reached the end of the dirt roads, and then the next major milestone: crossing the equator at Nanyuki.

Part Five

South of the Equator

Day 20: Sololo to Log-Logo

I slept better for the rest of the night but was still plagued by diarrhoea in the morning (even if I felt much better after a trip to the outhouse), as well as a cold. Initially I thought it was just a stuffy head from the stifling room, but all in all it had been a week of feeling weak, and I was craving some smooth tar and a settled stomach.

My wish was partially granted to start with. I skirted the edge of Turbi forest and bore left, heading south again. The road descended on brand-new smooth roads. They were so good it was hard to imagine they would ever end. In an hour and a half I made 42km and reached the first place for breakfast. I'd left at around 6 a.m. and no one had been up and cooking at the roadhouse.

At this new place they also seemed unprepared for breakfast, but did offer tea and bread, which turned out to be chapattis. Martin, the Kenyan driver, left and came back ten minutes later with a clutch of eggs, which he gave to the worker to cook up. While I was keen to remain as unsupported as possible, these not insignificant bits of help were much appreciated. The moral support was certainly very welcome. After the chaos of Ethiopia, I could see that north Kenya was going to be a very barren stretch.

The tea was very white and very sweet. Ed explained that they made it only with milk, as I would a hot chocolate. A skin formed on it as it cooled and I figured it would either curdle or cure my stomach.

It had been a cloudless start, but as I tried to counter my nausea and ram breakfast down, the heavens opened and the wind picked up. The water ran off the roof in waterfalls and blew in the open sides of the roadhouse. Ed stood by the door surveying the downpour, but I moved my chair further in, looking for sanctuary and dryness. I felt so rotten inside I just wanted a bed to curl up in. The rain battering off the roof in waves driven by gusts of wind did nothing to stoke the embers of my enthusiasm. I stayed longer than I needed to, hoping it would subside. Ed and Martin seemed to think I was some kind of cycling hardman who wasn't affected by such inclement conditions, and their keenness to crack on definitely made me commit earlier than I would have alone.

Back on the road they dropped the canvas side to the Land Cruiser so the policemen were in the dark, but in the dry. The rain stayed torrential for a few hours, but I zipped along with the helpful tailwind. Once in it, the rain was quite refreshing. This was the storm that was breaking the night of stifling mugginess.

It was fortunate that I found myself being fast-tracked by the wind as ahead lay one of the most desolate landscapes you could imagine. The Kaisut Desert lacks the striking colour and interest of sand dunes. In fact it is nothing like the desert of our imagination other than being barren and hot. This is a tract of land with an utterly homogeneous character and without boundaries, a rutted volcanic cinder field. Lime deposits and the sandy-coloured pumice lend the only highlights to the broken ground. Only the very sparse scrub and the ribbon of tar made this expanse look like planet Earth. It certainly came as a surprise so soon after dropping out of the mountains of

Ethiopia. As I wrote in my diary: 'This morning I cycled through amazingly boring lava fields after breakfast – lots of herdsmen but hard to know where they were going.'

These herdsmen were the nomadic Rendille people, walking their animals as they had for millennia, although the suggestion of real pasture out there is very misleading. Tall and willowy with straight hair, they were distinct and proud-looking people. I didn't stop close enough to see, but they also have blue eyes. As I flew past, I scanned the horizons for where they could be heading, what they could be feeding their animals on – mainly cattle, but some camels and donkeys. It was a vast and inhospitable stretch, yet surrounded by greener and wetter terrain. I couldn't figure out why anyone would choose to live there. I passed possibly a hundred men and boys but never more than half a dozen in a group, each with a small herd.

It had dried up and the road had turned due south by the time I started to climb, gradually to begin with but eventually rising a kilometre from the desert floor to the town of Marsabit. In total contrast, this was a cool, green realm swathed in cloud, dense mist-shrouded rainforest and moorlands that are home to elephant, greater kudu (antelopes), baboons and buffalo. From the lunarscape of the desert floor, an old volcano rose ahead of me like a mirage at the end of the drying road.

My speed plummeted and it was a tough slog uphill into the wind. Ed, Martin and the police had been getting a show of speed that was unsustainable all morning and commented on the sudden change of pace. I felt pretty weak with my queasy stomach, especially after having eaten so little food. It was an immense relief when a few kilometres before Marsabit they pulled alongside and said that a hotel they had stayed at on their way north was just ahead, and that we should stop there for lunch.

Ed had news that the chief of police for the north had been in touch saying that he needed his men back. There was no explanation for what was happening up in Moyale, but they were to return immediately. Ed was relaxed about carrying on without them, but conscious that our agreement was to include armed police. He could stop in Marsabit and recruit some more, but this would almost certainly involve a long break, long conversations and tea-drinking, as he put it. Having a vehicle with me seemed enough of a security blanket, a means of escape if a situation did happen. Ed had more presence and seemed a tougher cookie than the two local police put together, so I felt quite happy under his sole watch.

Jirime Hotel and Resort sits in its own farmland, and it looked very impressive with its modern red roof and lawns, certainly compared to everything to the north. It was in fact very basic. Lunch was stodgy but plentiful. Unfortunately, I still couldn't face eating much.

Before setting off again I was keen to work on the bike. It had taken a hell of a beating the last week, I was nearly halfway down Africa, and it made sense to work away in daytime rather than under torchlight. Sitting on the concrete near reception I used the chain tool to push a link out, and pulled the chain off. The theory was that by changing it before it was completely worn out I would not need to change the cassette, the block of gears on the back wheel, as well. If they got worn out together then a new chain wouldn't fit on the old block. Feeding the new chain on is a simple enough task, but not one I have done often. For someone who has cycled so much, I remain a lousy mechanic. Halfway through I called Gav, my mechanic, to check which way the chain should face – writing to the outside. It must have been an odd call to take on the shop floor in Edinburgh. Pushing the new link pin through, you then have to snap the end off to make it flush with the links. It was a satisfying bit of maintenance, and I set off proudly checking through my gears, enjoying the lack of gritty resistance. Whether it was psychological or not, the bike felt faster, definitely smoother.

In the middle of Marsabit the road ran out and I found myself in a bustling market town with no need to stop. On the dusty potholed road out there were lots of vehicles, animals, people and general busyness. So I nearly missed an amazing sight coming the other way – a vintage car, what looked like a Rolls-Royce, with big external wheel arches, skinny tyres on spoked wheels and a roof cage that was packed high, with the slogan 'Spark Your Dream' across the front. It turned out to be a 1928 Graham-Paige, an American car I had never heard of, and it was being driven by the Zapp family from Argentina. So far they had been on the road for fourteen years during which time their four children had been born. Candelaria and Herman had an incredible story of fortitude and daring to tell, of living their dreams. It's a story I took great strength from as I pedalled on south. Here's how she put it:

> Everybody has fears – just like us. You have to try so that the fears do not block you. So go for your dream with your fears because you will never be able to go without fears. Start, do the first step, and see what is going to happen. Usually when you do the first step, you'll think why didn't I start before? People always feel like they are not prepared. They say, 'First I have to have all this money, I have to have this and that.' But if it's your dream, something that you really really want to do, then you are already prepared and you will be able to do it. Many people ask us how we can possibly finance travelling, but if they would sell their expensive car, they could travel themselves for two years.

In contrast to their openness and relaxed nomadic travelling, I was a fairly closed book on a mission. I regretted, even at the time, my obsession with progress and my impatient nature when surrounded by such hospitality and treasures to explore.

About 20 miles out of town I was descending fast on the dry, rutted dirt roads when the front tyre blew out like a gunshot. It exploded with such force that a quarter of the tyre was outside the wheel rim. As I took this apart quickly, a Triumph motorbike made light work of the gravel and dirt, working its way uphill. The couple onboard, a man driving and a woman on pillion, stopped on the other side of the road, took off their helmets and gave me a beaming hello. Marsabit seemed to be a Mecca for travellers and I had hardly seen any foreigners since Khartoum. They explained that they had driven from Cape Town and were full of the joys of the road. In contrast I was very grumpy and a bit short-tempered, trying to fix my bike and make up for lost time. They wanted to stop and chat but I didn't have the patience to engage in small talk about the road ahead – the road they had travelled. They got the message and headed on. I had been pleasant enough, I thought, but I'd made it clear I was in a rush.

Once I had fixed the tyre, I freewheeled downhill, slower than before, trying to nurse the bike over the tough roads. That was when I kicked myself for being so antisocial. Alone, I wasn't in a bad mood; even on this tough stretch I was loving the changing landscapes, the big miles, the challenges. But whenever I met people going at a different pace, travellers wanting to unwind and reminisce, I seemed to feel this rising panic, the walls going up around me, the need to disappear back into my race. I was aware of how this must come across, but I was afraid of losing my motivation to keep going at pace. This obsessive momentum was distracting me from pain, illness and my greatest fears, injury and failure.

It was a very slow and tough stretch, and I could not have ridden more carefully. There was no doubt that I'd underestimated just how tough the unpaved roads in Africa would be, and had built a bike that was a tarmac speed machine in the hope I could slip through these untarred sections painlessly and without losing too much time. Eleven punctures was a ridiculous tally. Luckily, nothing more serious had happened. I was surprised no spokes had broken.

Forced to proceed at this far more sociable pace on dirt roads, I could take in people better, and there were a lot more of them around now. These were mainly Samburu, and they are hard to ignore: proud, athletic and dressed like peacocks. The men go bare-chested with brightly coloured cloths wrapped round their waist, feathers in their braided hair and ornate beads round their arms, which are always carrying a spear or machete. The women are equally brightly dressed with fabulous strings of beads round their necks and in their hair. It looked like formal attire, a huge amount of effort and jewellery, but Ed assured me this was their everyday attire. Most of all the men looked utterly ripped, as lean as you could imagine, muscular and tall. What a handsome race – lissom, imposing, and quick to smile.

I finished the day in the near dark, at Log-Logo. Without any streetlights it was quite a confusing scene of headlights and people on the road as I scanned the buildings on either side, all of them set quite a way back into the dirt, for somewhere to stay. A young lad eventually guided us to a small rest house with half a dozen rooms that we would never have found as it wasn't signposted. Ed seemed a bit more on edge here, a bit more concerned about opportunist crime. I wasn't too worried; once my bike was inside the room little harm could happen. Ed talked about himself or Martin sleeping in the Land Cruiser. But in the end Ed cleared it of all the valuables and everyone slept in the rest house. Martin couldn't help as he had come down with food poisoning. His condition put my own dramas into perspective: he was in a bad way, struggling to keep driving and obviously in a lot of discomfort.

The lady who showed us the rooms brought a tray of rice and goat stew. I have no idea where it appeared from as there was no kitchen attached to the rooms. I ate ravenously, my appetite fully returned.

A very stinky outhouse stood about 20 metres away and there were other concrete houses scattered around. I sat outside before sleeping as the room was too hot to bear, and people were wandering past all evening. I woke many times during the night in that windowless box, dripping with sweat, each time pulling the ill-fitting door open with a creak and sucking in lungfuls of cool night air. My stomach was also doing somersaults again. Twice during the night I sat outside on the plastic chair in the dirt, maybe half an hour each time. The moon was high and I could see clearly, even though it was the middle of the night. People were still up, walking between houses. At one point I watched a boy sitting outside a house playing with a wireless radio. I could hear the crackling of changing stations.

It had been another day of great contrasts, and a triumph at 130 miles, considering the long sections of climbing and dirt.

Day 21: Log-Logo to Isiolo

On my third and final day with Ed I needed to reach Isiolo, only 120 miles away. Today, the last day of April, would also be my last day of dirt roads. It would then be a fresh new month and tar all the way to Cape Town.

Martin was in a bad way, really struggling to drive. Ed took over for most of the day and Martin curled up, in a world of discomfort. I wasn't that bad but still had stomach cramps and some sort of milder poisoning from the food or dirty water. I was tired of being unwell; my energy levels felt shot now and I had lost a lot of weight in a week. This was not sustainable. I craved good roads and a healthy appetite.

We were now in the land of thorn trees and cracking, parched grass. I had been warned about African thorns, but for all my tyre woes I never got a thorn puncture. The surface was tar-macked after leaving Log-Logo for about 10 miles, but then it was back to dirt roads. I was just waking my legs up, getting spinning before the off-road battle recommenced when my chain started to slip. I shifted up and it worked fine, shifted down and it slipped, shifted down more and it gripped again. In the middle of the cassette block, something was wrong. When I stopped to look, the issue was obvious, but a new one to me: the fourth sprocket was out of place, floating freely between its neighbours. I was carrying a chain whip and sprocket tool mainly so I could take the brake discs off if I broke a spoke or if I needed to change the whole cassette. But I had only once taken a cassette apart, a fortnight before leaving for Africa. The words of Owen the mechanic haunted me now: 'I will show you how to take this apart, but you will never need to do it.'

A Shimano Dura Ace 11-speed cassette has separate sprockets except for a set of three in the middle that come as a fixed unit. It was the middle of these that had broken free. There was nothing I could have done, but I didn't know that, assuming it was an indi-vidual sprocket that had somehow come loose. Using the bonnet of the Land Cruiser for a table, I carefully dismantled the cas-sette. It was a caked mess of oil and dirt. I doubt many road bike cassettes have been so abused. I had to be able to put this back together and was nervous about that. Ed seemed concerned about the breakdown but impressed with my mechanical ability. He needn't have been – I was winging it. Once I realized the break was unfixable, I carefully reassembled everything and got back on the road.

My relief was so great that the gears still worked and I could carry on that I was less worried than I might have been about los-ing a sprocket. I soon found that this really meant I'd lost three gears, as the floating sprocket meant the chain wouldn't sit happily in the neighbouring sprockets either. So I had my easiest gear for steep hills and my fast gears, but on gradual inclines I had nothing so would either have to grind out too big a gear out of the saddle, or slow down and spin a very light gear. I was very surprised by this break, but it wasn't the end of the world. I wondered if it had had anything to do with the new chain, but there was no sense in putting the old one back on. The damage was done if the two events were related.

I called Una back in Scotland, and she got hold of KOGA. The plan was quickly made to send a replacement cassette to Arusha in Tanzania for Monday. I was amazed a parcel could be sent from Holland to Africa in four days and over a weekend, but delighted too. If I was outpacing the schedule and couldn't afford to hang around in Arusha, the back-up plan was for a second package to get to me in Zambia.

I was ready for the final 55km off-road. This could take five hours and make the push to Isiolo a tough target. Seeing oil drums up ahead, with yellow painted arrows heading off the edge of the tar into the dirt, I prepared myself for battle, but when I drew near I saw that the road straight on had recently been laid and was perfect, just closed. After weaving through the stones piled up to stop traffic doing just what I was doing, I had the new surface to myself, running parallel to the dirt road. With each stretch, each corner, I expected it to come to an end, so I loved each kilometre of bonus tar, watching the Land Cruiser bump alongside me, creating a tail plume of dust at this speed.

After 20km the top layer of tar stopped and I was down to a compacted base layer, but this was equally fast: no one else had been on it since a road roller. Then this ran out and the next section was covered in clear tarpaulin. The entire width of the road had been laid in huge strips – a vast amount of plastic, obviously a protective layer prior to the tarring process. This was held down with thousands of stones, which must have been a horrible manual task to place and later clear. I assumed my luck had run out but ventured on to the tarp, just to see what it was like. There was a group of workers and I stopped and asked if I could carry on. They waved me on enthusiastically. The plastic was wet with condensation on the underside, so when I glanced back I saw that I was leaving a clear track along the unmade road. Progress was a lot slower as I had to weave furiously around the maze of rocks, but it was still much quicker than the dirt road. After a few miles of this tarpaulin my luck did run out: I met another group of roadworkers who told me in no uncertain terms that I had to get back on the dirt road.

The last 25km to Merille was corrugated and slow, and I punctured again. But it was only 25km so I could easily count it down. Pulling up at the first food place I could find, I parked the bike outside the 'Modern Hotel' – a misnomer on both counts. It was a single room with some tables and chairs where I could order rice, beans and goat stew. The goats were definitely local: five of them were walking around inside and outside the 'hotel', eventually settling down out front – my very own guard goats. I sat inside and ate their relatives. Nature to plate in less than 10 metres.

A small girl, maybe seven years old, came padding in wearing a T-shirt but no pants. She was filthy but had a wonderful smile. Her father, who had served my food, gave her a plate too. I sat there eating hungrily, thinking about the life she would grow up to lead, how she would be working in a few years' time. I thought of Harriet and the life I hoped she would lead. This girl looked happy and already tough, but my fatherly instinct wanted to scoop her up and give her better prospects. Even as I thought this I realized how I was subconsciously judging, making grand assumptions about material wealth and happiness. I just couldn't help but see children in a more protective way since having my own.

Merille Bridge marked the start of the tar and I could have dropped down and hugged it. Except there was a group of teenage boys crowding around, being pleasant enough but keeping me wary. Quite a few stray dogs were taking an interest in my bike as well, so I was keen to get clear of the town. The bridge went over a parched riverbed that looked a lot smoother than the road I had just completed. I experienced a feeling of utter elation at only having asphalt for the rest of Africa.

The road swung south-east and for the final 50 miles of the day I slowed into the wind, despite having a gradual downhill. Ololokwe Mountain dominated my view as I skirted its mammoth sheer granite cliffs, rising out of a canopy of shrub savannah to its completely flat top crowned in lush green vegetation. It looked like another ecosystem up there, like Marsabit, in the clouds.

Archers Post lived up to its Wild West name, a street full of wood-fronted shops surrounded by little more than dust and sparse shrubby trees. Most signage was home-made and it felt like a frontier town. It was sorely tempting to stop as I felt seriously weak. My legs were fine but my head hung on the bike; I felt lethargic and lacking in focus. My Garmin watch then ran out of batteries and I stopped at the roadside to charge it off the battery pack for twenty minutes. I would never normally stop for such an excuse, but in truth I was feeling broken. Those final miles with Ed weren't triumphant and I limped into Isiolo in the steady rain.

It was a much bigger town than I had expected, the largest since Rastafarian Shashamane. And I had my guard up. Whether the throngs of men on the main thoroughfare, the vehicles and the sudden noise deserved my suspicion or not, in the late-afternoon light, in my shattered state, I felt all eyes were on me. I just wanted to find my hotel room to hide in.

Nestled between a few shops, a stairway led up to the hotel reception on the first floor, which I carried my bike up to. I was concerned about being dripping wet and muddy. But a Muslim man, dressed elegantly in brown and gold and sporting an impressive beard, welcomed me in a warm, fatherly manner and immediately showed me to a large room. It is amazing how a caring gesture and the relief of reaching the end of the day's ride can make one's spirits soar. I had been in the mental doldrums for a few hours, but there was a lot to celebrate. Good roads ahead, past the area of security concerns, and now pretty close to the equator.

There were quite a few parts that I'd had couriered out to Kenya that I didn't need, and I had about fifteen minutes to unpack, repack, and get Ed and Martin on the road again. Having new kit was another reason to celebrate, but I didn't need spare sunglasses, so these I gave to Martin, who was utterly delighted despite having battled without complaining through forty-eight hours of horrendous food poisoning. I sent a parcel back with Ed including the maps I had used, and the worn cycle jerseys for charity auctions, but opted to bin the bib shorts: I wouldn't want anyone bidding for them. After a heartfelt thanks to them both, they set off for the long night drive back to Nairobi.

Alone, wonderfully alone, I celebrated my new-found freedom with my first shower in six days, then headed out for dinner, finding a Barclays Bank, a Chinese restaurant and lots of other international reminders, utterly unlike what I had seen in the hundreds of miles I had just cycled through. Chicken and chips – my first chips in Africa – and then the same again. I felt human at last, and crawled into bed at 8 p.m.

North Kenya would be the only stretch where I opted to have a security escort, which turned out to be an expensive option for some peace of mind. There hadn't been a whiff of danger between Moyale and Isiolo. But Ed had been easy company and good moral support, especially as I'd racked up at least a puncture a day on those unpaved, broken roads.

Day 22: Isiolo to Juja

From Isiolo the road climbed immediately and relentlessly for 40km – 1,500 metres of ascent, which was never steep but a horrid gradient nonetheless because I no longer had my easy climbing gears. It meant spinning away furiously and making slow progress or cranking out my big gears, out of the saddle, for most of the first three hours. I kept forgetting where the broken sprocket was, so intuitive is gear-changing, but the crunching chain on metal teeth immediately reminded me. Despite this I actually felt really good after my first proper night's sleep since entering Kenya.

Nickson Mwaura is a Kenyan cyclist who first contacted me in 2009. He was doing well in his local mountain-bike races and had aspirations to cycle internationally, so I offered to fly him over to compete in the seven-day TransWales race. He did so wearing my Artemis World Cycle jersey and created quite a stir, but understandably struggled in the Welsh cold, mud and rain. Nickson lives in Nanyuki, the closest town to the equator on the Trans-African Highway, and had been in touch all along, really excited to meet up at last. Over the years I had sent him quite a lot of cycling kit and advice to keep him going and he seemed to do quite a lot to help his community, so I was happy to help.

But when I reached Isiolo, Nickson had called again to say that he had arranged for another friend to cycle with me in the morning. I wasn't yet out of the mental doldrums when he called and in as polite a way as I could I asked if he would please, please tell his friend *not* to join me. Necessarily antisocial, and the right move: those first three hours of climbing were pretty grim and I would have really struggled making small talk with a complete stranger. It was a time to dig deep within, not to be chaperoned.

I was climbing up to the plateau that lies above Nairobi and is dominated by Mt Kenya, which although 600 metres lower than the more famous Kilimanjaro still rises to 5,200 metres and dominates the landscape. I caught glimpses of it, a volcano eroded to expose a snow-sprinkled core, in the distance at dawn, but the horizon was soon shrouded in cloud and rain, which I hoped would stay to the east.

The countryside went from arid, sandy scrub to lush, rolling hills with neat fences and tended crops. I could have been in England. This really was a very different place, and not just in terms of its geography. At the very top of the climb I found a small whitewashed farm shop with picnic tables spread out across a lawn where they served me chips, fried eggs and strong black coffee. The shop next door was an incredible surprise, just like any farm shop in the UK, full of trinkets, oddities and quaint stuff for the house: cookbooks, mosaics, kitchen utensils, fridge magnets and local craftware. This was a whole new world, more like the Cotswolds than the Kenya I had come to know.

On the road I started to see Range Rovers and other expensive vehicles. What surprised me more, which was a daft thing to be surprised by, was the sight of white people, lots of them. Other than Ed, Colin, Jonathan and AR I hadn't seen white people since Egypt.

The road went up a bit more then ran mainly downhill into Nanyuki. From the unfenced, barren wilderness of the north, I now found myself in a land of tourist lodges, ranches and, oddest of all, signs for organic restaurants. This was expat Kenya, and of course home to those who had been here too many generations to consider themselves expats. I had crossed an invisible line, out of tribal Kenya and into a melting pot of cultures. With this change the roads also got gradually busier, partly due to the holiday weekend, the Friday exodus from Nairobi northwards into this idyllic countryside.

My plans to film the north of the country for three days had, as I said, fallen through in the weeks before the start due to the huge quotes and daft security requests. But an old school friend, Philip Maciocia, had recently relocated from Cape Town to Nairobi and was helping out a lot, partly because he had ridden a motorbike along much of my route from Nairobi to Cape Town, and also because his girlfriend Alice was a camerawoman and was free to come out and film. It was only a day, but this would be the only filming until I reached mid-Zambia.

Alice was twenty-nine and had grown up between these parts and England, her mother a local pilot. Straight away I noticed the light canvas shoes, the head-to-toe fashion – another telltale sign that this was no longer the wilderness, the world where clothes were purely functional. My first impressions were wrong: Alice proved tougher than I initially gave her credit for, running around all day in deteriorating conditions to get the shots. It wasn't easy to keep track of me as the traffic worsened and then the rain started. At one stage Alice and her driver lost me for well over an hour, and I had no idea if they were ahead or behind. Nor did they.

I had last seen Phil in Nairobi the year before during the Commonwealth journey. He loved life in the African continent and had no intention of coming home to Scotland. I found him again late that morning, at the roadside with Alice and half a dozen friends. They were on a mass weekend exodus, heading to a house further north near Lewa. They were all around my age, clean-shaven, well dressed, and they cheered and clapped as I pulled up. I was sweaty and dirty but it was only next to friends to whom I could relate that I suddenly felt self-conscious of this. Phil apologized for not having managed to track down a new USB battery pack for me. Hearing this, one of his friends dashed back to his car and gave me his pack. A real gent – thanks, Alex Perez-Fragero. After a few pleasantries there wasn't much more to be said on the roadside and I was desperate to make up for my slow start.

Just north of Nanyuki I saw Alice set up at the roadside beside a big group of people. I wondered what was going on, and then spotted a big yellow sign: THE EQUATOR. In the madness of the traffic and the filming I had forgotten about this milestone, this ceremonial halfway point on my journey.

Pulling over, I surveyed the scene: a motley crew of tourists surrounded by locals selling tat. People were politely jostling for position in front of the sign for their photo. As I arrived a well-to-do Indian family were taking their turn, followed by a bizarre-looking man dressed in a white suit wearing a panama hat and carrying a cane. He was flanked by a few other men and I am sure was very wealthy and powerful, but he looked like the cliché of a drug dealer and a bit of a chump to me. I paused for the mandatory snap, said a few words to camera, then raced off into the southern hemisphere.

Nickson had been texting all morning, very keen to meet up, and as I raced through Nanyuki itself I scanned the roadside for him. I wasn't sure I would recognize him from his photos but was relying on the fact that I was hard to miss. Disappointed not to encounter him but unwilling to lose any time I kept going, and was well south of the town when he called. He was coming to find me. Sure enough, half an hour later a fairly battered white car pulled alongside. It was lovely to finally meet the man, a keen outdoor enthusiast obviously doing a lot in his community. We had known each other via calls and emails for six years so it was fairly unsatisfactory to stand on the busy roadside for only ten minutes catching up. He wanted to take me out for lunch and suggested a few places up ahead. I would have loved to but was seriously behind for the day and desperately wanted to keep going. As we stood there I could feel that rising irrational annoyance: yet another kind soul wants to show me friendship

but all I want to do is race on. Momentum, fast miles, they were
my fix. I once again apologized and took off.

Instead of lunch, I stopped at a petrol station and found Fruit
and Nut chocolate, Oreos and Red Bull – the first foods like this
since Sudan. By late afternoon I was on a three-lane highway, a
million miles from the dirt roads of yesterday, and on the main
artery into Nairobi. The heavens were open again and the conditions were absolutely torrential. Thankfully there was a hard
shoulder, which I took refuge on, but trucks in the slow lane still
hit me with wave after wave of water. I was comically wet, and it
was fun and miserable in equal amounts.

The hard shoulder of a motorway didn't feel like a place for
bicycles, especially in the limited visibility, but it felt a lot safer
than the preceding 50km had. This was single-lane and the tar
didn't have any run-off, so the road dropped off the edge. Traffic
pinned me to the side of the highway. At one point I instinctively
cycled off the edge, maybe a half-foot drop, slamming on the
brakes and skidding to a stop. Was I getting twitchy or had that
lorry actually been closer? They were all too close to tell. There
was no sense in looking back to see what was coming as the traffic was constant, so I'd had to react quickly. It was horrid. I was
really concerned for my safety but just tried to get through fast,
hoping with each turn the road would improve as there was no
prospect of the traffic lessening. In this 50km stretch I passed
four crashes, all involving more than one vehicle, three of them
involving trucks.

This motorway madness was mainly downhill and the fast
finish compensated perfectly for the slow start. Bang on 150
miles, my first target distance for a week, I took a slip road
off and, still in the bouncing rain, found the nearest hotel. I
was just 30km north of downtown Nairobi, a stupendous result,
and I was very much back in urban civilization. The north
had been sparse, wild and rough going. This felt like a new

chapter. I checked into a modern-looking hotel and paid by card – another first for a long time. I found my well-appointed room and . . . the electricity went off. Maybe this wasn't so different after all.

Alice had done a great job and she stayed for a while to back up all my footage and Garmin data. She also agreed for her driver to come back in the morning and guide me past Nairobi. Another capital, another myriad of route options, and I wasn't there for the experience: I needed the fastest route south.

Dinner was a rather lonely affair surrounded by a packed terrace of families enjoying the May holiday weekend. I was the only one eating on my own which I didn't normally mind at all, but seeing all the children and revelry made me feel more alone than usual. Between the tables, light came from burning piles of logs which gave off an intense heat that certainly wasn't needed. It looked atmospheric, but though we were at nearly 2,000 metres, higher than you might imagine being so near the equator, the evening air was still hot and humid.

The electricity had come back on after a few hours, and after dinner I managed to FaceTime back home. Seeing Harriet and Nicci was wonderful. The idea of speaking every day and video-calling regularly simply hadn't been the reality for the first twenty-one days on the road. There just weren't the telecoms, but neither was there the time. When I did call it was often late, after Harriet was in bed, and I was shattered. My conversations with Nicci were practical catch-ups on everything since we'd last spoken. Nicci could never really know how much time I spent on the bike thinking of them back at home, wondering what they were doing. Having Harriet in my life had completely changed my mindset on the road; my heart and head were no longer entirely in the moment – I was split between home and away. It was an odd evolution from the way I used to think on expeditions. I was glad for it, despite the distance. The constant thoughts about Harriet and her unborn brother or sister were powerful fuel to my fire, to live this journey and make it a success but also to finish and get back to them.

I had plenty of time to think that night as this proved to be a club hotel: the tables were cleared from part of the terrace, the fire piles stoked and the music cranked up until 3 a.m. Right outside my room. I lay there, a mosquito net hanging low over my face, staring at my hand-washed kit that was hanging off the frame of the four-poster. I was so tired that I was actually indifferent to the noise, and just lay there for hours. I was in the southern hemi-sphere, I was in May, the month I would finish the ride, I was back on good roads. I should make Tanzania tomorrow. I was nailing this. I eventually dozed off snug and contented with these positive thoughts alongside those of home.

Day 23: Juja to Longido

I woke to rain at 5.30 a.m. and ate an entire packet of chocolate Hobnobs while sitting on the bed, listening to the downpour. A wander around the local mini-market after dinner the night before had been another first since southern Sudan, and was a dangerous but enjoyable half hour after such a big day. Spoilt for choice after such basic rations, there was no way I could get down the amount of food I had bought. Which was daft as it just meant weighing down the bike. My post-dinner snack had involved sitting in bed working through three medium-sized tubs of ice cream. I hoped the hotel cleaner would appreciate the unopened jam, bread, five bananas, whole cake and large tinned pineapple I left behind.

There was a knock at my door just after 6 a.m.; it was Alice's driver, whose name I never got. It was still bucketing down so I was dragging my heels a bit. By the time I had faffed the final prep the rain was stopping, so I set out with a lot of sitting water on the roads, which soon made me as wet as if it were still raining. Considering how urban the surroundings were, the road was also very muddy.

After just 5 miles, before I expected it, the car turned off left. This was the eastern bypass that would take me around the entire city. I was glad to have a guide: I would probably have missed the turn because it wasn't clearly signposted. And it was the first half hour of the day so I was staring at the front wheel, hurting and trying to wake up properly – the normal routine. Soon after that an SUV pulled alongside and someone called to me from the passenger window. Whoever this was, he was very excited to see me. There wasn't much traffic, but it was a dual carriageway so I suggested he pull up ahead.

Felix was his name. Dressed in jeans and a vintage cycling jersey, with a scruffy short beard, he was a young Belgian expat and avid cyclist who had been following the expedition GPS tracker closely and had come out to help me through Nairobi. My lead vehicle was some way ahead and I watched it disappear, unaware that I had stopped. A few minutes later the driver returned, looking for me. Felix had only wanted to stop me for a photo and to ply me with some sports gels, a banana and a few bars. He didn't ask lots of questions, didn't want to delay me.

'You are smashing it, man,' he said. 'Wow, keep going, I think you can do this in less than forty-five days. I just want to get you through Nairobi fast.'

I pointed at the car stopped up ahead on the hard shoulder with its flashers on and thanked Felix, telling him I already had a support vehicle. He acknowledged this but still stayed with me for the next half hour, just behind with his flashers on, enjoying his support role.

The road took me out past Jomo Kenyatta International Airport to the east of the city. I looked through the high-security fences at the fleet of Airbuses and Boeings and wondered how long it would take to fly to Nairobi from Cairo. It had taken just over twenty-two days to cycle. Then came the critical turn-off, the junction at Athi river. I didn't want to head south-east down to the coast at Mombasa, although my last time there had involved a party and a night spent sleeping on the beach in a hammock, all of which flitted appealingly through my mind as instead I took the 100-mile Namanga road due south towards the Tanzanian border.

Three hours' sleep left me drowsy on the bike. As soon as Alice's driver turned back I found the first petrol station and downed two cans of Shark energy drink, four Snickers bars and a Cornetto – a solid fix of sugar, caffeine and calories. I was buzzing for a few hours then inevitably was very tired again. For so much of my route I hadn't had a choice in terms of what food I ate, but now that I was back in the land of the plentiful I had to be more disciplined. I found that the more tired and hungry I was the worse my food decisions were, inevitably at the times when I needed to be most careful about eating better.

The industrial suburbs of the ring road gave way to wide open arable farmland which then became rolling grasslands with sparse trees. About 10 miles from Namanga and the border post, I stopped. There was a massive wall of black cloud travelling north, blown by the wind I was battling into. I was hungry again, so I thought I could fix both by finding food and letting the storm pass. My first attempt was fairly unsuccessful. A roadside sign for MAASAI ECO LODGE carried a restaurant symbol so I slowly tackled a 500-metre dirt track to find a manicured group of thatched huts that looked more like a conference centre than a tourist lodge. I found the dining room where there were a few well-dressed waiters setting the whole room for a meal, but there were no guests around. They could do lunch, they said, but it would take an hour.

I was about to leave when I saw a basket on the sideboard with four small pasties in it. 'Can I have these?' I asked. The waiter had turned back to folding napkins and seemed surprised. But he dutifully took them away, heated them up and served them to me with a bottle of Coke. I still left feeling hungry. This visit had wasted about half an hour but would see me to the border if I didn't find anything else.

About half an hour later, and still in the dry, I did find a restaurant open to travellers. A seriously welcoming young man dressed in a grubby dishdash brought me a huge plate of beans, rice, meat and yoghurt. He took my bike off me, wheeled it into the bar area and showed it off to his friends there as if it was his own. I tucked in greedily, amused by his enthusiasm.

But my plan only partly worked: soon after I set out, the heavens opened and I rolled up to the border soaking.

Shortly before Namanga an overlander bus had passed me and I had seen quite a few safari tour vehicles. Not far to the west stretched the vast Serengeti, and to the south-east was Kilimanjaro, the summit of Africa, so this route was a tourist highway. I was certainly expecting a very different border to Moyale four days earlier.

The border seemed to be under construction, or being redesigned. There wasn't much town to be seen – a school, a small church, some municipal buildings and a few houses. The road was dug up after the Kenyan passport office and I ended up carrying my bike across the construction site and over a wall to get to the Tanzanian border. There must have been a proper way for vehicles but I couldn't see it and nobody stopped me.

There was a fifteen-minute queue on the Kenyan side, but that is because it was genuinely busy. When I reached the front the well-dressed official was efficient and friendly.

'Where have you come from by bicycle?'

'Moyale.'

'You have cycled all the way from Moyale?' he exclaimed, in disbelief. 'How many weeks?'

'Just four days,' I laughed.

'Four days!' He also laughed. 'That is not possible,' he added, but it wasn't said as an accusation. 'Where do you cycle to?'

'Cape Town, eventually.'

'And how long will that take?'

'About three weeks, I hope.'

He didn't respond, just chuckled as he stamped my passport and handed it back.

On the Tanzanian side there were no questions at all and I was photographed, fingerprinted and rubber-stamped in a matter of minutes. The rain had stopped and once again the border somehow defined a noticeable change in scenery. There was no town at all on the Tanzanian side and I was immediately into the most beautiful descent through a tree-filled landscape, passing the odd herd of goats being grazed by young Maasai.

I can't have been the first person to cross that border and think that Kilimanjaro was pretty close, much nearer than expected. But what I was pedalling towards was actually Mt Longido, a mere 2,550 metres but nonetheless a prominent rocky summit that stands proud on a desolate plain that stretches to the horizon. Being so big in its surroundings, I overestimated its height – or maybe that was me being daft and sleep-deprived.

The road skirted its steep, rainforested flanks and I reached the small town of Longido by 5 p.m., where I came to a stop. Ahead lay over 50 miles to Arusha, the region's capital, but the map looked completely desolate between here and there. I approached a stall owner, and after checking he spoke English asked if there were any hotels ahead. 'Yes, yes,' he reassured me after a confusing bit of back and forth. 'Maybe twenty kilometres.' I wasn't convinced but thanked him and carried on, stopping again at a checkpoint where the barrier was open. A man in his fifties, wearing a black suit, was talking to a few policemen in a very relaxed manner. As soon as I pulled my map out and started addressing the police, he butted in. It turned out he was a local politician, and from his manner, quite the man about town. His was certainly the only suit I saw. There was absolutely nothing ahead, nowhere to stay, he assured me. I told him what the stall owner had said. 'He knows nothing,' the politician said. 'He has not travelled twenty kilometres in his life.' He had no idea which stall owner I was talking about so it was a damning indictment of the worldliness of his constituents. But he was correct: the road ahead was utterly remote and there was no way I could reach Arusha by nightfall.

It turned into my earliest finish since day 1 in Egypt. The politician, whose name I never learnt, walked me across a dirt path, giving half a wave – a fatherly acknowledgement – to everyone we passed before we stopped at a large round building called Tembo Guesthouse. It turned out to be a very well-kept abode, definitely catering for tourists and founded by some Canadians. I seemed to be the only guest, and the politician left me with a firm handshake and a 'bon voyage' – quite the smooth operator.

To make myself feel better for stopping early I justified it like this: it looked like more heavy rain was on the way, I was desperate for a big night's sleep, and I had a stinking cold. I had only covered 135 miles, but had made it past another major city and across another border. I was making excuses, even relishing the basic luxury of the guesthouse, and I felt like I was being weak. The internal doubts about my decision to stop early nagged me the entire evening.

There is no mains electricity in Longido, only power from a private generator, so there was a strict rule on a fast shower. But it was a shower all the same, and then it was back to the main road to find dinner. By this time there were a lot more men around, all of them Maasai, dressed in deep-red robes, many with huge fresh loops in their ears, others wearing striking silver earrings. They were all tall and willowy but with the ruggedness of men who lived their entire lives outdoors. I joined the throng and managed to buy some electrical tape from a stall. The daily rains had made my handlebar tape split.

The first place I found, a small café, was a very simple set-up with half a dozen tables and an open kitchen at the back. But this was not a shack; this had been designed and was very clean and tidy. Most impressive were the staff, who were the only other people there: two young ladies who were laughing and singing as they cooked, while a matronly lady sat in the café and barked orders at them, but in a familiar, well-meant manner. I loved sitting there, writing my diary, watching these ladies being completely happy and entirely themselves; one of them even did a dance behind the counter which was greeted with hilarity by her friend. It wasn't something I had witnessed for a long time. After a few minutes one of them bounded through with a bowl of warm popcorn. I hadn't ordered it, but what a delicious surprise. Dinner was ugali, which is cornmeal porridge – so, a different variation on the popcorn – alongside beef stew and beef empanadas. It was all absolutely wonderful, and made all the better by my singing chefs.

By 7 p.m. I was back at the lodge and in bed.

Day 24: Longido to Ndareda

I woke quite a lot during the night with a cough but still felt like a different person after resting until 5.30 a.m. After dinner at the cheery café I had picked up some home-made baking, a doughnut and a cake, which turned out to be stodgy and filling. Doughnuts in Tanzania don't have much sugar, if any. A few packets of choc cream biscuits finished off breakfast and I pushed the bike out by six. There was no one around, and after I crossed the yard to the gate, I found it shut. I was locked in.

I left the bike and walked the entire perimeter, looking for a gap or somewhere I could climb out, but it was over 10 feet high and not even a rabbit could escape. Returning to the main metal gates, I had the idea to look inside the whitewashed gatehouse to see if the keys were hanging there. It seemed a bit excessive to have a gatehouse, no matter how small, for a guesthouse in a rural village. Poking my head inside the opening that acted as a window, I was surprised to see a man asleep on the floor.

'Hello,' I called.

The man woke immediately, and jumped to his feet. Far from being annoyed, he seemed positively excited to see me and very chatty. 'This is my office,' he exclaimed proudly, gesturing back at the tiny gatehouse he had emerged from. He walked proudly with me all the way back along the side streets until I reached the main road. 'My job is security,' he explained.

I gave him a tip as I got ready to leave, and teased him, saying, 'You can go back to sleep now.'

'No, no, I am security, I stay awake,' he responded.

The road headed south and then bent east to reach Arusha, so the side wind became a headwind. The wind had been pretty constantly from the south-east for a long time now. The first three hours were a slog, averaging 20km/h, and I really had to work for that. The terrain was gently rolling, mainly grasslands but lusher than what I had left on the Kenyan side. Oddly, this stretch reminded me a bit of the Scottish Borders, which is exactly what I was thinking when a lorry passed in the opposite direction with the livery 'Tam Ross Haulage' and the saltire flag. Bizarre. How did it end up here?

Then I passed a herd of zebras, and the Scottish illusion was gone. Apart from camels and baboons, this was my first sighting of a proper 'African' animal. On the right side of the road was the large group of zebras and on the left, only a hundred metres apart, was a smaller gathering of donkeys. There was no mixing, but they looked pretty similar, apart from the zebras having stripes and being a bit larger, of course.

The turn-off to the capital of Tanzania, Dodoma, came just before Arusha, a dog-leg back south-west, but I was surprised to see it as soon as I did. The road off to the right was very small, but the sign definitely said DODOMA so I dutifully followed. It soon petered out into a dirt track, but this was well compacted and easy to ride. I asked a local farm worker on his bicycle if I was heading for Dodoma. He confirmed I was, but I soon realized this wasn't what the map showed. I reckoned I was on a tiny rat run to cut off the loop into town. In any case it was beautiful: I found myself passing vineyards and manicured estates under a boulevard of ancient hardwoods that cast dappled shadows over the road. It was slow going, but I was lost in the moment, enjoying being off the Trans-African Highway, exploring a back road. This eventually emerged opposite Arusha airport at a T-junction and I turned right, immediately benefiting from the direction of the wind, which I had been battling. My only concern was that I had deftly but by accident missed Arusha, was now heading back into the countryside having covered 50 miles, and could feel an intense hunger. I pedalled along, hoping each corner would reveal somewhere to eat but soon realizing that each corner was in fact taking me further away from guaranteed food and therefore losing me more and more time. I wasn't carrying any supplies whatsoever.

I was on the verge of turning round, worried it could be a very long way before my next meal, when I reached a surprising sight. On my right was a whitewashed boutique shopping mall with manicured lawns. Except the car park was worryingly empty. I turned in and found that everything was shut except for an American-style diner. I couldn't believe my luck. It just seemed so incredibly incongruous.

The manager was a redhead. I stared at him as if I hadn't seen a redhead before (my wife and daughter have red hair). Everything about this place seemed out of context, but what a welcome refuge it was. It turned out it had only been open for three days – what a stroke of luck! I tucked into a full cooked breakfast with two extra servings of toast, two cappuccinos and two orange juices. It was simply amazing, accompanied by fast wifi. The diner was a very hard place to leave and I spent an hour there, far longer than a normal meal stop. But I left with my energy and morale on a big high which, along with what was now a tailwind, made for fast miles.

The road slowly descended into more arable land and I zoned out, eating up fast miles. My left knee was twinging again but it was just tight, nothing to worry about. I put it down to not having those normal climbing gears so I was pushing a lower cadence, grinding out bigger gears than normal. I didn't get off my bike for 100 miles – that's the power of a good meal. And I reached Babati, which was my target for the day, by 5 p.m. after almost exactly 150 miles.

My route turned off towards Singida, and I could see the road slowly rising out of view. I pushed the bike along some wooden planks over an open ditch, and under some trees to a row of stalls. After asking a stall owner for two packets of shortbread, two packets of chocolate biscuits and a Coke, I dug out the map to consider my options. I could either finish here, having achieved my target for the day, and then start tomorrow with a big climb, or carry on to the next town 23km away. There was enough day-light, but it looked like it could be climbing all the way. There was no saying what I would find there either: Ndareda looked tiny on the map, and I would be assured a decent hotel in Babati. Not for the first time I fought between the comfortable and safe option and the ambitious and uncertain one. Meanwhile the stall owner didn't want to give my change back. At the second time of asking he gave me some money, blowing cigarette smoke over me at the same time, but there was no way it added up. That decided it,

I wasn't staying in Babati. I'd been looking for any reason to tip the balance of my internal argument.

Sure enough the road did climb, up and up and up. It was a lovely gradient though, one that I would have really enjoyed if I'd had all my gears. As it was, it was pretty much two hours out of the saddle, but every metre gained was one I didn't need to climb in the morning. The views back were breathtaking; as the light yellowed the road called me onwards and upwards. I was passing small wooden houses and animal pens made from bound branches – back into smallholdings and subsistence after the industrial-scale farming of the lowlands.

I was still climbing and on a big sweeping left when I reached Ndareda, which looked very small and basic, a village of huts on the hillside. I was committed to staying here – there was nowhere else to aim for, and I certainly wasn't going back – but the first signs weren't good. A group of young men on the roadside shook their heads. A bit further on a stall owner told me that there was no guesthouse, no motel, nowhere to stay. I was trying to think of English words they would recognize. I knew there wouldn't be a hotel here but I had to find somewhere, even if it was someone's house, so I turned back and followed a dirt track towards a cluster of stalls. I was drawing a lot of attention, but no one approached me. Then, as I dismounted and walked over to another stall owner, a young man came forward from the crowd and introduced himself as Musa Yusuph Chakulanga, a teacher.

Musa led me down a narrow dirt path, followed by his friend, another local teacher. I asked what his friend taught, and he told me English. Musa was a maths teacher. I hoped his maths was better than his friend's English as he couldn't string a sentence together. Musa, however, did speak good English.

We arrived at a doorway to a small courtyard. The lady inside spoke urgently to Musa in what I assumed was Swahili. After a minute we carried on. Further down the hill we stopped at another doorway, this time leading straight into a small building, and a man looked at me silently before saying something to Musa. He walked on.

'They see the colour of your skin and they want the best,' he remarked by way of explanation.

'I don't need anywhere special,' I protested. 'Just somewhere safe, with a bed and some water.'

The third place we stopped at was behind metal gates, a cobblestone courtyard and four rooms behind padlocked doors with very small windows with metal bars on them. The man didn't seem certain about giving me a room, but Musa insisted, and for the princely sum of 8,000 shillings – about £2.40 – I was given one with electricity and even an ensuite toilet and shower. By this time it was dark and Musa left me, saying he would be back in half an hour to pick me up for dinner. I hadn't asked for this but was grateful. It is always exciting at the end of a day on the bike when your luck turns fast and you find a bed and dinner.

Following Musa by headtorch back up towards the road, we entered a low tin shack where about twenty men were sitting behind rows of blue plastic tables, almost like in school, except they were all watching a rather fuzzy picture on the television. It was Manchester City versus Tottenham. By the entrance a few ladies were cooking over an open stove. The three of us – myself, Musa and the English teacher who didn't speak English – sat beside each other in silence as everyone seemed engrossed in the game. Along with the others we were served rice, a meat stew, some greens that looked like spinach, and beans, all in a big round prison-canteen-style tray. This was accompanied by a big plate of chips. I don't follow football, but this was a link to home and I found it comforting getting caught up in the excitement of my fellow diners, all of whom were clearly supporting Manchester City.

It was only afterwards, as we walked around the village in the dark, Musa showing me where to buy bread, bananas and biscuits for the morning, that we got talking. He had recently married but his wife lived in Dar es Salaam, the biggest city in Tanzania and its former capital. Musa was trying to save up enough money so he could leave his job, or get relocated by the government to a school there so they could live together. Despite the hardship of life apart, not to mention conditions in this small village, Musa was optimistic for the future. He wanted me to leave with a good impression of Ndareda, pointing out the school, all the shops and details about its way of life, all in an unfussy and charming way.

It had been a cracking first full day in Tanzania – nearly 2km of ascent but almost 170 miles in the right direction. I sat in bed writing my journal and doing the mileages. Those poor days in southern Ethiopia and north Kenya had hugely impacted on the fast start in Egypt and Sudan, but I was still firmly on target for a forty-five-day finish if I could keep averaging over 150 miles a day.

The turn-off at Babati meant that I would be doing extra miles, however, looping a long way west to Singida on the B143 while the main trunk road, the A104, carried on due south, far more directly to Dodoma. My route was an extra 90 miles, nearly two-thirds of a day's riding, not to mention all the climbing up and over. However, in this case the B road was a lot better than the A road: from my research, it appeared that the short route was still under construction with long stretches of corrugated dirt. It was still a tough call going an extra 90 miles to stay on tar, but with my already broken gears I simply couldn't risk clattering the bike over 160 miles of difficult roads.

Day 25: Ndareda to Manyoni

I didn't travel far before looking for a second breakfast, and the village of Katesh looked like the only place I might find food before Singida another 60 miles up the road. A man was sitting cross-legged in front of an open fire with a broad metal bowl and I watched him making chapattis. I assumed it was his son running around serving. I asked for eggs, at which he ran out on to the road, returning a few minutes later clutching three. His father broke these into the chapattis as they fried, which turned out to be delicious and very filling.

'Do you have coffee?' I asked the boy.

'Yes, sir.' He came back a moment later with a sachet and a mug. 'Would you like coffee in tea?'

'No, in hot water, please.'

'No, no water,' he explained.

'OK,' I said hesitantly, and watched him empty the sachet of coffee into the mug, hoping the tea was very weak. It wasn't, and the hot cocktail inevitably wasn't very nice.

It remained hilly until Singida, interesting scenery, and a decent tailwind made the final descent a real thrill. The town itself was a giant's playground of rocks, strewn all over the place or piled on top of one another. The area has some of the continent's oldest rock art, and as I cycled past I was drawn to their vast scale, as if they had hailed from the mountainside and partially embedded in the earth, hugely prominent, completely bare. Some buildings lay in the shadows of these huge rocks, lending them an even bigger scale.

My headline for day 25's journal simply read 'Tough day mentally – very boring scenery and slow going', which summarizes the rest of the day. There was a little more to it than that, but I did struggle to pull my spirits up, battling the wind as the road curved progressively west. This left me pedalling downhill at 12mph in a barren scrubland. The only thing that broke up this stretch were lots and lots of speed bumps. They came in sets of three or four in a block and were really tough on the bike. I held my breath for punctures, but got away with it.

For the final three hours, now heading south again, the skies grew dark and the heavens opened. I was glad it had been mainly downhill as it was a serious push to make town by dark over some pretty rough tar. I wasn't the only one who'd had the idea to skip the dirt roads and I was kept on edge by hundreds of trucks thundering past. There was a small hard shoulder, but the trucks seemed to keep their wheels inside this to allow other vehicles to overtake. One gave me a real fright, coming very, very close. There was nothing I could do but hammer on, hoping to reach town by nightfall. By the time I reached Manyoni I had my lights on. What a relief to crack 157 miles.

Manyoni sits near a coming-together of routes, and on the main road it looked like a transitory town, a truck stop, with wide pavements and numerous eateries and places to stay. I ducked into Manyoni Star Lodge, which stood out with its lit-up frontage and painted gates. Dripping wet, I felt a bit self-conscious stepping into the narrow entrance hall, which had a reception counter down one side and a TV blaring out a Wild West film on the wall to my right. What immediately caught my eye was a large sign propped up on the end of the counter with a handwritten list from 1 to 9 of the rules of the lodge. These included 'Married Guests must show their marriage certificates', 'Money or other valuables must be handed to the concierge' and, lastly, 'Noise and quarrelling are forbidden in the hotel'. It finished with a scribble in green pen reminding guests to 'Feel at home'. It was like being shouted at then being asked if you are having a good time!

I am sure the receptionist was just bored, as opposed to shifty, but there was no way I was handing over any valuables to him. On the sign-in sheet it asked for my 'Kabila Lako', my tribe. I paid £2.50 for a room and dripped my way another few metres to the door right in front of me. Ironically it was so close to reception that it was me who ended up asking the receptionist to turn the volume down. The furnishings were quite girly, with a candy-pink mesh curtain hanging from a four-poster bed made up with bright purple linen, but I couldn't have cared less: I was out of that relentless rain.

I found dinner in a shack next door. In the bucketing rain and thick mud I didn't explore further. The lad running the kitchen must have been in his early twenties and was very enthusiastic about getting me fed and looked after. He sent off another boy to get me something to drink then set about cooking on a cut-out oil drum. I explained that I was seriously hungry, and without further prompting he cooked a whole chicken and two chip omelettes. Admittedly it wasn't the world's largest chicken, but it was still a veritable feast, and the chip omelettes were a complete revelation – inspired, delicious, and a total treat with a bit of spicy sauce which he said was home-made. All this for £6, too, which is a lot for a meal in rural Tanzania, but I would have paid ten times that I was so hungry and it was so good. It was a wonderful way to end a pretty rubbish day on the bike as the rain continued to fall in small waterfalls off the tin roof.

As I devoured my food, my cook sat down opposite me with lots of questions. He asked all about my cycle, where I had been, where I was going. 'I would love to travel, I would like to see other countries, but I need money,' he said. 'You have to eat three times a day – this is too expensive for me.' He seemed resigned to this fact, as he sat there playing with two mobile phones.

Day 26: Manyoni to Chipogolo

It was 80 miles to Dodoma, 80 miles mainly east. What a glorious milestone Dodoma was: from there I would start heading south and west all the way to Cape Town. For this final easterly tack, though, my old bipolar friend, the wind, was back with a vengeance. Today we were not friends. But I was also suffering from a lack of decent food. After just 10 miles I stopped in a small village and tried three places, but none was serving food yet. It was just gone 7 a.m. The fourth I tried was a small wooden stall with dried biscuits and not much more. But I spotted a large round piece of Tupperware which was steamed up on the inside. A group of a dozen teenage boys and younger children were standing around, but there was no one older in charge. I gestured to the plastic tub and was presented with five fried bread balls, which I wolfed down with a bottle of Coke. They were delicious, but pure stodge. It turned out that they were called kaimatti, a flour dumpling.

One of the boys was carrying an infant on his back. It was asleep when I arrived and I watched its blissful slumber, its head fallen to the side out of the blanket swaddle. The boys were all talking about me as I perched on a narrow wooden bench, but I paid no notice, tucking into the fried bread and being reminded of Harriet. Then the baby woke and caught sight of me. His reaction was one of sheer terror, the sort of horrible panic a parent never wants to see in their child. He was terrified of me. I guessed he hadn't seen a white person before and he fought and wriggled to get away. Rather than comforting the poor baby, the teenage boys thought this reaction was hilarious and brought him closer, trying to put him on the ground next to me, making the baby scream more and more. This wasn't a normal little upset but a panicked and hysterical screaming. I told them not to but they took no notice, so I quickly packed up and left before they could torment the baby any more. I felt terrible as I cycled away; it was a horrible reaction, a father's nightmare. And I felt very lonely indeed, thinking of family but feeling a million miles away.

Two dry chapattis, a bottle of Fanta and six packets of biscuits finished off the morning's diet. No surprise, then, that I felt woeful, like I was riding along with a flat battery.

Late that morning I did something for the first time on the

ride. I stopped. I planted my feet wide, put my hands on the bars and dropped my head, closing my eyes. I just couldn't face carrying on. I could feel myself swaying slightly as the din and gust of a truck passed me by, but I kept my eyes shut. After a few minutes I opened them and squinted. Everything seemed very bright. I knew I would carry on soon, that this wasn't a major crisis, but for the time being I just had to stop. I couldn't keep battling. For ten minutes my world came to a halt. I felt pretty terrible in a physical sense, but it was wonderful to give my mind a rest, to stop tormenting myself to ride fast – to just stop.

About 30 miles from Dodoma I found myself in a huge valley, back in those hills I had crossed the other way the previous morning, but now much further south. Ahead something caught my eye, some cyclists descending fast, but they were a good way off and it took quite a few minutes for them to draw close. When they did, they slowed, then swung across the road. I was at a loss for a moment who this could be, but then remembered.

A few months before I left for Africa a Scot called Ross Methven had got in touch via Facebook to offer his assistance. He had cycled Nairobi to Cape Town recently and taken a broadly similar route to mine, albeit more slowly. I had then met Ross in Edinburgh and he had proved to be a seriously helpful contact. He had put me in contact with the Dodoma Cycling Club and their captain Joshua Malanda, who had advised me to take the detour via Singida.

This was no mirage, this was none other than Joshua and his team-mates coming to chaperone me into Dodoma. My spirits soared. They were brilliantly welcome and exactly what I needed at that moment.

I hadn't expected Joshua to come out and ride with me, but I knew that he had been contacted to pick up my new cassette, which had been expressed out from the DHL office, and to meet me in Dodoma with it. I couldn't wait to fix my gears; it would make all the difference in these hills and when I was into a head-wind. But the last I'd heard they were being held in customs at Dar es Salaam and were therefore unlikely to arrive in Dodoma in time for me. This was the same package that had been destined for Arusha, but I had got there before it arrived so it had been redirected. It looked like this might happen again. There was no problem sending packages quickly to Africa, as I had found in Khartoum; the difficulty was signing them out from customs. That is where you hit bureaucracy, unexpected costs and delays.

All three riders wore red- and white-patched team kit, and Joshua had a small rucksack, which his dreadlocked ponytail hung over. Aged fifty-five with a scruffy moustache and goatee, he could have been a decade younger, kind-featured but very wiry. He rode a hybrid bike with flat bars, while the two younger riders had road bikes. One of them had surfing shorts on and no helmet, but it soon became clear that these younger riders were seriously strong and they left Joshua and me far behind on the hills. I didn't even try to hold them, preserving what little energy I had. Joshua was the wiser, more experienced cyclist, and very steady on the bike. That is until one of the youngsters swerved in front of him to avoid a rock in the road and clipped his front wheel. Joshua fell hard across the tarmac, grazing his elbow and knee, but without any annoyance or complaint he picked himself up and carried on.

Joshua had arranged for a national TV crew to meet and interview me on the outskirts of Dodoma. I was so relieved to make the city and so grateful for Joshua's support that I didn't mind the slight delay as we stopped right by some traffic lights on a busy junction. Reflecting on a morning of baby-bullying and boredom, I have to admit I fibbed slightly in answer to the excited questions about my day so far. But I could also reflect on the warm welcome I'd received from so many people, not just in Tanzania but ever since Cairo, with some obvious exceptions in Ethiopia.

I didn't need to go into Dodoma itself and was resigned to the fact that I wouldn't get the DHL parcel with my new gears. It being a very long holiday weekend, Friday through to Tuesday, sealed this fate. But Joshua felt responsible because he had been given the task of getting my new gears, and he insisted we go and check. I couldn't very well on the one hand say the gears were important but then say I didn't want to go and see if they were there. But the truth was I knew they wouldn't be there, and if they were they wouldn't be handed over, so I was willing to cut my losses. I decided to call Scotland for an update. I couldn't get a connection. My mobile network provider EE had at that moment decided to cut me off as a precaution because of the higher than usual international usage. So with no means to communicate we detoured into Dodoma, stood in line at the DHL parcel depot, were told what I already knew and lost an hour. This wasn't Joshua's fault, he was trying his utmost, but it was bloody annoying after the morning's tough slog.

After climbing out of the city my domestiques turned back. They had got me out of a tough spot and I had enjoyed their company, especially Joshua, who without any prompting had seemed to understand the battle I was facing and fallen in beside me, not asking 101 questions like normally happens, just quietly supporting, chatting amicably.

The road wound up through the hills and steadily became more interesting, or was it that I was appreciating it more now that I had passed another milestone, another capital city, and was no longer being wind-blasted? I stopped at the first hamlet where a stall by a garage was selling chips, which were pre-cooked and cold but still delicious to a hungry cyclist. Once again I handed over a big shilling note and had repeatedly to ask for change. In the end my cold chips cost nearly as much as my hotel the night before. This was becoming a bad habit in Tanzania.

Like the night before, I was left pushing it really hard in the final hours to make the village of Chipogolo by dark. There were quite a few small hamlets, but no obvious places to stay. And I was carrying only a few packets of biscuits so camping out wasn't an option, although it was dry. I hoped I was getting south of the rainy season by now.

Only a few miles out of town, my back tyre punctured. It was annoying and bad timing, but didn't seem serious until I found a rip to the sidewall. Déjà vu from day 1, and I was left trying to place a patch on the tyre as well as the inner tube. In the fading light on the dusty roadside this was a real faff.

A pick-up truck pulled up on the other side, heading north, and two young men stepped out.

'Are you OK?'

They were well dressed and spoke good English.

'Yes, fine, just punctured,' I replied.

'Can we give you a lift somewhere? This area isn't too safe to be out at night.'

I thanked them and explained that I just needed to make Chipogolo. They told me they had just come from there and assured me I would find a good place to stay. They kindly stayed with me, using the truck lights to help with my repairs.

It was pretty much pitch dark when I arrived just before 7 p.m., using my bike light and headtorch to navigate. It didn't help that there was no mains electricity and no streetlights, so although there were plenty of people, vehicles and a few animals roaming around, apart from the searching headlights of passing cars everything was in darkness.

I stopped a couple of teenagers who led me down a dirt track to a guesthouse that had a few faint light bulbs running off batteries. There was no humming generator so the place was silent.

It would all have been a bit unnerving if you were skittish of the dark. Arriving late and trying to secure an abode and food was certainly tricky. It was no place for an active imagination.

My tiny room had a light, but it was so dim I still needed my headtorch, and there was no electricity from the plug socket and certainly no water in the shower. Walking back towards the main road, I found a stall to buy some water and biscuits for breakfast and a hut with two women cooking who gave me rice, beans and meat. As I waited, I scribbled:

> No way to communicate as phone cut off. Pleased with today's mileage considering wind and delays with Joshua. Must get better food in mornings – not just biscuits. Tanzanians very hot with money! Almost always have to ask for change and often correct them. Shopping this evening – put bunch of notes and coins on counter for them to take correct amount and they took it all!

Day 27: Chipogolo to Kisolanza

It was still dark when I wheeled out and the busy little village of Chipogolo was asleep, so I never really saw what it looked like. My main mission for the morning was to re-establish coms; I needed to get my phone working somehow. Every day for nearly four weeks on the road, wherever there had been a signal there had been multiple calls back and forth, mainly with Una, who was back in her role at base camp, pulling in messages from a much wider team. Behind the simple act of pedalling as far as I could each day there was an impressive amount of logistics going on.

By the time I reached the village of Kisima I had already eaten five small packets of biscuits, but I stopped when I spotted proper breakfast: a man frying chapattis on a blackened metal

frying pan over hot coals – a makeshift barbecue. He was bare-
foot, sitting on a plank of wood next to a few small redbrick
buildings with blue tarpaulin roofs, not only cooking but looking after his son. On the bench opposite was a big pile of fish,
which were not on the menu and didn't look very appetizing
lying out in the sun.

It wasn't hard to spot this place, even though there was no
restaurant, as a group of young men were milling around, and
another group was on the roadside nearby standing around their
motorbikes. This was a Tanzanian thing, and I had only just
worked out that these men were not petrol-headed delinquents
but the local taxi rank. One lad being served his chapatti was
wearing a jacket back to front – the uniform of the Tanzanian
moto-taxi driver, a practical step to create a windcheater. It certainly wasn't cold enough to justify a jacket otherwise.

As usual, I stood out and everyone stared at me, but there was
no hassle, no intimidation. I asked the chef for some eggs and
chapattis, then realized that by asking for eggs I was going
expensive, going for the deluxe option. I would already be seen
as rich just for being white and being a traveller, but ordering
eggs, well, that confirmed it.

I sat next to the jacketed lad on a broken plastic chair and
broached the subject of using his mobile for a quick call if I paid
him. He handed it straight over to me without question. I explained
that I was calling Europe and it may be expensive. I hit the keypad
and the screen came to life showing a naked white model in a pro-
vocative pose. The lad seemed pretty pleased about this; it was
probably the reason he was keen for me to see his phone. But there
was no credit on it, the line was dead. I gave him 10,000 shillings
and asked him to go and buy some credit. He seemed delighted at
this and disappeared off on his motorbike. As I ate my breakfast
I wondered if I would ever see him again.

Ten minutes passed and I was about to leave when he sped up

and proudly presented his phone. I was surprised and relieved to get through to Una, give her the all-OK message and explain the phone issue, which she could then sort. I gave the lad another 5,000 shillings for his honesty and left, well fed and back in communications.

After a few overcast and cooler days, today the sun was shining and it was dry and windy. My warm-up miles were kind and fairly flat, skirting Mtera reservoir until the road crossed on top of the dam wall. Without stopping I pulled my phone out midway across and took a photograph of the view across the Great Ruaha river, which to my right was a huge expanse of water and to my left was little more than a stream.

When I reached the far side, two soldiers stepped out of a sentry tower and one of them waved me to a stop with one hand; the other held his assault rifle.

'No photo, why do you take photo?' he shouted as I came to a stop.

'Sorry, I am a tourist.' The adrenalin was pumping as I remembered Anselm Nathanael's treatment in Egypt. 'I will delete the photo. I didn't know.' I made a show of deleting the image, although I didn't, and pushed off again before they could say anything else, only glancing back after about a hundred metres to see them still standing in the road, staring after me.

Ahead lay the impressive tree-lined peaks of the Uluguru Mountains, but I was spared the climb for a good few hours as the road contoured around to the west, following but out of sight of the lake shore, to the town of Izazi. From there I started a stunning, gradual, winding ascent. Teams of roadworkers, under the watchful eye of Chinese engineers, were building drainage and shuttering for concrete works at the roadside, giving me a regular audience for my efforts. A few cheered and others waved, but most just watched me silently. The views that opened up to my right as I climbed were over a sparse, semi-arid forest, vast and breathtaking emptiness. I would have assumed this was uninhabited, but on the way up I passed a few tracks off to the side with rudimentary signposts to remote villages. The road was impressively wide, hemmed in only by a crash barrier, but without any markings and made of pretty rough tar. It was the most beautiful cycling in Africa so far. It maybe wasn't as high or as rugged as the Ethiopian Highlands, but I had peace to enjoy the climb this time, despite spending most of the time out of the saddle.

The descent was glorious too, and once again I discovered I was seriously hungry. I pulled in at the next village for a massive portion of rice and beans. The young lad there was obviously used to the company of travellers, this being the only place to eat on this remote stretch of the Trans-African Highway, so rather than race off to get my food he started trying to teach me Swahili – a conversation he had obviously had many times before, I am sure to the adoration of his audience. However, as rude as it was, I was too hungry to care about learning Swahili and stopped him after a few minutes, insisting he go and get my food. He did so, and to his credit lost none of his enthusiasm, sitting opposite me as I ate, still trying to teach me a few words. I was his only customer and I dutifully repeated 'Karibu' (welcome) and 'Kwaheri' (goodbye), among others.

Reaching the larger town of Iringa, I also met the Tanzam Highway, the larger trunk road from Dar es Salaam on the coast to the Zambian border. With this the road quality improved and I started to come into more farmland, but still spent the afternoon in a landscape predominantly of trees. The most impressive of these were the baobabs, with their massive trunks, like stout elderly statesmen plonked along the highway. I could see that some of these trunks, measuring many metres across, were hollow inside. These huge vessels for water and shelter are the perfect adaptation for these drought-plagued parts. Every part of the tree can be and is used and its 'bread fruit' is edible. Even without being told, I could see that this species must have a special place in the locals' lives – not for nothing is it known as the tree of life. I even stopped to walk around one, to explore its vast cork-like and warty trunk. This was one of the few times I stopped in the entire Cairo to Cape Town race because something other than food caught my interest at the roadside.

I had been told by Phil Maciocia about a wonderful place to stay, the Old Farm House at Kisolanza Farm. According to my estimates it would be at 138 miles, which I could just about justify, although ideally I would have liked to go further. It actually came nearly 10 miles earlier than that; my sums had been off, and I stood at the road sign, done in old English calligraphy, fighting the urge to carry on. Una had already been in touch with Mark Nightingale, the Englishman who ran the camp, who had initially said they were fully booked. But once Mum explained what I was doing, he said that Al Humphreys had also stayed there years before and that of course they could find space for me. By the time I had clattered down the long dirt track to the main gates I was questioning if this was a good idea. But I definitely needed one big night's rest to shake the stinking cold that was lingering – another excuse for stopping early, as it was only 5.45 p.m.

Inside the gates I was met by the sight of German tourists wandering around sipping on cans of beer, huge overlander trucks parked up with tent awnings, and an array of thatched-roof buildings. Mark met me like a long-lost friend and showed me across the camp to a small thatched house which he was gifting me for the night. This was incredibly kind and not at all expected. It normally cost $120 – definitely a price for the tourists, considering my average night in Tanzania so far had cost less than $5.

Mark had walked the length of Europe, much of Africa too, and ended up here nearly a decade before. He had stayed ever since, helping to build this amazing refuge for travellers in the middle of the remote central region of Tanzania. He explained that it had been completely open until recent years, when some night raids forced them to build a fence and employ security. My house had all the luxury of a hotel with the rustic charm of an African bush camp. This was as close as most travellers got to the real Africa, and it was a wonderful place, a long way from staying in village dwellings and eating off the stalls of street vendors. Mark left me to it, saying he would see me at 7 p.m. for dinner, and I wandered around my new abode with a wide grin, absolutely delighted with the luxury, the homeliness, with my incredible luck. No regrets for stopping now.

Dinner was a magnificent three-course meal served by candle-light in a large thatched house. Wooden tables were made up with red and yellow cloths, like the shawls I had seen tribesmen wearing, and a fresh bunch of flowers. A waitress offered wine or beer, which I was sorely tempted by. Soup, followed by a steak, cooked rare, with greens and a dozen new potatoes, and then a crumble and ice cream. An explosion of interesting fla-vours compared to my staple of flatbread, beans and rice. I wished I had someone to share it with. It is only ever during odd moments of luxury that I have that craving for company, to share the memory. I couldn't help but listen to a father and son on the next table planning their safari for the next few days, amused by their comments about the hardship of early starts and the lack of electricity. In their minds this was truly roughing it. In my recent experience this was living like royalty. To crown it all off, Mark came through afterwards and presented me with all the leftover desserts 'as a midnight snack'.

As I was about to leave, someone from another table called me over. I had spotted this man and his friend earlier as they arrived around the same time in a Red Cross decaled Land Cruiser. He introduced himself as Benson, and once he had asked where I was cycling he revealed, quite casually, that he had done the same trip, a long time ago.

'Really? When?'

'In 2003, with Tour d'Afrique, the first time there was a record on the route.'

Benson had ridden with Michael Kennedy on the original record, and here he was at a bush camp in the middle of Tanzania, en route south with his medical work. What a brilliant coincidence. We spent twenty minutes swapping tales about the route then and my journey now. So much had changed; it was as if each of us was describing a completely different continent. I could have stayed a lot longer because it was wonderful to hear Benson's stories and benefit from his enthusiasm for my ride, but I was shattered. It was 9 p.m. when I crashed out in the luxurious kingsize bed. There was nothing 'expedition' about this night. It was wonderful.

Day 28: Kisolanza to Mbeya

At 5.30 a.m. there was a knock on the door of my cabin and I jumped up to find a man standing there in the darkness holding a large wooden tray covered with a white tea towel. After turning on the porch light, thanking him with a tip and asking him to leave it on the table outside, I eagerly settled down to see what I had. Four freshly boiled eggs, a big pile of warm bread, butter, jam and a cafetière of coffee. Dressed in just my shorts, my toes curling into the cool earth, the campsite asleep around me, first light seeping through the branches, it was the breakfast of the trip, one of the best of my life.

Luxury slows you down: it was 6.45 before I got on my bike. I wasn't on a mission to go anywhere and it took a good hour to get back in the zone, to build the momentum again. When I did get back into the right mental gear I committed to doing at least a 270km day to average out yesterday's total. Not having to stop to find breakfast certainly helped me make up for lost time. I thought about how much faster I could go if all my meals were

taken care of, and of the quality I had experienced at the Old
Farm House. I reckoned that at least a few hours each day were
eaten up in the pursuit of calories, and a pile of biscuits and
Coke was often the best I could find.

For the first time in Africa I was riding through managed forests, huge areas of softwood that reminded me of parts of the
Continental Divide in the US. Then I entered a region of sun-
flowers, which felt like Provence. A sidewind to Makambako
changed into a tailwind when the road turned due west and I
finished with a massive push, absolutely flying along to reach
Mbeya by nightfall. However, this change of tack also spelt an
end to the hard shoulder and any generous width to the road,
and this was a major truck route. The regular crashed and broken-
down trucks reminded me of the danger; a few near misses and
being run off the road again made me even more wary. Some of
the trucks looked like deathtraps: one that passed me had no
windscreen and what must have been a broken suspension, as
one side of the cab drooped alarmingly to the right, into the
middle of the road. Along the side of tarred roads throughout
Tanzania is a dirt track where walkers, animals and most cyclists
go. Apart from around the cities of Dodoma and Dar es Salaam
it is unusual to find a cyclist on the tar. Quite simply, there is no
such thing as road share in Tanzania. The trucks assume you
will get out of their way, just like a donkey and cart would.

Despite my caution, my spirits were high for most of the day.
It is amazing what recovery and good food do to morale.
I stopped at 60km for a stocky meat soup, an omelette and
chapattis, then rode for another 100km before looking for lunch.
This restaurant was fairly large and partially outdoors thanks to
a large canopy with an open front to the road. About a dozen
people, all men, were scattered between the tables as I sat down
on the plastic garden-style furniture.

A guy in his early twenties came straight over to me and I assumed he was staff, even though he was holding a bottle of beer. He wasn't, but was obviously known to the staff. He asked what I wanted and said that he would order for me. He then sat down and started telling me his story, pausing to drink beer.

'I came to the city to beg the government for money to go to university, but they wouldn't give me any,' he explained.

'What were you going to study?' I asked.

'Law.'

'At which university?'

He faltered. I wasn't trying to catch him out but this place didn't look big enough to be a university town and I could see where this conversation was heading. He carried on talking about his life when my food arrived. I felt a bit sorry for him. I didn't doubt he had big plans, like we all do, and I am sure he had faced a lot of setbacks in his young life, but the truth of his situation was that he was getting drunk in the middle of the day. From his over-familiar manner with the female employees, I could tell he spent a lot of time in the bar.

Then the inevitable line came: 'You could make my dreams happen – you could pay me.'

He was sitting directly opposite me and his manner was over-confident. He saw me as a captive audience. It wasn't a conversational line. I had a full mouth so I took my time before looking at him and responding.

'I am sorry, but I cannot pay you. I don't know you and I am a traveller. I am not carrying much money.' I tried to make this sound friendly but firm.

He leant forward so that we were looking directly at each other. 'You are rich, you can send me money.'

'No.' I deliberately kept my reply short.

He reached across and grabbed my wrist. 'Give me money!'

It was more demanding than begging and I realized that if I didn't quickly escalate the situation then he would.

Jumping to my feet, causing my chair to fall over backwards, I twisted away the wrist he was holding and in one motion caught his wrist, turning it sharply inwards and then up. He shrieked in pain as I stepped around the table and pushed him a few steps backwards, still jamming his arm upwards, painfully. I must have been nearly a foot taller than him. The adrenalin was coursing and I found myself bellowing in rage at the desperate drunk.

'Don't you ever threaten another tourist! Next time a cyclist comes in here, don't see them for money!'

It was a nonsensical shout, but he got the message. I released my grip and he backed off quickly, sitting down a few tables away.

I returned to my chair aware that everyone in the restaurant was watching. I was shaking with adrenalin, livid but also ashamed of the outburst. Then, without a word being said, an older man, maybe in his sixties, came over from another table and sat directly opposite me; without acknowledging me, he lifted his paper and carried on reading. There was no way this man could break up a fight, but he was definitely neutralizing the situation. I felt silently reprimanded, branded a troublemaker. Trying to calm down, I finished my lunch in fast, angry mouthfuls.

Back on the bike I definitely sped up, fuelled by the cocktail of emotions. I had received a largely warm welcome throughout Tanzania so this alcohol-affected youth had definitely let down his team. I was sorry I had reacted violently, but he had seen me as an easy target and the moment he put his hands on me I felt I was out of options. Then again it had happened so quickly I couldn't honestly say that I had thought my reaction through. A trigger had been pulled, and I had reacted in rage. It didn't make me feel good at all. Like any tussle, the idea may be heroic, but the hangover is a feeling of shame.

For the final hour and a half to Mbeya the road rose quickly so I was left with an uphill slog. It was hot, sweaty work and I was hurting, but I also felt really strong, pushing hard past the planned 270km mark. By the time I reached the town my lights were on. I'd been on the go for twelve hours, and rather than carrying on to downtown I stopped at the first place I saw, the Mbeya Golden City Hotel, a modern three-storey concrete construction whose entrance had been softened by miniature manicured hedges and statues of a lion and cheetah. It wasn't as posh as this suggests and the room I was given was just bigger than a single bed, with a bathroom that was the same size. It also had a desk with an old computer and printer, as if during the day this was someone's office. I unplugged this and wheeled it into the hallway, which allowed me to carry the bike over the bed and store it in the bathroom.

With more than 2km of ascent and a solid 15mph average, it had been a very long day, I thought as I tucked into a Chinese dinner. The only other guests were a couple of Chinese engineers who sat at the table next to me talking earnestly, I assumed about their work. I didn't suppose it was a coincidence that they had checked into a hotel with a Chinese kitchen, and it certainly made a pleasant change to my diet – not that I'd had much to complain about for the last twenty-four hours. I was still salivating after the perfect breakfast I had had that morning.

From here it was just 100km to the Zambian border – only three countries left now, with five countries down after four weeks on the road.

Day 29: Mbeya to Isoka

Covering this many miles each day meant that the changes in daylight hours were obvious. I set out just before 6.30 a.m., and it was completely dark. At the border to Zambia I would go back an hour, so this was the equivalent to a 5.25 a.m. start; but then it would be dark by 6 p.m. from now on, meaning my days would have to start at 5.30 if I was still to take advantage of all daylight hours. The first hour was a fast descent, which was a lot of fun in the dark, and I raced quickly towards the Zambian border at Nakonde over some big rolling hills. My only stop was briefly for a second breakfast, a standard sitting of omelette, goat soup, three chapattis, a can of Red Bull and a litre of fruit juice.

Tanzanian exit checks were very easy after a bit of a queue. There was a bit of indignation around as I wheeled my bike into the packed passport office. I was also acutely aware of how much I smelt, so wouldn't have been surprised if it was that that was causing offence.

The man behind me in the queue was a prop-forward of a guy wearing chinos and a shirt.

'I saw you yesterday,' he started enthusiastically. 'Wow you are travelling fast.'

'Yes, I am racing to Cape Town as fast as I can,' I explained.

It turned out that he was an engineer from Lusaka and was returning home. He had studied in Germany and visited Scotland, and had fond memories of his time in Edinburgh. By the time we reached the front he was insisting that I come and stay with him in Lusaka, and he took my map and scribbled down his contact details. I had already made it clear that I was going as fast as I could and didn't have the heart to tell him there was no way this would happen. So I left him with a thanks – and, one never knew, it could yet be useful to have a contact and postal address in Zambia's capital city.

On the Zambian side was a large office and a lot of people milling around, inside and out. As the passport queues were all inside, I wheeled the bike in and parked it neatly against the wall. Fifteen minutes later I had made it to the front where the border guard, a smartly dressed man around my own age, beckoned me to the counter.

'I am not serving you until you take that vehicle outside,' he said. 'This is an office.'

'It is valuable and I don't have a lock,' I told him. 'The bike is not doing any damage. If you can please do my passport I will move it straight away.'

It was a large hall with a lot of people and luggage making a lot more mess than my bicycle. There was no way I was leaving it out of sight for that long.

'No,' he said.

He signalled to the man behind me, who pushed forward and handed over a pile of identification papers.

I retrieved the bike and wheeled it outside, considering my options. Spotting a well-dressed man with his family, I took a risk and offered him 5,000 shillings if he could please watch my bike for five minutes. Back inside, I walked straight back to the front of the queue and placed my passport on the counter, which was then stamped and returned without a single glance or word.

Welcome to Zambia!

I thanked the kind man who'd watched my bike and set off.

There were two out-of-service ATMs in Nakonde so I ended up changing what little Tanzanian money I had left with a street vendor before finding some lunch. From the waitress who served me breakfast to the engineer, the border guard and the money changer, it was immediately obvious how much better everyone spoke English here.

Zambia was also flatter, but the first 10km were not promising. Sections of the road looked as if they had been mined. There was just no explanation for why huge sections of tar were missing, leaving big holes in the dirt. I weaved my way through these using the entire width of the road to find a smooth path. The big trucks couldn't do this. For them these craters posed a serious obstacle so I was much quicker than them for a while. Then the roads improved and they all lumbered past me.

On the roadside there was nothing but six-foot-high grasses for the next 100km; I had no idea what communities or fields existed behind. The only regular activity I saw was groups of men selling live chickens, normally in pairs, advertising them by holding them upside down by their legs. I obviously looked like a promising customer to many of them, someone rich enough to buy live poultry, for I had quite a few shaken roughly at me as I pedalled past, accompanied by market trader shouts. The roads were wet. It wasn't raining, but it remained overcast and humid, a storm brewing.

When I reached the first small community on the roadside I dug out the map to learn that the main town of Isoka, my destination, was actually 3 miles off route. This was a bit of a blow. My thoughts for much of the preceding hours had been to get money out, stock up with food and head on, probably to camp for the first time. I didn't want to stop early at 135 miles. But the impending storm was making me question this wisdom. I asked a guy at the roadside who confidently informed me there was a guesthouse in Chinsali, 20km ahead. Perfect, I thought, and raced off. But a doubt niggled, and just 200 metres later I stopped again and checked with an older man.

'Is there a guesthouse in Chinsali?' I asked.

'Yes,' the man replied.

'And how far is that?'

'A hundred and two kilometres.'

That was very exact. And a bit confusing.

'Another man said it was only twenty kilometres,' I said.

He did not respond to that, just pointed at a massive road sign standing about 10 metres away: CHINSALI 102KM. I felt a bit daft, not just for the question but also for being about to carry on to this town armed only with a packet of chocolate biscuits, some cashew nuts and no money. The first 100km had been so barren I had to assume the next section would be the same. I had no sensible option but to stop my Garmin, end the day's ride and sidetrack into town for the night.

Isoka turned out to be in a deep valley with a cracking descent, which was a fun finale to the day, though I did keep wishing it would end as I would be climbing back out in the morning.

Limset Lodge was the recommendation of a number of locals; it was on a dirt track 500 metres back up the other side of the valley. By the time I reached it the rain had started to fall and the red earth was turning to a sticky clay. Limset looked more like a large family home than a guesthouse, and I was met in the living room by three people who looked like family. I asked them for a room and a teenage boy said this was 140 kwacha – less than £17. He showed me down a corridor to a room which had a shower and then another which had a bath, asking which I would prefer. I chose the bath, but he then explained there was no running water. As I went back to fetch my bike, a man who I guessed was his father arrived and took over. I handed him the 140 kwacha and he corrected me, saying it was 150. 'I was quoted 140,' I told him, at which he turned on his heel and walked off, calling for his son. I could hear his raised voice in the next-door room and felt bad that I hadn't just paid the extra 10 kwacha, or £1.20.

The father appeared fifteen minutes later with two large buckets of boiling water. It was very shallow in the bath and I needed to wait for it to cool, but it certainly soothed sore limbs and a bruised backside.

Dinner was served alone, not just because I was the only guest but because the lights went out, so I sat in the small pool of light from my headtorch. The son was back on duty and served up nshima, a cornmeal stodge. This was the same as the ugali of Kenya by a different name and came with a stocky soup to add some flavour. Then came chicken which was as tough as old shoes, a fitness test for my jaw. I asked the chef about the power-cut and he explained that this happened every Thursday evening for a few hours, but he had no idea why – maybe the government saving money. This wasn't a great explanation: it was Friday. Before finding my way back to the room I asked him about breakfast and he was not enthusiastic about the 5 a.m. request.

'Can I please have some eggs and bread?'

'I cannot cook eggs.'

'But do you have eggs?'

'Yes.'

'Perfect, see you at five a.m. I will cook. Thanks, and goodnight.'

Day 30: Isoka to Mpika

The rain had carried on all night but was stopping when I walked through the kitchen and found the son feeding a dog some scraps in the yard. He dutifully presented me with two eggs and left me in the kitchen where I threw together an omelette without any oil or but-ter, making a mess of his pan. I left it to soak by way of apology. It was a pitiful breakfast but I wolfed it down and got going, stopping at the ATM again as the most it would let me have each day was 1,000 kwacha, the equivalent of about £120. I had been told that Zambia would be a big step up in cost and today I was meeting Tim and George, the South African cameraman and his Zambian driver, so my daily outgoings could be about to triple.

It took twenty minutes to climb back up to the road. My legs were inevitably tight, and I was generally sore, but I felt like my strength was growing. South of Nairobi and through Tanzania had felt like a bit of a recovery ride after the illness and broken roads. A low immune system and the cold had been inevitable

Above: Tim Chevallier was another key player in capturing the Africa Solo story and a wonderful companion on the road, helping me, amongst other things, to find a replacement for a broken pedal (**right**).

Below: Having difficulty fixing the new cassette after cycling for three countries with a broken sprocket.

Above: My KOGA was a constant source of fascination, and the best-dressed man in Lusaka certainly appreciated it. I was struck by how vitally important the bicycle still is throughout the African continent (**left**).

Below: Crossing the Zambezi river. What a wonderful way to enter a new country, just downstream from Victoria Falls.

Above and right: Botswana then brought an abundance of wildlife, and unforgettable moments with elephants on the road and racing alongside giraffes (**below**).

Above: A dot in the Great Karoo, a seemingly never-ending horizon of scrubland, taken by drone cameraman Glen Thomas.

Below: In the zone and racing hard for the finish.

Above: At the top of Bainskloof Pass, where I felt like King of the Mountains, before a reckless descent.

Left: A police escort was on hand through Cape Town, where the sense of relief is etched all over my face a few miles from the finish (**below**).

Above: Reunited with family at Mouille Point. What a tough ride it had been for those at home. What a different perspective on these challenges being a husband and a father gives me.

Below left: A world record to celebrate, and Mum's first long-haul flight to be at the finish line.

Below right: Home-coming celebrations with Granny, Jessie MacLeod.

after all that, but now I was through the other side, feeling deeply fatigued but with a growing resolve to push my average speeds, to stay on the bike longer each day.

The Muchinga province, the biggest in Zambia, has a population of fewer than four people per square kilometre, the same as its southern neighbour Botswana and similar to the likes of Australia and Canada – and I can vouch for the fact that those countries are vast and almost empty outside the cities. Ethiopia, by way of contrast, is about twenty-five times busier, which sounds a lot, but to witness these extremes is staggering.

I had planned for this to be a rural section of the route. The other option at this stage was to be further east, on the shores of Lake Malawi, heading for Lilongwe. But between the two options of similar distance and road quality, I had plumped for one less border crossing and quieter roads by coming through Zambia. Along the road there was almost nothing except tall grasses, some trees and the odd clearing for subsistence farming. On the roadside the options for commerce were charcoal or chickens. Huge hessian bags of charcoal, elaborately heaped and crowned with a framework of twigs and rope, were stacked at regular intervals. Many of the trucks that passed – and these were the main road users – had charcoal bags thrown on top or strapped to the back of their loads.

Tim appeared mid-morning just like Colin Cosier had, already set up on the roadside filming. He was a tall, confident, athletic-looking man in his sixties with a head of grey hair and a kindly expression. George was a small Zambian man who seemed shy; I soon learnt he had quite a nervous disposition. Tim had been very understanding about all the changing logistics in the build-up to the ride. I had originally planned to fly him into Kenya as well, but had run out of the budget to do this. But he was scheduled to be with me for at least three days in Zambia and then I would be with him again for the final stint into Cape Town.

Back at Christmas time I hadn't known a single cameraman in the African continent so I had taken a varied approach to finding them – something I had never had to worry about when working with the BBC. First I went back to the BBC and used their list of preferred camera operators in each country. This is how I found Robbie Wright in Cairo. But none of their South African options had been available, suitable as expedition camera crew, and within budget. So Tim had come through an unlikely source – Facebook. A lady called Claire from Thorn Tree Safaris in Zambia had dropped me a message asking if her company could be of any help. She explained that they had assisted a number of other cyclists with their journeys through Africa. So I asked her for recommendations, saying that I could use Thorn Tree as fixers for a vehicle and driver. Claire and Tim had worked together before, she told him about the Africa Solo journey, and Tim got in touch. Not only was he interested, available and within budget, he turned out to be one of the best and most appropriately experienced cameramen I have worked with. He reminded me of my great late friend David Peat, who gave me my apprenticeship in documentary making, someone with a real passion and knowledge of the art. Tim's most recent documentary, which he sent me instead of a showreel, was about Chris Froome training at his winter home in Johannesburg.

Despite being two-thirds of the way down Africa and on target for a forty-five-day finish, I still didn't feel that the filming was going well, and it worried me. We had some great stuff in the can from the start, Sudan, Ethiopia and a day in Kenya, but my own footage was almost non-existent. This diary-style filming had always been a huge part of my focus on the world and Americas cycles, but here in Africa I was pushing much harder, and as much as it bothered me every day, I just couldn't find the time or energy to get the cameras out to film, even for the most interesting moments. I was always in such a rush. The best I was achieving was chatting to camera at the end of some days, reflecting on what had happened, which was better than nothing but not nearly as powerful as filming in the moment. So on meeting Tim I was relieved to be with a cameraman again, even though I remained concerned about what we could cobble together afterwards.

It came as a surprise to learn that Claire at Thorn Tree Safaris had supported Keegan Longueira not as a filming fixer but as a support vehicle, like Midhat had in Sudan. Keegan's ride was reported as a self-supported ride, so the shine was coming off it slightly for me as I kept learning of the help he'd had. This may be unfair, the truth may have been lost in the social-media communications; it hopefully wasn't intentionally misleading. Both supported and unsupported attempts are valid, but you should be open and precise about which you are doing. I make no bones about the limited support, not least of the moral kind, these film crews were giving me, but I was still riding as unsupported as possible. I had been in touch with Keegan a few times on Facebook and he seemed a good chap, mainly motivated by his faith.

Claire had sent me an itinerary detailing full support, including driving me at the end of each day to interesting experiences and guesthouses. It was a tourist's sightseeing itinerary as much as it was allowing for my daily mileage targets so it had taken quite a bit of negotiating to peel this back in terms of scale to just providing a vehicle to carry Tim and his equipment. By that stage Claire said her services as a fixer therefore weren't needed and she would send George, one of her safari drivers, instead.

It was a punishing day physically as the tar was rough. It's something you wouldn't notice in a vehicle, but on a bike over twelve hours, the constant vibrations on my arms, neck and backside were pretty painful. Tim commented at one point on how flat and fast the roads were; later, after tracking alongside me to film close-ups of my hands on the bars and my backside in the saddle, he noted how debilitating the surface was. This isn't something a non-cyclist will understand easily as it's something you'd barely notice over a few minutes, but over hours and hours it wears you down, becomes agonizing. Despite the discomfort I felt strong and kept my average speed close to 25km/h.

I was also in regular contact with home, trying to figure out if my replacement gears would be arriving the next day. I had now travelled more than 1,500 miles with a broken cassette. Admittedly I had cycled past two attempts to DHL me the new part, but stopping for either of these would have meant losing at least a day.

There wasn't much to think about in the world around me, not many visual stimuli. But there were again quite a few crashed trucks, some of which seemed to have been run off the narrow road. The occasional villages were all built around a church and a school. Each school had a placard on the roadside with an English slogan, like 'Suffer the Present and Enjoy the Future', telling of a tougher way of life than when I was educated. None of these villages seemed to have anywhere open, it being a Saturday.

By late morning I reached the first reasonably sized place, the wonderfully named Two Leopards, and after asking a few people on the roadside I was quickly directed to a fast-food stall with home-made beef pies and hot dogs in puff pastry. What a welcome break from ugali, rice, beans and goat. I relished this, and I appreciated losing no more than fifteen minutes on the stop.

After covering 270km, I could barely get off the bike. Harking back to the supported/unsupported question, even though the vehicle wasn't carrying any kit or supplies for me that day, it was undoubtedly easier to motivate myself not to take breaks, so in this sense their moral support did make a difference. I was off the bike in total for less than thirty minutes all day and finished with my lights on. The road had got very hilly again, back up over 1,700 metres on a few occasions, then finishing with a cracking descent to 1,400 metres. I had long looked forward to the route getting flatter in Zambia but now that I was here a few people were telling me the flatlands wouldn't happen until Botswana.

Tim and George had stopped at Mpika on their way north and had a terrible time in their hotel, with noise all night, so they'd scouted out a better option, which turned out to be an American-style guesthouse, a drive-in with doors on the outside, inhabited mainly by foreign engineer contractors by the looks of the trucks and men in the dining room. It took ninety minutes to cook dinner, which wound me up to the point where marching into the kitchen for the third time I started serving up the rice myself from a pan. The chefs were not impressed but I had lost my patience and humour so wasn't trying to make friends any more. Zambia was not painting itself in glory when it came to cuisine.

Both Tim and I felt a bit awkward that George left and went to sleep somewhere else. We didn't know where and we didn't know his situation well enough to insist he stay.

Day 31: Mpika to Serenje

The village of Serenje, 230km away, was the only sensible target for the day. After that there would be nowhere to stay for a very long way. As always I had the option to camp out, although I had managed to avoid this for an entire month so far. Also, the cassette package had been delivered to Thorn Tree Safaris and someone would be driving out to meet us en route, so I had some servicing to do. Not something that I wanted to undertake in the dark, camped in the bush.

The road continued south-west past Lake Lusiwasi and just south of the Lavushi Manda National Park, a vast forested area that used to be the domain of the black rhino. As in so many of these pockets of untouched wilderness, poaching has taken its toll. The road was also cutting close to the border with the Democratic Republic of Congo, which I would be within just a few miles of at one point on day 32.

In mid-morning a white Land Cruiser passed with a canvas roof box and a Kenyan number plate. They gave me a toot of the horn and then pulled in a few hundred metres up the road.

'Would you like some coffee?' said the driver in a thick Dutch accent.

Would I? What perfect timing. There was nothing out here and I could do with a short break and some caffeine. The elderly man had on a safari-style shirt and a white cloth cap, but best of all was his very fine grey moustache. His wife, who turned out to be Brazilian, poured me a very strong black coffee out of a flask into the lid. The trucks were thundering past so we sheltered on the passenger side. It turned out that they had passed me yesterday and been surprised to see a cyclist. They were even more surprised to see me again this morning, so far down the road. They were on a long loop from Nairobi to Namibia and back again. We pored over the map together, sharing knowledge of the road ahead as I greedily downed their magnificent brew.

There was no Two Leopards fast-food counter today. Instead I pulled up for lunch at Sunduus Restaurant, a faint-yellow concrete building with handwritten signs inside and out. These included an advert for 'Halal Feed' and the warnings NO SMOKING and NO BEER. The young man serving there was wearing a body warmer despite the heat and I checked he was happy to be filmed before following him into the kitchen area. His helper, a teenager wearing an Arsenal jersey, was working on a round table rolling out dough. Pots were cooking on a makeshift indoor barbecue, metal baskets of hot charcoal. My choice was a soup and some meat, but as he threw this on to a frying pan, I had to question the description. There were cut-up pipes and organs, a mixture of bloody grey offal.

'This looks like offal,' I said, picking up the metal spoon and giving the food a stir. 'There is no meat there?'

'Maybe I can mix more together and give you just meat,' he offered, taking the utensil from me.

'If possible just meat – sorry to be fussy,' I laughed.

He scraped the half-cooked offal back into the big pan of raw meat and liquid then started picking out bits of meat to start frying again. As usual there was no cutlery, so the technique was ripping off sections of chapatti to scoop up the cooked goat. I was joined as I ate by some locals and we chatted through the distances ahead, trying to get a sense of the road and its potential points of supply. I loved how enthusiastic everyone always got when I pulled a map out, how more and more people crowded in, adding their experiences and opinions.

It was a tough decision to finish at 4.30 p.m., but keeping in mind it was now completely dark by 6 p.m., I had little option. The town was a few kilometres off the highway, like so many in Zambia, I was finding. It turned out to be the right decision as Serenje had no electricity until late in the evening, so from the moment I stopped and found a room I had less than an hour of daylight to rebuild the gears.

In the car park as I pulled in I was met by a Japanese man on a mountain bike. He was delighted to see me and I was surprised to see him. It was a cheap Raleigh mountain bike and he was wearing a cycling jersey, a sweatband, white sunglasses and lycra shorts. He seemed very out of place. (Pot. Kettle. Black.) In broken English he explained that he was a teacher, sent to this little town for a two-year voluntary work placement. What an impressive commitment; what a remote place to be sent. He explained that he loved cycling and wanted immediately to sit down and carry on chatting. I sensed that he was pretty lonely.

But I had to make my excuses. I said that if he came back later when I had finished fixing my bike then it would be great to talk more.

It didn't take long to break the chain, unlock the cassette nut and take the broken part off. Then I unpackaged the new cassette, cleaned a month's worth of grime off surrounding parts, and started slotting it neatly on. It was wonderfully satis-fying, like a game of Tetris, sliding the progressively smaller sprockets on to each other. I then laid the old chain and new chain across the table and cut the new one to the same length. Putting the wheel back into the frame, I could then feed the chain through and link it up, spinning the chain tool closed so that the link clicked into place. All that was left to do after that was snap off the bullet head from this link. Within fifteen min-utes the job was done, to my immense relief.

I was working outside in a pathway at the back of the hotel, outside my room. Tim was filming the whole process so I was doubly relieved it had gone so smoothly. At that moment the Japanese man turned up and asked what I was doing. I explained about the need to change my gears and got to my feet to spin the back wheel, moving the shifter, and checking they smoothly ran up and down the new cassette. This went perfectly, but when it came to changing between the large and small chain ring at the front, the chain jammed in the derailleur. This was a mystery, as I hadn't touched the front derailleur.

For the next half an hour I fiddled with the limit screws, tried every set-up I could think of, but the chain kept jamming. It just wouldn't move smoothly between chain rings. The Japanese man was very keen to help and asked to have a go. As soon as I let him do this, he settled down, peering closely at the gearing. I soon realized that he didn't know what he was doing, so after a few minutes I politely asked to get back in there so I could keep working. But he stayed, asking lots of questions. I was getting more and more fraught and made three calls to Gav in Edinburgh to chat this through. Eventually I had to ask the over-friendly Japanese man to leave me to it, and told him that I couldn't meet him after all, I had too much on. His face dropped and I felt bad, but I was seriously worried about the bike and he was being a pest. Tim stayed fairly quiet throughout; he could sense my worry and didn't seem surprised when I asked the enthusiast to leave. Gav's final suggestion was to stop fiddling with the gears and just take the bike for a ride; the chain might need to be under tension to shift smoothly. By this time it was pitch dark outside and I was not in a good frame of mind, exhausted and panicking about having an unrideable bike, but I wheeled it out on to the street.

The chain tool had been stored in a dry-bag alongside my puncture kit and spare inner tubes, strapped on to the left side of my front fork. I had Salsa Anything cages on each side so that I could carry extra water, extra food, extra anything if needed. They had spent most of the ride lying empty, but during the regular punctures in Ethiopia and Kenya I had got into the habit of keeping all this repair stuff handy rather than packing it away within the saddlebag. This dry-bag was held on by a compression strap.

I was in such a rush and it was so dark that I didn't notice this strap was hanging down between my front forks. I pushed off and pedalled down the street, about to change gear. Bang. There was the most horrendous noise of grinding metal and I was thrown into the handlebars as the bike slammed to a stop. What the hell? Peering down at the front wheel in the light of my torch, fearing broken spokes, I saw the stupid thing that had happened: the strap had wound into the spokes, pulling the cage round and into the wheel.

Amazingly, the wheel had taken it and the spokes were fine. The cage had snapped off at its two brackets but it only took a minute to untangle the mess. Kicking myself for being so stupid,

I placed the cage on the dirt at the roadside, planning to fix it back on afterwards – very much a secondary priority to these gears. I set off again down the road and, hey presto, the front derailleur changed flawlessly. I can't describe the relief I felt. I beamed from ear to ear, laughing out loud at the tizzy I had got into. I only went 50 metres down the road, then turned round and kept checking the changes as I pedalled back to the site of my stupid accident.

Stopping to pick up the cage before going back inside to tell Tim the good news, I found it was gone. I got off the bike, laid it by some paving stones and walked up and down the roadside, scanning with my headtorch to find it. Then, looking towards a shack off to one side, I caught a glimpse of three or four boys who immediately dashed out of view as the torchlight landed on them. It was hard to believe they would have had time to get to the roadside and back in the time I took to pedal down and back up the road, so I discounted them and kept looking. But after another five minutes had passed I had to give up.

On the grand scale of things that could have gone wrong that evening, including having broken gears and broken spokes, some kids nicking my cage was much more preferable, but still avoidable. They must have been incredibly quick in the dark to spot me putting it down then dash out and grab it while I was just metres away. Nevertheless, feeling hugely relieved, I wheeled the bike into my room, admiring the gleaming new gears, and went for dinner with Tim.

There was still no electricity so we entered a very basic can-dlelit restaurant to find the Japanese man with his half dozen Japanese friends, all teachers, all volunteers here. This made me feel much better about having sent him away, and I could now make up for being abrupt. He didn't seem to have taken offence and quickly joined us. To give Tim credit, he had a lot more patience for working out what he was trying to say – the man's

English was barely understandable. But we went over and said hello to all his friends. They seemed cheery enough, then explained that they were a bit bored, that life here was very basic and a million miles from city life in Japan. I can only imagine, but all credit for sticking it out.

Dinner took well over an hour to arrive, and on top of the day's exhaustion and stress I was aware that I was poor company. I sat there, trying to engage in small talk and struggling to contain my hanger – that hunger-induced anger that makes conversation difficult. Eventually, after asking the young man for food for the umpteenth time, I gently took his arm and steered him into the kitchen. This was becoming a bad habit of mine but I couldn't find any other way to speed things up. In the kitchen there were pots over an open fire and all the food was ready, the staff were just sitting around. They didn't like me in their kitchen so they soon brought out our food. Omelette, rice, chips and chicken – it was a good feed in the end.

The electricity was back on and I was caked in sweat and dirt so I needed a shower. But I was too exhausted even to think when I got back to my room, falling on to my bed in my clothes and straight to sleep.

Day 32: Serenje to Chibombo

It was 3km back to the main road in the first light of dawn. I was zipped up in my jacket for the first time since the rains as it felt chilly; in truth it was 15°C. The change in the road came immediately, a graded tarmac with a proper quantity of tar, not just lots of gravel. As a result my speed was immediately up on the day before, even though the gradients remained similar. The road also developed a better hard shoulder so I was afforded that refuge, and a peace of mind that meant I wasn't wincing with every truck that passed. By the time the day properly came to life the landscapes were also changing, no longer subsistence farming and smallholdings but big farming countryside, looking more like ranches.

The tailwind, the perfect road, gears that worked – all my dreams were coming true. It was taking some relearning not to stand up every time I hit an incline: for three countries I had been compensating in this way for not having the full range of gears. I was 7,500km down Africa and fixated on the final third. By lunchtime I was on an absolute high, having flown all morning, and in need of fuel. My plan at the start of the day had been a big 270km, but I was now thinking even bigger than that.

The congregation of trucks and people led me to the Food Court and more fast food, but I didn't care as it *was* fast and it was big calories. I just wanted to keep the momentum up and stuffed my helmet with more supplies for on-the-go eating. So far on this ride south my helmet was being used more as a bike basket than as a form of protection – not something I would advocate, but the truth nonetheless. The server in the Food Court wore full whites and a chef's hat, which made a big change from the typical uniform of football jersey and flip-flops. He came round the counter, sat down opposite me, leant forward and asked quietly, 'So, how does it feel in here when you cycle?' With both hands, he'd gestured in a V shape between his legs. I laughed, surprised at the question and amused by his hushed urgency. But it was perfectly valid. And the answer doesn't sell endurance cycling.

After 125 miles, at Kapiri, my road, the T2, met the T3 coming in from the north and I arrived at a T-junction being controlled by traffic lights. This might seem unremarkable, but I had hardly seen traffic lights since Cairo. I don't know why seeing such a normal, everyday object amused me so much, but it made me laugh. That says a lot about my tired mind and high spirits.

I thought that by turning south I would lose the helpful

tailwind, but it just kept coming and I made it to the larger town of Kabwe by 4 p.m., having already covered 160 miles. There was no need to carry on. Except it was only four o'clock and I was flying. And the day before had been short.

This part of Zambia was more populated, more developed, and I was seeing more places where I could stay, so I took the risk of carrying on. But I did hedge that risk by asking Tim to drive ahead and phone back if there was absolutely nothing. This was crossing the line in terms of having a support vehicle, but I justified it by reasoning that if I hadn't had the vehicle I would have carried on anyway. Sending Tim ahead was a peace-of-mind thing.

On the outskirts of Kabwe I passed a few more guesthouses, and each was a triumph, a few more kilometres' progress. I remembered the kilometre marker for each in case I needed to turn back. But there would come the point when it would be too far to turn back and I just had to hope there was another guesthouse ahead. It was an exciting game of stick or twist. I kept on twisting, hoping not to go bust and end up in my tent! It seemed unbelievable that I had made it a month down Africa and still not slept in it. It was always there as a back-up, but I was carrying so little kit that having enough food and water for a decent overnight stay in the bush was far less appealing than finding a proper abode. So my obsession was always to search out an evening meal and a good night's sleep.

I didn't hear from Tim for a long time and it was getting dark by the time he reappeared. I was absolutely hammering it, low on the tri-bars, time-trialling at the end of what would be a 195-mile day. I was nearly 15 miles from the last place I could stay so wasn't willing to turn back. To my immense relief there was somewhere ahead. By the time I pulled on to the dirt track to the Tecla Hotel and stepped off the bike, my legs were shaking and I was more than a little bit dizzy.

Day 33: Chibombo to Chisekesi

I thought I might suffer in the morning for that fast finish, and I was incredibly sore. At home I would have called it overtraining and taken the day off the bike. At 5.30 a.m. I walked like John Wayne from my bed to splash water on my face. It was dark outside and ahead lay at least twelve hours of riding and an ambitious target of 180 miles.

One big psychological boost was pulling on new kit. North Kenya was the last time I had done that. And now the nights were a lot cooler there was no way I could hand-wash kit as it would still be wet in the morning so I had done thousands of miles in the same kit without even rinsing it. The new bib shorts felt tight compared to the worn-in sets and didn't have that damp-nappy feel from weeks of chamois cream.

It was a relatively cool 16°C as I pedalled out. The south of Africa was now in winter and I was starting to notice the difference in the mornings as I left the equator far behind. It also now felt like I had left the afternoon rains behind. Not far ahead was the Zambian capital, Lusaka, another major milestone, and I didn't get off my bike till I reached it. The road ran straight through the city; there wasn't any need for a guide here.

The only issue was poor George. As we approached Lusaka I was communicating with Tim through the open window of the Land Cruiser. The plan was to get into the city and find somewhere to eat. It was mid-morning and I was seriously past second breakfast. Tim was also keen to capture some of the bustle and me tackling it.

As the traffic thickened I was often quicker than the vehicle, but stayed behind them most of the time, trusting that George knew where he was going. But after we stopped at one garage that didn't have food and another place that wasn't suitable, I took the lead, beckoning them to follow me instead. I could cut through and find somewhere to stop. Tim was finding it quite challenging to get George to drive alongside me for anything more than a few seconds. He would lose his nerve and race on, or hit the brakes and drop back. I could sense the tension. Then George suddenly spotted a place on the left where he thought we could stop. He immediately turned towards me without indicating. I reacted instinctively to avoid being flattened and walloped the side of the vehicle with an open palm. George straightened up and hit the brakes as I squeezed through the gap at the edge of the road. I was raging for a few minutes, but calmed down once I'd realized it wasn't malicious, that George was stressed out of his tree.

Fifteen minutes later, during which time the Land Cruiser kept well back and just followed me through the traffic, I spotted a shopping mall off to the left and pulled into a fast-food café at the front. George looked terribly upset and I did my best to reassure him. This was not his idea of a tourist drive and he obviously thought that I was one horribly bullish customer. Tim also needed to unwind from the unnecessary stress of the drive through Lusaka. But we were soon laughing about it.

The perfect antidote, as I sat there eating a pile of chicken pasties and chips, was an elderly local man in a very fetching purple suit, shirt and tie with thick black-rimmed glasses who took a keen interest in my bike. First he quietly gazed at it from the next table, then he got up and peered at and touched every part, fascinated. He even picked up my helmet and tried it on, which was an act of bravery in itself considering how utterly minging it was. We chatted a bit, but he was mostly interested in exploring the bike. He was a lovely, gentle man with a lot of style; I think his name was Chris Ekesi. I couldn't pull off a purple suit in my thirties so what would be my chances in my seventies?

The ride out of Lusaka was uneventful and I was now in fairly uninspiring cattle country – ranch lands. Soon the T2 would carry straight on south towards Zimbabwe so I turned right on the road to Livingstone and Botswana. Once again I had made this decision as it meant two fewer border crossings. At the junction there were a few hundred metres of small banana stalls, local ladies selling bunches. I bought three for the equivalent of one penny and the lady was very excited to sell to me, or at least excited by being filmed. She grabbed me round the waist, doing what so often happened when we asked people if it was OK to film – posing as if it were a photograph.

I was now on a much narrower road, which made me nervous, and it was not as smooth, but I did pick up a helpful wind. I had been warned about a cracking climb and had built it into such a monster in my mind that I couldn't believe my luck when it was over just as I settled into my rhythm. It was completely clear, not a cloud in the sky, and by now around 30ºC, so any climbing would be an intense and sweaty business. It didn't help that a callus under my right foot, right where the cleat sat on the shoe, was causing intense pain. But within twenty minutes I was over the top and enjoying the breeze of the descent.

I was in a strange place mentally for most of the day, fairly zoned out, and I didn't listen to any music. In the big empty spaces of Africa, where the roads were quiet and safe enough – since Tanzania, in fact – I had been putting on my headphones more often, even though it's not strictly recommended when cycling, but not today.

I covered steady miles all day, barely stopping, so I only had to push for half an hour into the dark to reach the Mayfair Guest House. The change in accommodation in Zambia was marked. Most places now had road signs in English selling their 'luxury' to travellers, as opposed to the often unadorned local guest-houses I'd found in Ethiopia, Kenya and Tanzania. By 'luxury',

I mean advertising the likes of Friendly Aura, Amicable Staff, Tasteful Menus, Quenchable Drinks and Cost Bedding. What more could you need?

Thanks to these back-to-back big rides I was now dreaming of reaching the border town of Livingstone the next day. I reflected to camera: 'There's something quite exciting after a big day on the bike – riding from first light, and then chasing those final miles. That's the marginal gains. That's where you really break the records. You know, anyone can sit on their bike during the day, but first thing in the morning, last thing in the evening, riding into the dark, that's the margins. I can probably make Livingstone tomorrow. Which would be amazing. I think that's another 180 miles from here. Hah . . . I can't think about that right now. I need food, a shower and bed. But then I can really start to think about Botswana. It's flattening out nicely as well – good roads. Great day.'

Part Six

Elephants and Mammoth Days

Day 34: Chisekesi to Nona Lodge Camp

I had always seen Lusaka as the start of the final chapter, the sprint to the finish through Botswana and South Africa. It was just under 3,000km from Cape Town and from here on I knew the roads would be of good quality. My confidence was also growing to push into the night, so for the first time I didn't feel limited by the twelve hours of daylight.

Tanzania had had the most dangerous roads in Africa, owing to the kamikaze trucks and lack of hard shoulder. Kenya had felt like a recovery ride after the food and water poisoning in Ethiopia, and the fast miles of the Sahara in Sudan felt like a distant memory. Zambia was now almost over, and the road arrowed south-west; the Zimbabwean border and Lake Kariba were on my left horizon all day. Ladies lined the roadside at regular intervals selling the sweetest bananas I had ever tasted. Half the size of the monsters we find in UK shops, I would eat half a dozen at a time.

In the middle of nowhere, while passing more vast cattle ranches, I saw a figure on the road up ahead and initially thought nothing of it. While there weren't nearly so many out here, the sight of people walking down the roadside can happen almost anywhere in sub-Saharan Africa. But as I drew closer I noticed the cart and the western clothes. Slowing to see who it was, I was amazed to pass a Japanese man, bent slightly forward, walking purposefully and towing a small cart. I gave him a big wave and shouted 'Hello!' before carrying on, bemused.

Tim wasn't far behind, and he stopped briefly. This was Masahito Yoshida, who was on a walk from Cairo to Cape Town. He didn't speak much English and told Tim that he was in too much of a rush to stop any longer than a few minutes. He was walking, and in a rush! On his behalf I was concerned about what lay ahead, the big wildlife reserves with lots of young bull elephants and lions, not to mention the 100-mile gap between water points. Here was a man with a cart walking the same route I was cycling. That put my trepidation into perspective.

Mid-morning, I finally worked out that the rhythmic clicking that had started early in the day was coming from my pedal. A bottom bracket can grumble for weeks without causing any real issue, but seeing the grease starting to ooze out of the SPD bearing told me that I would soon be pedalling one-legged if I didn't replace it.

Ahead lay Livingstone, a Mecca for outdoor enthusiasts and the last big town until Francistown, over 500km ahead. I was on a long, fairly straight but hugely undulating road and quickly chatted this dilemma through with Tim as I pedalled alongside him and he hung out of the window. We agreed to turn to social media in the hope that someone would know someone in Livingstone who could help. I was pretty certain that no bike shops in this part of Africa would stock mountain bike-style clip-in pedals, but there might be a member of the public who could help. Tim also agreed to race ahead to Livingstone and start asking around. Once again, this was definitely more than just using a vehicle for filming, but I justified it by reminding myself that there was no difference in the eyes of Guinness

World Records between supported and unsupported rides. It was my own conscience, not their rules, I was wrestling with.

Within an hour word had gone round on Facebook and Twitter, and quite a few smartarses came back saying there were plenty of options to get a replacement pedal in Livingston – that being Livingston (without an 'e') near Edinburgh. But it was also surprising, not to mention more useful to me, how many people had connections with Livingstone, Zambia. An RAF pilot friend based in Cyprus had a good contact. One of my cousins, based in Switzerland, also knew of someone. It was incredible how quickly word went round. As I pedalled along, updating my social media, I was reading about new connections and new ideas every few minutes. But it was Tim's Facebook network that got there first. A friend reposted his message and a local helicopter pilot who had no prior knowledge of who I was or what I was doing got in touch. Within minutes of this message coming in Tim was en route to his house, but the chap was about to race off to work – another sightseeing flight over Victoria Falls. Just as Tim arrived in his driveway, Ignatius Lindeque handed over the pedals off his own mountain bike.

By the time I limped into Livingstone a short while later my pedal had completely shorn off and I was holding it on by pushing my foot sideways into the crank, which was neither comfortable nor sustainable. But my delight and relief at this act of kindness by a complete stranger was overshadowed by a very near miss, a van that turned into me amid heavy traffic. My panicked reaction was to wallop the side window, which resulted in an irate driver. I took the verbal abuse with dignity, as a lesser evil to being run over, but the incident left me physically shaking.

As the adrenalin settled, I dug out the map and tried to figure out a plan for the night – my daily game to try and eke every possible mile out of the day. Stopping in the town was the easy and safe option, but that isn't how you smash world records! My route headed due west out of Livingstone; straight on and I would soon have entered Zimbabwe. Instead I planned to follow the north shore of the Zambezi river, and then turn south into Botswana.

On the outskirts of Livingstone I crossed a cattle grid and passed a security lodge and an ominous sign that warned of wild animals. From here on I was in a nature reserve and I immediately started scanning the roadside excitedly, expecting a lion to appear at any second. The normal evening focus on finding a place to stay was heightened by the chance of a wild encounter. There were quite a few grand-looking gateways to my left, long driveways to large tourist lodges set on the banks of the Zambezi. But I pushed on, hoping for something closer to the road and more likely to accommodate an impromptu one-night booking.

At dusk I found a small German-run guesthouse, the only place I had passed on the roadside, and was shown to a hut with small round doors and a thatched roof. Tim was given a similar hobbit hole nearby. To my delight and surprise the porter who showed us our rooms was cycling a very old carbon-framed Koga Miyata bike, given to him by a Dutch cyclist over a decade ago. I have ridden KOGAs since my round-the-world cycle, and for a relatively small brand it is amazing how they pop up across the planet. This must have been one of their original carbon frames, with metal lugs.

Claire from Thorn Tree Safaris lived nearby and pitched up to say hello, along with her sons. It took some explaining that I hadn't opted to stay at hers, that every mile counted, which was why I'd carried on past Livingstone. It had been worth it to push through 180 miles. At least being just 15 miles from her place meant poor George could go back to stay there overnight. I could see that he was finding the whole trip very stressful.

As patient as Tim was being, theirs was a strained relationship. George was simply unable to drive alongside me at a steady pace for filming for any more than a few seconds, and passing vehicles and busy towns brought on some very erratic driving. On a few occasions when Tim asked him to stop or slow down, he simply took off, kept driving until he calmed down. The constant urgency, the fast meals, the quick conversations and decisions – all of this was upsetting for his laid-back approach. No doubt well suited for tourist drives, George was way out of his depth in a race like mine.

The German guesthouse owner made Tim and me a cracking dinner, finished off with a pancake dessert in the shape of Africa, with a glacé cherry at Cairo and Cape Town and a drizzle of chocolate sauce along my route. It was a delicious and calorific touch.

I was up late, replacing the pedal, changing my tyres, fixing my bike and going through kit to see if I could lose any further weight. This was my final major resupply point. By 11 p.m. I had a suitably satisfying pile of 'non-essential' kit that I hoped the porter would find good use for to go with his Koga Miyata bike.

Day 35: Nona Lodge Camp to Nata

I left at 5.30 a.m., aiming to reach the border 50km away by dawn. I would have left a bit earlier but poor George didn't wrap himself in glory again by sleeping in. Of course I could have pedalled off and Tim could have caught up, but I had been strongly advised by Claire against riding alone in the wildlife reserve in the dark.

Ahead lay Chobe National Park, an area with an abundance of wildlife. I was so looking forward to it. However, cyclists also talk about it as running a 300km gauntlet of elephants. I had been told

quite a few scare stories about young bulls mock-charging and trying to tip cars, but couldn't find consistent advice. Some said
I would be lucky to see anything in the distance while others
recommended a full escort of park rangers. Keegan had taken this
option, which I declined, though I conceded it might be unwise to
be completely alone.

The original plan was for Tim to turn back at the border but he
was absolutely loving the filming, thriving on the frenetic pace of
the journey. Most of all he was passionate about trying to film some
wildlife, so he had offered to come along for another day at no extra
cost. He was certainly invested in the journey for the right reasons,
and I agreed that it would be wonderful to film elephants, although
I wasn't optimistic. In a month of cycling the only wild animals I
had seen were zebras and baboons. Unlike the Africa of our imaginations, you have to look pretty hard to find the so-called big
game – a phrase I dislike for its hunting connotations.

A few cracking climbs made those first hours slower than
planned, but I soon reached the village of Kazungula. The great
Zambezi river flowed wide and brown, deep foliage overhanging
its banks. Passport checks were brief and within minutes I was
wheeling down the concrete slip and on to an open barge. As we
cast off I thought back to documentaries about the great migra-
tions of wildebeest that crossed this exact river. The barge's
engines fought against the fast current as we glided towards
Botswana, and I leant on the railings, enjoying this most satisfying way to enter a new country. Midway across we briefly entered
Zimbabwe, and a few hundred metres downstream was Namibia,
so I was looking at the confluence of four countries.

A family of baboons was swaggering confidently across the
car park next to the landing stage. I skirted them to go to customs
and passport control, which I cleared quickly, before all the
vehicles. Beyond this there were surprisingly few houses and I

realized the community lived on the Zambian side of the river. Surrounding the car park, however, were shops, including a Barclays Bank and a Shoppie supermarket. This was a step-up in development; it could have been a mall in any small American town. No more roadside shacks and informal vendors. I parked the bike and asked the security guard at Shoppie to watch it while I walked around, wide-eyed at the incredible choice.

By the time I'd reclaimed my bike and tipped the security guard with a doughnut, Tim had still not appeared, and I couldn't reach him by phone. I could, however, call Scotland. Una relayed to me, after a call with Claire, that their Zambian phones didn't work in Botswana, so I took some reassurance from this; they could still be stuck at the border. I decided I had to carry on, hoping they would make it through and then catch up. It was well over an hour before they did, by which time I was starting to think they had turned back. This wasn't an issue, except for the fact that I might have had to rethink cycling into the dark in a wildlife park without an accompanying vehicle.

I set out with a plastic bag hanging from each brake lug – a feast for the road which may have slowed me for a while, but I quickly worked my way through the lot. There was a small town 100km from the border, Pandamatenga, but that would make it only a 150km day, so I was committed to carrying on, even with another 200km to the next town. Wild camping in these parts was not an option. But this first push into Botswana proved slow going, around 20km/h. Any normal day and this would have been bearable, but with today's big target I would be riding until nearly midnight.

I arrived in Pandamatenga in the early afternoon and wasn't in great spirits. It had been a real battle. My choices for the day were 150km or 350km, and nothing in between. I also hadn't seen much wildlife and was starting to believe it was all an exaggeration.

Carrying on felt like madness, but I just couldn't face stopping. In truth I was in a bad state physically: my cleats had continued to cause calluses to form on my feet, which were very painful when I pedalled, and my neck and backside ached deeply. None of this was new, but the scale of the task ahead of me that day and the monotony of the wilderness had me in a big mental slump.

After a few hours of this, really battling the mental doldrums, barely lifting my eyes from the road in front of my wheel, I caught sight of something. A few hundred metres ahead an elephant appeared from the foliage on the right and lumbered slowly into the road. Rocking slowly from leg to leg, it moved silently, gracefully for such a giant. I slowed, mesmerized. It entirely ignored me, carrying on into the bushes until it was gone.

The pain disappeared. I suddenly felt alert, and my spirits soared. I pedalled on with renewed gusto, craving another glimpse.

Tim had missed this encounter as he was some way back, but he didn't need to wait long for another. The foliage thinned in one area to reveal a small watering hole, with only a few sparse trees along the roadside, and there, playing happily, oblivious to me, was a whole family of elephants, including some calves. What magnificent, peaceful animals. I had seen a group of them before from a vehicle, but there was something very different about being so close, on my bike. I felt no discomfort now, and as I left them behind my speed increased involuntarily.

This speed stayed with me, and I stretched over the tri-bars, peering into the trees for more glimpses of African wildlife. There were lots more elephants, including some crossing the road. Then something else: the slow, elegant craning of a long neck as an adult giraffe heard me coming. After considering me for a moment, it decided I was a threat and turned on the spot, breaking into a canter. But I was already at 30km/h and pulling alongside. Its gangly legs ate up the rough ground less than 20 metres away, its hooves rhythmically thudding into the earth. For a mesmerizing ten seconds we raced parallel to each other, keeping perfect pace, neck to neck, the giraffe by the treeline on my left with Tim filming out of the window to my right. And then, in a second, it darted left into the trees and was gone from sight.

'Did you get that? Tell me you got that!'

I spun around to see Tim lowering the camera, also beaming. What a magical moment. I pedalled on, thinking mainly of Nicci, wishing she could experience that one day, riding alongside a giraffe in flight.

Nothing in my body had changed, but these wild encounters really had somehow neutralized the pain I was feeling and completely dispersed my mental clouds. I wish I knew what effect this is and how to control it without the need to keep bumping into elephants and giraffes.

At sunset I paused, took my light which normally sat on the handlebars and mounted it on to my helmet. Tonight I needed to see more than a pool of light on the road. I still had 50 miles to go. It was a wonderful few minutes, that stop, eating a packet of biscuits and looking up and down the empty road. There was almost no traffic, so having the camera car there was a comfort. I don't think Tim would have missed this; he was as much a kid at Christmas as I was. George seemed indifferent to the ellies, and it was clear he was still not enjoying these back-to-back long days. Ah well. I gave him a few words of encouragement, and got back on the bike.

For the next three hours, darkness crept in. It wasn't as instant as further north, and with no light pollution I left my front light off as long as possible, letting my eyes adjust to the gloom. In the last light I met some more elephants; I could just see their huge silhouettes in the road ahead. Slowing, creeping forward, I could see another on the roadside. Tim wasn't far behind, and I considered my options. They were slowly walking now so I kept going, speeding up when I was about 10 metres behind the last one. Glancing sideways, they barely registered me, and I soon lost them in the dark. Then another, this one right on the roadside to the left, on my side of the road. Tim came alongside me and I darted to the far right, keeping up my speed, then pegging it for about 50 metres. The elephant just stood there, lazily flapping his ears at me. My heart was flapping like a hummingbird's wings as I pulled alongside the vehicle to see if Tim was having as much fun as I was. It was now too dark for him to film, but he was certainly still loving the close encounters.

And another elephant, and another. My light was now on and it was very hard to see them until I was very close. As my eyes were now failing to pick out the periphery, my ears seemed to tune into every noise – the cracking of wood underfoot, the rustling of branches.

At points there were at least 10 metres of open grass verge before the trees and I felt relatively safe, but in other sections the trees and dense brush closed on the roadside and my active imagination went into overdrive. Time-trialling into the night, I was fixated on all the wild beasties that could be just a few metres away, just waiting to pounce . . . so I found myself cycling right down the middle of the road, joining the white dots, fearful of moving to either verge.

As I nervously scanned from left to right, occasionally spotting huge grey outlines but frightening myself more with my imagination than any real encounters, I laid down my fastest intervals of Africa. My bravado from the day before – talk about how I would happily cycle this without a vehicle – had evaporated. Claire was right: not at night-time. I was back as my ten-year-old self, afraid of the shadows. But it was wonderfully exciting. The air grew chill, the stars came out, and it was slightly easier to see again.

Barely a car passed me all evening and I sat at around 22mph, which was a serious effort considering it was a 221-mile, fifteen-hour day. By the time I reached the lights of Nata and safety for the night I was on a complete high. I was exhausted, but I knew I would be unable to sleep for hours as I thought back on my wild welcome to Botswana.

Tim was on a similar high, and in awe of my riding from 5.30 a.m. until nearly 10 p.m., barely pausing. As we checked into a cheap motel we recalled each encounter. His enthusiasm and our bond on the road again reminded me so much of my great late friend David Peat, the man who filmed the world and Americas cycles with me. A very similar age to Tim, both men had that infectious love for being utterly lost in an experience and the thrill of capturing a journey. I felt drained, but buzzing, and most of all starving. Once we had room keys we raced straight out.

At the crossroads in Nata, a few hundred metres from the motel, was a choice of restaurants, all still open. A fast-food place seemed the easiest and I quickly ordered two meals.

I had meant to ask Tim to bring his camera. This wasn't for the documentary, but on the bike that afternoon I'd had the idea to film my phone conversation home: it would be amazing to watch back in years to come, when my children were old enough to understand. While I had been pedalling furiously into Botswana, Nicci was visiting the hospital for her twelve-week pregnancy scan. I had been desperately trying to call her all afternoon, but there had been absolutely no signal.

Waiting for our food, I sat in a booth next to Tim, with George opposite. It took a moment to connect, the phone rang briefly, and then Nicci answered.

'Hiya, how are you? How did it go?' I asked excitedly.

There was a pause.

'I am sorry, Mark. I am so sorry.'

I heard a world of pain in every word.

I felt numb, and stood up. I walked aimlessly around the restaurant. I closed my eyes, knowing but unable to understand. This situation had never crossed my mind.

Nicci was upset, of course she was, but she had had hours to stop crying. She seemed more worried about me. Her incredible kindness. I was a million miles away when she was told our baby wasn't alive, and her concern was for me.

I was short of words, but assured her I would be fine. She had her parents and Una nearby and would need them, not just for the emotional support. In the morning she had to go under general anaesthetic for an operation. Unlike a miscarriage, Nicci had had no indication that anything was wrong until the moment the doctor put the ultrasound scanner on her tummy and looked into her womb. She saw a void, a black space. Nicci's mum had been there and optimistically thought she saw something, but Nicci said she knew straight away. The best guess was that the foetus had stopped living after about eight weeks.

By the time we hung up, I returned to a cold meal. Without having to say anything, Tim put a hand on my shoulder as I sat down. I put my head in one hand and closed my eyes. I felt lost, close to tears, numb.

Back at the motel I called home again. Nicci was showing amazing resolve. She wanted to cushion the crushing news by saying that she was now coming to Cape Town for the finish. The plan had always been for me just to fly home. Flying out while pregnant and with a toddler in tow had seemed like an unnecessary mission, but now there was nothing stopping her. Indeed plans were already in motion.

I wanted to close my door and be done for the day, but Tim was turning back in the morning so we still had over an hour of backing up data and sorting kit. It was gone midnight by the time

I collapsed into bed. I messaged Nicci one last time, knowing she would be asleep. Wishing I was with her.

Day 36: Nata to Shashe Mooke

After about five hours' sleep I woke to my alarm. Every other morning, no matter how sore, I was out of bed straight away, shaking my head, talking aloud, anything to bully myself into gear quickly, to get on the bike as fast as possible. This morning I lay there, in the dark, aching, just staring at the slither of streetlight coming in through the curtains. I could not have cared less about riding my bike. I was awake despite being exhausted – there would be no dozing off again – and the nightmare of what had happened came flooding back. I felt utterly deflated, with little interest in carrying on.

Giving up wasn't an option, though. That would prove nothing. But after the elation of yesterday's ride, the momentum I'd been building towards the finish, finding motivation was tougher than at any point since Cairo. I had just lost one of my biggest inspirations, my daily thoughts about our unborn son or daughter and his or her part in this journey; more importantly, back in Scotland Nicci was waking up alone to go into hospital for a major operation and I was over 8,000 miles away riding my bicycle. It felt irresponsible and downright daft.

By 6.15 I had wheeled out to the nearest petrol station, which had a Wimpy restaurant attached. What a bizarre juxtaposition it seemed, modern America living next to the wildest part of Africa. This was the first fast-food chain I had seen since Egypt, and the first wifi since Kenya. I sat with Tim and George eating a huge breakfast at a very leisurely pace. I seriously could not be bothered to start cycling. Yesterday's thoughts of smashing out another 200-mile day were long gone. I sat there until 7.30 – over an hour of food and procrastination. A trip to the bank wasted a bit more time, then finally I waved goodbye to Tim and George. The plan was to meet up with Tim again somewhere near Kimberley in South Africa.

There wasn't a cloud in the sky all day and it was surprisingly cool to start with. The road turned further towards the south-east, heading for Francistown, and I found myself on a very barren stretch, devoid of wildlife and for much of the time devoid of people. For the first 120 miles I ate only a couple of packs of biscuits and some yoghurt – there was little else to be found, and I didn't have much of an appetite after the morning's feast. I was very sore and mentally struggling, but I did bully myself not to get off the bike. The road was flat and fairly fast so I just kept it steady, wishing time away. At one stage, along the roadside for many miles were hundreds of men and women hacking down thorny bushes and dragging them into massive piles. It looked hot, prickly, incredibly tedious work, but I got and gave many waves and hellos – a welcome bit of camaraderie. It would have been ideal for Tim to stay with me another day. I felt very alone.

My route passed very near Marobela Village, home to the young Nijel Amos, the 800 metres sprinter who among others had inspired me to get back on my bike. As I pedalled towards Francistown I ended up thinking about him quite a bit, the boy who was trained on a grass track and who went on to beat the world record holder David Rudisha. I needed a bit of perspective on my own mental battle and I ended up thinking what it would be like to grow up here believing you could take on the best in the world. It was a chain of thought that distracted me from pointless self-pitying.

There was a long, gradual drag up to Francistown, Botswana's second city, the capital of the north and a gold-rush boomtown in the nineteenth century. The wind was against me, but from the city I would cut south-west again, so the battle would be short-lived. The outskirts seemed to be in turmoil and I was taken on a meandering diversion route that meant I didn't experience the city at all, but instead got to see the industrial suburbs before being dumped neatly on the A1 south. The only issue with this was a lack of supply stops. The only fuel of the afternoon came from a petrol station and its array of junk food.

Twenty miles further on, also on a highway being rebuilt, I reached Shashe Mooke and just couldn't face carrying on. It was only 5 p.m. and 37 miles to the next small town – a distance I could easily cover in a couple of hours. But I had absolutely no appetite for night riding and felt done in. After grabbing some fried food from a garage, I booked a crappy motel and was asleep by 7 p.m. Thanks to the flat roads I had managed 135 miles, so it wasn't a disaster, but it had been the toughest day mentally on a bike that I could remember. It made the food poisoning, breaking bike and terrible roads in Ethiopia seem appealing, because the difference today was that I really didn't want to be on the road in Africa at all. The world record just wasn't important any more, and Cape Town felt a lot further away than it had when I triumphantly raced into Botswana the morning before.

Nicci's operation had been successful, but she was staying in for observation. We spoke a bit, but I couldn't communicate well. It certainly wasn't helpful for me to share my struggles. I just needed a big night's sleep and to sort myself out – to get back in the zone.

Day 37: Shashe Mooke to Dinokwe

Being winter in the south, it was remarkably cold now in the pre-dawn hours, hovering around 6°C. I shivered in my lycra shorts, wishing I had acknowledged my research which showed that Africa wasn't all scorching hot. But there was something about this cold darkness that brought me back to the here and now, got me back into the journey. It made me crack a smile for the first time since Nicci's news – it was that feeling of being up against hardship and loving it. Just me, my bike and the road. I was sure the ten hours of sleep had helped as well.

I left before 6 a.m., crossing the road to the garage in order to turbo-charge the morning with a breakfast of a few pies and a Red Bull. When it did warm up it was another bluebird, a cloudless and beautiful albeit quite boring day. But boring was good; I had long been looking forward to the boring flat roads of Botswana. The roadworks stopped but the old, disused road still ran parallel, all the way to the town of Serule. And so for 40 miles I had a road to myself, rather than battling the trucks on the new road. Only a few farm labourers on their bicycles joined me, and on the sections where the tar had broken or had had piles of dirt dumped on it I slalomed whichever route was fastest. It was fun, pedalling past obstacles as if in a video game.

A pinch puncture after hitting a lip of tar finally convinced me to get back on to the main road, but it had been a good run. This happened right by a stop where a Portakabin was manned by two policemen sitting on plastic chairs either side of the road. They were stopping nothing, and they ignored me as I set about changing a puncture within a few metres of them. Their determination not to acknowledge me was comical; they seemed bored to silence, frozen by lethargy. Poor chaps. As I finished I gave them a cheery 'Hello, how are you?' which merited a nod of the head, nothing more.

The next town, Palapye, turned out to be a big place with a long strip of fast-food diners and malls whose car parks were full of pick-ups. Botswana has major power issues which mean the entire country is plagued with blackouts. This has impacted lots of infrastructure, but Palapye holds the key to a lot of the country's electricity supply, hence it has doubled in size in recent decades, obviously taking inspiration from the layout of American towns.

I took advantage of the fast and plentiful food with two Wendy's meals and another stuffed on to the bike for the road. A great idea, until the bag split and my Apidura saddlebag and the back of the bike were smeared with mayonnaise – an unusual chain lube!

Mahalapye, another 50 miles further on, was also bigger than I'd expected. I was there by 3.30 p.m. after 130 miles. It was the last place I could see of any significance for another 120 miles, until the capital, Gaborone. Stick or twist?

I couldn't stick. Not after yesterday's woeful mileage. I couldn't leave today short of 150 as well. But ahead there really wasn't anything to aim for, so I committed to my first night in the tent. About time: I hadn't unpacked the handlebar bag for thirty-seven days now, since leaving Cairo. After ordering two meal deals and four packets of biscuits, and tying an extra litre-and-a-half bottle of water to the Anything cage on my front forks, I was ready for a night in the sticks.

All day the railway had run parallel to the road, and as the light started to fail another very long cargo train made a slow pass. Trains crossing the African plains are a vision that evokes emotions of great journeys, history and ambition; there is something unavoidably romantic about that heavy industry. Thirty miles out from Mahalapye I was in no great rush, just starting to look for a place to camp. It was barren and open so finding a place to hide wouldn't be easy. Then, off to the left, I spotted the small hamlet of Dinokwe. There certainly wasn't anywhere official to stay there, I doubted there was even a shop, but on the spur of the moment I slowed and turned in.

I crossed the railway tracks just as an old banger of a saloon car was approaching. I waved it down. The driver was a dishevelled-looking young man holding a bottle of beer. His passenger looked like his girlfriend. I paused; my gut told me not to trust him. Throwing caution to the wind, I said, 'Hi, is there anywhere here to stay? I have a tent, but don't want to use it. Is there a guesthouse? Do you know anywhere?'

The driver paused, looking like he wanted to drive off, then appeared to reconsider.

'OK, follow me,' he said.

With that he spun the car round and led me back towards the houses. The road soon ran out and he started driving across the earth, which was so fine and dry that it was impossible to cycle. I jumped off and ran after him to keep up, pushing the bike as the tyres sank in. He eventually parked under a tree at the edge of a sandy football pitch and joined me on foot. His passenger stayed in the car. Still swigging from the bottle, he was definitely slightly pissed, but shook my hand and fell in beside me as we walked across the pitch and down lanes of sand between some houses. He seemed a bit nervous, maybe excited, and introduced himself as Ivan.

'You can stay at my house,' he told me. 'Well, it is my parents' house. I was leaving to check my cows at the station and can stay at my girlfriend's. You can have my room.'

'Wow, thank you. That's perfect.'

His mother, grandmother and sister were all at home, a simple construction, its tin roof and bare brickwork contrasting with a stunning carved wooden door depicting elephants. It was a work of art. Across the yard was a smaller building with a metal door – his bedroom – and another was the village shop, although you would never have known from the outside.

Ivan unlocked the padlock on his door, let me in and quickly said he had to leave. I gave him 150 pula – the same as the motel the night before had cost, about £9. He hadn't asked for anything but was visibly delighted and ran off to give his mother 50 pula.

The room was very sparse and a real tip, with a broken mirror across the floor, but it had a bed and electricity, which was all I needed. I took my picnic dinner outside, and a chair to sit on. Granny reappeared and shouted fiercely at her granddaughter to get her a chair as well, then placed it in the sand nearby. She was a very large lady wearing a loose frock of rather thin material so that when she sat down you couldn't help but notice her huge breasts resting across her tummy. She had a kind smile and to begin with said very little. We just sat there as I ate.

When I arrived with her grandson, she had said nothing, so I'd assumed she didn't speak any English and asked him to translate when I thanked her for letting me stay. She spoke perfect English, and we ended up chatting for nearly an hour. She was South African, and loved and missed the West Cape, making an annual drive there to sell clothes in the markets. She wanted to know all about my journeys and listened intently, nodding slowly as I commented on different parts of Africa. All the while the grand-daughter – or maybe she was a great-granddaughter because she seemed a generation below the chap I had met – played in the sand by the door to the house.

It was wonderful to be welcomed so openly by this family; there was no fuss, no issue of trust between us. I watched the bickering between generations – there was no being polite in front of me – and felt completely at ease. After witnessing this slice of normal family life I felt a whole lot better when I called to check how my own family was faring.

Day 38: Dinokwe to Mahikeng

There was only the slightest suggestion of dawn as I pushed the bike out. Ivan's sister was filling heavy buckets of water to carry back to the house, but she seemed shy and didn't reply when I said thanks and goodbye in a hushed voice. The rest of the village wasn't stirring yet as I retraced my path across the football pitch and found the road. It seemed like a longer journey in the dark.

Just past dawn I reached another milestone that I had forgotten about. It wasn't quite as monumental as the equator, and certainly not as much of a tourist draw at that time of the morning, but there was a big roadside sign for the Tropic of Capricorn. I cycled past it, not wanting to stop, because I would get cold again. But 50 metres on I grumpily admitted to myself that this was an important moment to document and I should return.

I pulled out my camera for a quick arm's-length chat.

I'm on the Tropic of Capricorn and, well, it's just before seven o'clock in the morning, day 38, and I never thought I'd say this on this trip but it's freezing, it's really cold. I never thought I'd stand on one of the Tropics saying that I'm freezing, but it's really cold. Just begging for the sun to come up and warm the day up. But another milestone. By the end of today I should be somewhere close to the South African border. This is a very, very empty stretch of road. I think I've got another 80 or 90 miles before I'll reach a shop, and I hope it's open, because it's a Sunday. Um, but, uh, most importantly, I hope it'll warm up soon. I can hardly speak, my mouth's numb. Cold, cold, cold! Right, onwards.

It was my own daft fault for being so minimalist with my clothing. I just hadn't believed it would get cold in Africa, but it was about 5°C and I only had lycra kit and a thin rain smock. It was fairly comical, pedalling along shivering, bleary-eyed, teeth chattering audibly.

The first 100 miles were indeed very barren but I did find some doughnuts and a Coke for breakfast. Rubbish, but calories. My right pedal, the one the helicopter pilot had given me, was starting to leak grease. It must have had a long and relatively gentle life until being gifted to me and after just three days' hard use it was already complaining. I put in an urgent call to base camp to get Tim to pick up another set in Cape Town and hoped I could nurse what I had for another 500 miles till we met again.

From the arid, flat emptiness of central Botswana I reached the outskirts of Gaborone, and was entertained for a while by an incredible airshow that was happening nearby. Helicopters, biplanes, fast jets and stunt aircraft all buzzed noisily overhead and I was oblivious to the passing miles as I enjoyed the spectacle. Then the road started very gradually to decline, and I was pedalling along quickly, hungrily, only thinking about reaching downtown and looking for lunch.

I was on a dual carriageway when a blue SUV drove alongside. The passenger window was down and a lady called across, 'Hello Mark!' The driver waved enthusiastically and someone was also waving in the back. It was a busy road and they were now going at cycle speed, so I shouted hello back and asked them to go ahead and stop.

By the time I caught up they were out of the car. They were Anoop, Swati and Neela Sharma, an Indian father, mother and teenage daughter. Amid the excited conversation I cobbled together the connection. Anoop had been following all of my expeditions right back to the world cycle. It was his birthday and all he wanted to do was come and find me, so the family had been out since early that morning driving up and down the road. The GPS map had given them a rough idea of my progress but they had still been searching for hours.

'We want to take you for lunch!' Anoop explained.

I hesitated for a minute, bowled over by their enthusiasm but concerned that this could become a recipe for losing a lot of time. I was on a mission to reach the South African border. Then again I had no idea where to stop and needed lunch anyway.

'Thank you,' I said. 'If it is en route that would be lovely. But I am sorry, I can't stop for very long.'

'I know, I know, you have to smash the world record!' Anoop said.

They drove off, but slowly, half in the hard shoulder so I could keep up. In the middle of the dual carriageway were streetlights, big enough to light up all four lanes. After 5km I was wondering how far this restaurant was. Then there was a loud creaking noise, something I didn't really pay attention to over the passing engines and tyres. But it did register, and it got louder, and then, as I drew level with one of these thick, very tall poles, I suddenly saw it falling. It happened in slow motion, from tee-tering slowly to crashing on to the road just behind me. There was a screeching of brakes and every car behind me was caught behind the lamp post, which now lay across the entire dual car-riageway, or at least our side of it. I was the last one through, and only by a matter of metres. I would have the entire road to myself for the rest of the cycle into Gaborone. (After that experi-ence I started noticing quite a few stumps where other lights had fallen. What a staggering safety risk.)

A few minutes later I saw the Sharma SUV pull into the middle lane and indicate right, towards a shopping mall. As I followed them in, I wondered if Anoop and his family had seen this staggering near miss. They must have noticed the sudden lack of any traffic. I asked Anoop excitedly, the adrenalin still pumping. 'Yes, we saw,' he replied, but there wasn't even a note of surprise in his voice. I guessed such crazy life-threatening occurrences weren't so unusual on a trip to the shops in Botswana.

We sat in the crowded outdoor seating area of a very nice Italian restaurant. I say very nice; it was utterly average, just modern. It felt like in the towns of Botswana I had left the Africa I had come to know behind and was back in familiar European or American suburbia. I immediately felt very self-conscious about my appearance and odour. My kit was filthy and it stank, which normally didn't bother me, but squeezing in beside this lovely family with other diners around me, all well dressed and fresh-smelling, I felt acutely out of place.

A pizza – a massive, generously topped and utterly delicious pizza – and two large mugs of coffee: I was in absolute heaven. I couldn't quite believe this was all Anoop wanted to do for his birthday lunch, as it was me who was having the treat. And they were lovely company. The daughter was shortly off to university, probably back in India, but they had lived in Botswana for a long time and enjoyed life here. They certainly found it quieter, less populated and frantic, so wondered how they would adapt if they ever did go back to India. They insisted this was their treat and that I should get going quickly. So after a quick photo I was back on the road.

As I pedalled out of the car park on to the linking road back to the dual carriageway, a road cyclist drew alongside me. I didn't see where he'd appeared from. This was the first roadie I had seen since Joshua in Dodoma and I was very surprised but happy for the company. After a few kilometres of pleasantries, me asking if he was taking the same road and the like, he introduced himself as Oteng Sebonego. I told him I was Mark Beaumont and he replied that he knew, that he had been following the journey on Facebook and had seen my video of the elephants from Nata. And I realized this meeting wasn't by chance, and he had been playing it cool. For the next 25km I had a pace man. The combination of a great lunch and Oteng's company certainly helped me pick up the pace.

Oteng had studied in the US and was now at home in Gaborone starting up a mobile-app company. He spoke passionately about what a wonderful place Botswana was to live, but how greed was creeping into what was the least corrupt state in Africa. This manifested itself most in the electricity issues. For

such a developed country, compared to its northern neighbours,
there were too many power cuts due to the massive water short-
ages in the south. The main dam was dry and the 450km pipe
from the north kept bursting and being tampered with. So
development in the capital was being stifled by the lack of basic
commodities. Oteng remained optimistic about his chances as
an entrepreneur, however. He was certainly a solid bike rider
and saw me through the hills south of Gaborone, turning back
once he'd got me to the top.

For what I thought were the last three hours I flew. Head
down, stretched across the bike, spinning powerfully at 35km/h,
I reached 287km and the border just as darkness fell. To my surprise there really wasn't any town here, despite the map showing
a place called Ramatlabama, only a petrol station and a few huts
along the main road. I had recently passed through a few other
towns but too far back to retreat; there was, however, a turn-off
and a sign for a motel. But with the border in front of me,
I thought it might be easier to cross at night and not lose any
time in the morning.

Passport control was a long, low building and it was deserted
outside as I parked the bike. I had no concerns about leaving it
out of sight this time because there was nobody around. Before
handing my passport through the glass, I asked how far it was
on the other side to a place to stay. The answer was 25km. It
was getting dark and I wasn't about to pedal into a new country
in such conditions, so I pulled back my passport and told the
young chap that I'd be back in the morning.

Retracing a few hundred metres, this time with my lights on,
I turned left and pedalled off in search of the advertised motel.
There were a few houses but little more, and after 3km I was getting concerned when I spotted a bar. Pulling on to the dirt, I
leant the bike on the wooden post holding up the tin awning and
approached three men standing outside. I tried to ask them but

couldn't make sense of their drunken gibberish. So I went inside, where the music was really blaring, into an empty bar. I could just about hear the barman shouting that it was another 15km into town for a motel – another 15km off my route. Argh. I fetched my bike to the bullish braying of the drinkers and pedalled back towards the border. I had lost half an hour and it was now properly dark as I re-entered the passport office and left Botswana.

After the urgency to reach the border in daylight, I didn't feel nearly so rushed on the other side. I had a generous hard shoulder, the road was deserted, and I actually enjoyed the thrill of pedalling into South Africa under the cloak of darkness. Mahikeng is a big place, and initially I went on a wild goose chase for fifteen minutes, following the first signs I saw for a hotel. I eventually found it, down some side streets, but it was shut. I shouldn't have been so eager: a few more kilometres and I was in downtown and spoilt for choice. Coming into town along the wide boulevard I encountered a series of traffic lights – another nod to American town planning. There was by now a fair amount of traffic and I was feeling a tad vulnerable, so imagine my delight when I came to a junction with a huge garage on one side and a swanky-looking hotel on my left.

Yaas! I am staying here! It felt like a week since I'd rolled out from Ivan's house and it was definitely quite a few days since I'd had a decent shower.

The Protea had a security gate, a covered driveway by the entrance, and the concierge had obviously parked the guests with the best cars closest, which added to the upmarket impression. I wasn't bold enough to wheel my bike across the polished floors and felt like a castaway as I made my way to the desk. 'Certainly, sir.' There was no hesitation. A staggering 1,500 rand later – about £66 – I had a room. It was the price of at least a week's accommodation from most of my journey through

Africa, but I didn't care. What a day it had been, and here I was in South Africa, a day before I expected to be.

Carrying my bike to the elevator, I found my room and was so famished that I threw off my cycling kit, put on my grubby shorts and white T-shirt and went straight back down to the restaurant. On the way in, a small sign stated that 'smart clothes' must be worn. I stole a quick glance around the mainly empty restaurant: most people looked like business travellers, dressed casually and eating alone. I thought I would be fine, but the waiter had other ideas. He sat me down, gave me a menu and left without a word. He returned a minute later, but when I started to place my order he cut me off, turned, and said over his shoulder, 'I need to check you have a room.' He could easily have asked if I was a guest and I would have shown my keycard. It was intentionally rude, but rather than be offended I laughed out loud, got up, walked over to another waiter and ordered. Calamari, chicken schnitzel and tiramisu – what a wonderful three-courser that would be. By the time the snooty waiter returned I was delighted to tell him I was all sorted. I watched with amusement as he made a beeline to his colleague to quietly berate him.

Just shy of 200 miles. What a wonderful day it had been, full of kindness from strangers, which wasn't going to be spoilt by this clown. Mind you, I was dirty and reeking – I was close to offending myself – so he probably had a point.

Day 39: Mahikeng to Kimberley

4.30 a.m. It was a rude alarm call and it wasn't easy to jump into action from the lap of luxury. The garage across the road fuelled me and soon I was too busy getting started, getting warm, to realize I was going the wrong way. I hadn't even dug out my South Africa map yet; I was working off a map of the entire southern half of Africa. As I left the last houses of Mahikeng I passed a highway sign for Lichtenburg, which didn't ring any alarm bells, followed by one for Johannesburg. I knew where that was – pretty much in the opposite direction to Cape Town. So I cut west, following my nose through suburbia, knowing that if I skirted the town I would bump into trunk road 18 to Vryburg. It eventually worked, but I lost a chunk of time.

Thankfully, the conveyor belt was back, the cracking north-easterly which fast-tracked the rest of my day. It was very welcome and I was in an indomitable mindset. Cape Town was between five and six days away if I covered 150 miles a day, but I was starting to think it might be possible in three or four if I really went for broke. My leg muscles felt tight but resilient, my body generally ached but there was nothing acute. This ability to continue increasing my daily mileage of course relied on having safe roads on which to ride into the dark.

Since entering Botswana my daily average had been creeping up. And since the crushing news in Nata, my mindset on the bike had completely changed. After initially feeling lost, almost wanting to quit, my focus had quickly hardened. The inspiration that had seen me through many tough points in Ethiopia and the north had gone, replaced by a cold focus, an obsession to eke out every possible mile each day. It was amazing news that Nicci and Harriet were coming to the finish, and my thoughts should have been with them a lot more, but they weren't. I felt like I had cut myself off from the outside world and was comforting myself with the discomfort of the ride. The bike and the miles were my only barometer for success now. For so much of the journey I had kept my focus short, distracted myself with thoughts of family. Now, well within the final week and into the final country, I was riding for the finish, under a thousand miles away.

Fields of maize hemmed in the highway and the wind through the heavy heads of grain sounded like a river. This added to the impression of speed and I kept it steady, kept it fast. For a long stretch a cycle path appeared alongside, not the dust tracks of East Africa but a proper concrete pathway. However, it dipped every 50 metres to allow for drainage under the highway and had rough joins, so that at 25mph it made for a pretty exciting ride. Despite its relative safety I soon gave up and returned to the highway, once again joining the many trucks.

Early on I passed a sign for a farm shop some way ahead. It looked so inviting that I pedalled along imagining coffee and home cooking. This motivated me for about an hour, until I admitted to myself that I must have missed it. By now I was passing huge excavation sites, man-made mountains of dirt so large that they dwarfed the gigantic dumper trucks that wound their way up the craters like worker ants. Full of gold, platinum, cobalt and other minerals, this area has a long and rich heritage both under and on top of the land. Vryburg, the 'Texas of South Africa', is the country's biggest beef producer, and by the end of the day I would be racing towards Kimberley, the diamond capital of South Africa.

Stella was my first proper stop after 70 miles and my first warm South African welcome. Although when I entered the small café I thought I would be lucky to be served. The lady behind the counter was arguing with a man, maybe a colleague or family member, who looked like he was trying to leave. Which, after a few curt retorts, he did. Afrikaans, to my untrained ear, sounded quite an aggressive language, lots of harsh syllables. It certainly seemed like a good language to be angry in, as opposed to the Italians who sound warm and passionate when in their fits of rage. I am guessing English sits somewhere in between these extremes.

I headed for the fridges and the biscuit shelf to give them time to stop fighting, but I needn't have been so timid: the lady turned on the charm the moment he left. A middle-aged white lady in an apron, she recommended a bacon, egg and cheese kitke bun, so I ordered two. They are made on sweetened bread, with the fried eggs left runny and the whole thing doused in a red sauce containing ketchup, but far superior to that condiment. She introduced this as a Johannesburg speciality, then explained that she had moved to Stella six months ago to run the shop with her husband, who was a cycling nut. She wanted to know where I had cycled from, but Cairo didn't seem to sink in as without pausing she carried on excitedly telling me about her husband's exploits pedalling around the district.

For the fifteen minutes I was in the café a crazy man stood outside. And I mean crazy in the proper sense of the word. It was very sad to see. He stood there wearing socks and no shoes, trousers that were in tatters and falling off him, and an open jacket with no shirt, and muttered to himself. The lady told me to ignore him and not to make eye contact. As I paid up, the conversation returned to him and she admitted she was really scared of him, wouldn't go outside when he was around. The poor man should have been looked after, not treated like he was a stray dog. He followed me to my bike when I went outside but seemed harmless, pretty much lost in his own world. I pedalled away thinking Stella was odd, although it was probably no quirkier than any other small rural town.

Some 30 miles later on an arrow-straight road I reached Vryburg and went on the hunt for some rear lights. My batteries had run out twice now and I didn't want to risk more night riding without any rear lights. I also needed an adaptor for South African plugs. This was an easy find. I was directed to a general store run by an Indian couple who took one look at the bike parked by the door and gave me the adaptor.

'No charge, have a good journey.'

I hadn't said anything about the trip so I thanked him for his kindness and took his directions to his friend's shop for bike lights. Unfortunately his friend wasn't able to help, but he did

try to sell me a camping lamp that I could strap on to the bike;
he even offered to come outside and fit it. The lamp was the size
of a kettle and a white light, so in almost every way inappropriate.
All he did have was a shoe-box of second-hand bicycle reflectors,
so I bought a few of these as a back-up plan.

On my way back to the crossroads where I had turned off
highway 18 to find these shops, I stopped at traffic lights. As I
waited I spotted a young black man admiring my bike from the
pavement. I called over, 'Is there a bike shop anywhere? I need a
new light.'

'Nah, no shop,' he said.

The light changed, I turned left, and a short distance later I
pulled into a garage forecourt to stock up on water and food
before leaving town. Leaving my bike under the watchful eye of
the forecourt attendant, I went inside for about five minutes.
When I walked back outside, the young man from the traffic
lights was there, with another guy around the same age. He was
standing by my bike and greeted me with an exuberant hand
clasp and shoulder bump. (I am sure there is a proper phrase for
this greeting, but it's not in my lingo.) His friend then pulled two
bike lights from his pocket. They were very cheap, one up in the
range from a Christmas cracker light, but they would do fine as
a back-up. The friend said nothing.

'He used to own a bike, these are the lights,' my new-found
buddy explained.

They looked brand new.

'How much?' I asked.

'One hundred.'

That was about £4.50, which seemed about right. Not that I
felt haggling was appropriate on a garage forecourt with these
characters.

'OK, thank you.'

It may have been perfectly normal, but it felt a bit dodgy. He had magically found these lights in the few minutes since I had met him. He deserved my business for such quick enterprise.

I was back on a narrow road with no hard shoulder. To the left of the solid line at the roadside was about six inches of tar, which I could hug, but I had to concentrate. There was no sense in riding wide as trucks constantly thundered past, paying no attention. This was not a time to own the road, to fight for my rights as a cyclist. One bus completely ran me off the road. Again reacting instinctively, I found myself bumping along the dirt, quickly coming to a stop and cursing impotently as the vehicle disappeared like a wrecking ball down the road.

I really flew the final hours of daylight to Warrenton and I was fairly resigned to staying there for safety reasons. It hadn't been a bad day, but I felt a tad disappointed. I had been dreaming of making Kimberley to keep my dream of a forty-three-day finish alive. It was another 50 miles ahead.

I pulled in at a general store and approached a farmer who was throwing some bags into the back of his pick-up. I explained the trouble with the trucks and asked if the road continued the same all the way to Kimberley.

'Yeah, you'll make Kimberley, no problem,' he said, 'there's a big shoulder all the way.'

I appreciated his enthusiasm, considering it was getting dark and I had already cycled 184 miles. If I had simply dug out my map I would have seen that I was at the end of the N18, and if this local was to be believed then the N12 was a much grander, much safer trunk road. It was a risk – if the farmer was wrong then this would be a very dangerous 50 miles – but I quickly ran into the store, stocked up on energy drinks, waffles and doughnuts, and excitedly pushed on into the dusk.

Maybe it was the caffeine and sugar, but I found myself hammering the pedals, committing to the pain in my saddle and feet rather than squirming around, and staring into the dark, hungrily eating up the miles. It was uncomfortable yet perfectly flowing, tough yet effortless.

Close to 8 p.m. I reached the outskirts of Kimberley, and despite its sparkling reputation, I found myself pedalling past township housing, homelessness, graffiti and litter. Entering any city in the dark can give a skewed impression, but this definitely seemed rough. Around the same time Tim was driving in from the south and he reported a world of middle-class wealth. Despite my concern my lights lasted well; perhaps inevitably, the cheap ones had lasted for all of half an hour.

The N12 got a bit lost downtown, or at least in the dark I managed to lose it, so it took a while longer to find the southern outskirts, which put me in a better position to get out quickly in the morning. It was already late so I didn't mind ambling along, exploring the city by night, asking a few drivers for directions and recommendations until I found a lodge.

At 232 miles, it had been the biggest day yet. I walked 500 metres from the lodge to a fast-food diner, which was a welcome chance to stretch my tight, weary legs. Just as an embarrassing tableful of food arrived, so did Tim, with some of his family and a driver called Frans. He had just made the long trip from Cape Town in eight hours and was staying over with family nearby. It was wonderful to see him and he was surprised and pleased that I had made it so far. His plan had been to continue driving north and meet me the following morning.

After welcomes and pleasantries, we eagerly discussed the plan.

'It's just shy of a thousand kilometres to Cape Town – can I do it in three days?'

Tim was already on the same page. No one else was thinking this fast. I had put a question out on Facebook, asking people to guess what day and time I would finish. Tomorrow was Tuesday, and the earliest guesses were coming in for Friday; most were thinking Saturday or Sunday. I was also causing problems for my family's travel plans as it now looked like I would arrive in Cape Town before Nicci, Harriet and Una.

But with no injuries, no breakages and a bit of luck I could average over 200 miles a day and finish Africa Solo in less than forty-two days. Tim's absolute belief in my ability meant a lot. Without a word, he'd already assumed I was going to push it seriously hard. This time round his driver also seemed up for it. Frans was a big ex-rugby-playing South African, still in his twenties and eager to be a part of this adventure.

They didn't stay for long. After giving me a box with new pedals they left me to feast and sleep.

Day 40: Kimberley to Victoria West

By sunrise we were already heading out of Kimberley in a south-westerly direction. I was in better shape than expected and it was reassuring to be tracking alongside the vehicle again, chatting away to the camera, getting my head into gear for the day ahead.

It's uh, on the grand scale of things, a short distance left, but it's still a huge, huge way to cycle. After you left me, Botswana got a bit more boring. You got the exciting bit with all the wildlife! After that, through the south, just never-ending farmland. I feel like I've been following this train line for the last week; I've always had a train line to my left. It was also pretty remote in southern Botswana, long gaps between towns, but, incredibly kind people. I'm starting to pick up signs for Cape Town now, which is a huge boost to the morale. I'm getting much less sleep because I'm riding later into the evening. So I'm not getting the same recovery, but I can really count the days down now. Four if we go at normal speed, three if I really push it. Let's see how

today goes. Yesterday was over 370km, about 230 miles, so the
legs are a bit tight this morning. I'm doing good though. I just
don't wanna . . . I don't wanna push it . . . too much. I've still got
to pace it. I feel my legs are so tight if I, if I really upped it, I don't
know how much more they could take. I can still do big miles,
but it's just about going steady for longer.

The early-morning chill soon gave way to gentle heat. The
winds were favourable to start with and the provincial roads of
the Northern Cape were light with traffic. I was closing in on the
Great Karoo, epic landscapes reminiscent of the vast horizons
of the Midwest, which I would cross until the road finally fell off
the high plateau down into the endless wine-growing valleys of
the Western Cape, and my ultimate destination. This vast area
of South Africa is as bleak as it is beautiful, a semi-arid desert
with sparse scrub that sustains sheep and some game. To the
north-west it merges seamlessly into the sands of the Kalahari
desert, and then into Namibia. In the days of early adventurers
and hunters, the Great Karoo was seen as an impenetrable
barrier to the interior of the country. But for me the transition
was fairly gentle, going from manicured farmlands around
Kimberley to huge expanses of grassland that gradually became
more barren as the day wore on, telling of lessening rainfall.

At one stage Tim and Frans disappeared to film some sable
antelope way off in the distance. It wasn't long before a vehicle
pulled up and a burly farmer asked what they were doing. Apparently there were rhino in the vicinity and he wanted to make sure
they weren't poachers scoping out his property. It was amazing to
realize this virtual wasteland was being watched over so closely.

The first hours were inevitably sore but after five hours I had
made 78 miles and crossed the Orange river, another milestone
that took me from the Northern Cape into Western Cape, the
final province. Before stopping in Hopetown for supplies I passed

a set of intriguing road signs, including ones for Edinburgh and Bannockburn. They seemed to be road signs to almost nowhere, little dots on the map, maybe only hamlets or farmsteads, but they were evocative links to home from which I gleaned further motivation.

I allowed myself only short breaks every three hours or so and the N12 stayed wide, smooth and fairly fast. But speed, as always, was dictated more by the wind than my legs, and this had now turned against me. The slightest cut of the road to the west and it became an absolute demon, my speed plummeting and the reading on my power meter skyrocketing. The previous day I had been sitting at 100 to 150 watts, just tapping along, but into that wind now I was doing 200 to 250, hour after hour after hour. That's energy-sapping stuff. But the road to Cape Town would swing increasingly to the west so I just hoped the wind would die down into the evening, because I knew it was the main factor that could break the new dream of a sub forty-two-day finish.

After Hopetown it was a long 80-mile push to Britstown, which as the name suggests was significant during the Boer War at the turn of the twentieth century. I had covered 158 miles and was hurting, but this was make or break in terms of whether I would finish in two days' time or three. It would have been so, so easy to stop; the cumulative effect of the past three, four, five, forty days was definitely catching up on me. But I pushed on into the night another 66 miles to Victoria West.

Much to my amusement, I came across a series of signs telling drivers IF TIRED STOP/REST.

As the sun set I clocked up 10,000 kilometres down Africa. Almost without fail I had seen the sun rise and set for the last forty days, and this one was by far the best sunset yet. Incredible! The sky was just like lava. It felt like a suitable celebration for 10,000km in the saddle. What a place to be for it. Just beautiful.

The final hours were a grind, though. Night-time miles definitely pass more slowly. By Victoria West I had been on the bike for about fifteen and a half hours, and to stay on target I would need to do the same tomorrow. It really was feeling like a long, straining sprint finish. All I could think about was the next hour, the next meal, the next sleep, and after 224 miles there was still the routine of wrapping up the day's events on camera, charging kit, showering and tending to sores, writing the blog, phoning family, eating dinner and preparing breakfast. I was shattered.

Day 41: Victoria West to Matjiesfontein

Up with the sparrows, I was back on the road in the dark and headed towards Three Sisters, 90 miles away, as my first target of the day. There I would link up with the busy N1, the national highway heavily utilized by traffic thundering through the Karoo. So in all likelihood the roads would get busier and I would be heading straight into that wind. But it would also feel like the final turn into the home straight. From there it was 350 miles to Cape Town.

It was a painfully hard day of fighting that blasted wind, pedalling, pedalling, pedalling, lost in the zone. It was a huge day of just cycling, cycling, cycling as far as I possibly could. The scale of the landscape around me did little to help any sense of progress. Once again I was transported back to parts of Texas, the Outback, the Atlantic coast of Patagonia and other equally vast horizons. For a cyclist, such vistas compound the never-ending nature of the road. These ribbons of tar exist only to get vehicles across these expanses; there's little reason for anyone to turn off or stop.

Eventually I passed through Beaufort West, Leeu Gamka and Laingsburg, where we quickly regrouped, had a chat, and decided to hammer on to Matjiesfontein. Tim was concerned about riding in the dark on the N1 but the choice was simple: if I didn't push those extra miles we'd have huge distances to cover the following day. So they drove alongside me on the shoulder of the highway, hazard lights flashing, protecting me from the trucks during hour after hour of night riding. It must have been criminally boring in that vehicle but Frans and Tim were stoic and completely up for the task.

Anticipating a late arrival, Tim rang ahead to the Lord Milner Hotel to ensure they kept rooms open. Matjiesfontein was barely on the map, but Tim and Frans seemed particularly keen to get there, and I soon discovered why. Set off the highway, alongside the railway line, this heritage village had been kept in the style of yesteryear, and the Lord Milner was every inch a late-nineteenth-century hotel.

The final hour's riding was a slow uphill slog, which made my arrival at the Lord Milner all the sweeter and the impact of the quaint shopfronts and grande olde hotel all the more surreal. I was given a royal welcome by the manager who sat us all down in an otherwise empty dining hall to be immediately served a three-course meal by maids in Victorian garb. After sixteen hours in the saddle and over 230 miles it was a wonderful finale. I was also up over 900 metres again, so looking forward to what had to be a descent in the morning.

Glen Thomas, a drone cameraman, had joined us to film the final push to Cape Town. A large, jolly man who had known Tim for decades, he had plenty of larger-than-life tales of derring-do. So I sat there quietly over dinner, utterly exhausted, as Glen jabbered on. My mind was in a strange place, full of a sense of closure; everywhere I turned it was counting down the final this, the final that. This was the final evening meal on the road. I had entered the final twenty-four hours. That had been the final night ride, not counting tomorrow morning's early start. My stomach had butterflies of excitement and my thoughts had clear tunnel vision to the finish. And yet I was utterly drained, ready to collapse into a heap and sleep for a week. There was still admin to be done, too.

It was gone midnight before I crawled into bed, setting the alarm for 4 a.m.

Day 42: Matjiesfontein to Cape Town

What a beautiful place not to see in the daylight. I stood under the ornate street-lamps outside the Victorian gates of the hotel and hoarsely chatted away to camera before saddling up and rolling back to the N1. It was 4.30. I was exhausted and hurting but also in a whirlwind of excitement. If all went according to plan, this was the final day.

I'd had no more than three and a half hours' sleep, but thanks to massive efforts since entering South Africa I was only about 160 miles from Mouille Point in Cape Town. The official finish point had to be on the Atlantic coast and Chris Trott, the British Consul General, had suggested the iconic Victoria & Albert Waterfront. But the V&A quoted a small fortune for permission, so Chris recommended Mouille Point, pretty much the most western point of Cape Town. It was further than the V&A so Guinness World Records were happy to agree to it.

It was another cold start, but Tim had brought out a Primaloft jacket and I rode the first hours zipped up and hooded up, again lost in my own world. More than ever I needed my little routines to get me through. At that point it was all about getting to dawn and then finding a second breakfast. I was still mentally protecting myself, still not wanting to overexert during the cold, sore hours.

As the sun came up, radio stations from South Africa and the UK started calling both my and Tim's mobiles, which meant a couple of short stops. I would have kept cycling but in the rolling hills the signal was patchy. The excitement was palpable, but it was a bit disconcerting to answer questions about how I felt, as if I had already finished and broken the record. The DJs were inevitably asking me to reflect on the journey but I was still so obsessed with the coming miles and keeping my focus on them that I wasn't ready to bask in glory.

All morning I was getting regular updates through Tim from Una that preparations were well underway for the finish, but there was still a long road ahead with a big climb and a tricky approach to Cape Town. For now I was still in the plains of the Karoo – perfect for aerial photography, and Glen managed to capture footage of me as a tiny dot in this vast open landscape. The perfect illustration of the loneliness of the long-distance cyclist. That isn't to suggest I was lonely: I felt like I had a massive peloton of support from the tens of thousands of hits on social media and the many hundreds of comments. And on the road I had Tim and Frans sharing this fast momentum with me, this obsession with getting to the finish. I could see that they were also tired – they'd put in a tough shift in the support vehicle – but their willingness and enthusiasm were unwavering.

Glen wasn't used to this pace; I was travelling a lot faster than he'd expected. So I would see him parked up ahead, but by the time he spotted me and got the drone airborne I was past him. Seeing him frantically racing around became a bit of a game. As much as I wanted him to get some great footage, this spurred me on to go faster to try and beat him to the shot.

The plateau of the Karoo that I had been racing across for over two days came to an abrupt end. Over the brow of a gradual incline, the road swept quickly downhill. Unlike anything I had seen since Tanzania, this descent just kept going and going. I hurtled dangerously fast wearing a wide grin all the way from the arid plateau into the fertile Hex river valley. Suddenly I was pedalling along this wide and spectacular valley surrounded by autumn colours, the fields around me covered by vineyards, until the sheer rocky sides took over. I was effortlessly eating up the miles, but there were about 100 still to go.

An unwelcome detour lay ahead. After the town of Worcester, the N1 cut through the Du Toitskloof mountains that surround Cape Town via the 3-mile Huguenot Tunnel, which I wasn't allowed to cycle through. The only alternative was to take the old route, up and over a mountain pass.

The predicted fierce headwind hadn't materialized that morning, to my great relief, but it put in an appearance when I turned on to the small provincial roads and headed for the Bainskloof Pass. I slowed to a painful pace, and my power output in order to keep going shot up. I couldn't stop myself from doing sums based on my new speed to work out how much later I would now finish. This was a bad habit throughout the ride – getting obsessed about my current speed and constantly extrapolating that to figure out the day's possible mileage and finishing time. Such short-term variables were hopeless to plan around, but it was impossible to detach myself from the numbers when the going got tough. On my left was the wall of mountains that I had moments before been heading towards. A quick sprint beneath them and I could have been through in less than ten minutes; instead I had a detour that would take me a few hours.

It was a relief eventually to reach the left turn on to the mountain pass. This took me from the equivalent of an A road on to a C road. It was narrow, fairly flat, and a fast sweeping start, crossing the river and following every contour. It was another world from the trunk roads I had been accustomed to since Gaborone, bulldozing the route of least resistance. Now the close-up scenery – the patches of forest, the strewn rocks, the fast-flowing river – gave the ride a drama that was completely different to what I'd enjoyed in the vast theatres of land and sky

I had been pedalling through for weeks. Apart from the odd tourist driving slowly past, or parked up taking photos, I had the road to myself.

Gradually the road steepened, and as it did so the noise of the river I was following increased; I was passing rapids and water-falls. Higher still, the road left this river in the bottom of the gorge and clung to a ledge, cutting a vulnerable path upwards, the left-hand side marked only by painted white stones and the odd section of crash barrier.

I don't know what got into me but I hammered it. Pushing myself back in the saddle and resting my hands gently on the tops, I spun a low gear fiercely, staring at the road in front, climbing like I was going for a mountaintop stage win in the Tour de France. It was euphoric, wonderful, and utterly pointless.

Tim and Frans had raced well ahead, keen to get a perfect vantage point. They made it over a small stone bridge, around some hairpins and through a section of massive overhanging rock formations. They assumed I would be miles back, so I watched with gritted amusement as Tim set up his tripod and Frans, who was on lookout duty, yelled, 'Here he is!' And with that I was past them, sprinting up the mountain, sweat dripping on to the road. I was tight and sore, but through the excitement of the fast climb I had the renewed energy of a horse bolting for home. They jumped ahead again and Tim set about filming out of the back of the car, tracking my climb. Having the target of a vehicle to follow only redoubled my efforts. I rose out of the saddle and for a few kilometres, on the steepest section of the climb, raced with complete disregard for the consequences.

I summited Bainskloof Pass gasping for air and dripping in sweat, but elated. I had left the river far below and up here there was a staggering contrast: on one side I was surrounded by swathes of green, and on the other far hillside were charred remains, red-dish soils and blackened stubble. A series of ferocious fires had swept through less than a month before, ravaging the vegetation; two firefighters had lost their lives on this mountain. Tim told me about this tragedy as we paused near the top. It was shocking to witness the scale of the blaze. I could clearly see how it had been fought from the gardens of some of the hamlets by the roadside.

The summit was too broad to give me a dream of a view down the other side to the Atlantic and to Cape Town. Besides, I was still over 60 miles from the finish, so my sprint to the top was somewhat premature, and one I would pay for, though never regret.

The descent was every bit as rewarding and I was much faster than the camera car, as good a driver as Frans was. Once again I hurtled past a baffled Glen, who was struggling to get the drone airborne, and I found myself laughing out loud, whooping with glee with the thrill of the descent.

I was throwing the bike around with abandon, tucking into the tight corners for the first few miles, when bang! I hit a rock lying on the tar midway through a sharp left. The bike twitched violently but I managed to catch it before crashing, then quickly ground to an untidy stop. The front had blown out. But considering the mess I had nearly created this was a small price to pay.

By the time Tim and Frans caught up I had the bags off the bike. Sitting cross-legged on the roadside, methodically and in no real hurry I fitted a new inner tube and pumped up the tyre. After my race to the summit and then kamikaze descent, this near disaster finally calmed me down. I wasn't annoyed or upset, I wasn't stressed or rushed, I was more amused at the frenzy I had worked myself into. And amazed by the absolute calm I now felt. I was full of sheer bloody relief that I hadn't broken the bike and thrown myself into the trees. Tim thought it was incredible and quite amusing to have a puncture so close to the finish. I don't think he realized how close I'd come to a whole lot worse.

I finished the descent barely pedalling, freewheeling without urgency until the town of Wellington, where I went from wilderness into traffic lights and congestion. It was my first inkling of the mayhem of entering Cape Town by bicycle during rush hour.

But I wasn't anywhere near Cape Town yet and, after the mental and very real milestone of the mountain pass, I mentally crashed with the realization. On the grand scale of even that day, let alone the 6,700 miles I'd covered since Cairo, what was left equated to nothing. Yet both mentally and physically I felt utterly finished. Back out in farmland and open roads, I could have cried I was so low. The euphoria of a few hours earlier and being King of the Mountains was long gone. I had fallen from that high into the foulest of moods. I felt angry and depressed.

Una called to say that unfortunately some of the cyclists who had hoped to come out and meet me couldn't, as I was a day earlier than planned. My reply was that I couldn't care less, I didn't want company. Cape Town was less than 30 miles away now, but what Una was talking about felt light years away. I was so grumpy and sore on the bike.

My expectation of freewheeling from the Bainskloof Pass summit all the way to Cape Town was obviously ridiculous. As we approached Durbanville the road rose again, then when it reached the town it cut steeply up, which my legs protested deeply about. On the outskirts we were met by another car driven by Jurgens Schoeman, who was Frans's boss from Live the Journey, a company providing tailor-made adventure tours. I had met Jurgens in Scotland just a month before leaving for Cairo when I was hosting the National Adventure Awards, which is how his company had enthusiastically ended up being involved. Jurgens' job was to lead us to a meeting point, which proved to be at the summit of this last climb. I was getting back in the zone by the time we reached a big lay-by, but was unprepared for the waiting party.

I had expected a motorbike and a cameraman. The scrambler was driven by a man called Anton Crone, a friend of Tim's, and the plan was for Tim to jump on the back of it to film the ride through Cape Town, as I would almost definitely lose a larger vehicle in the traffic. The cameraman was Antony Smyth, who was meant to take a few photographs out on the road and then race ahead to the finish at Mouille Point. But there were about a dozen people there, and as I stopped, everyone stepped forward excitedly to laud me. I wasn't ready for congratulations; my mind was a long way from the finish yet. I picked out Antony from behind his camera but didn't know anyone else. And then I noticed Nicci's friend Abbie. What was she doing here? Beside her was another woman on a bike, who turned out to be an employee of the WEIR group, one of my sponsors.

I greeted everyone quickly and could see Tim rushing to put the motorbike helmet on and get going. Everyone else seemed in a much slower gear, in celebratory mood.

'Come on, let's go!' I called out, feeling that rising panic from being delayed, then turned to the young man driving a pick-up who had dropped off the cyclists: 'These cyclists are with you, OK? I have to keep going.'

And with that I pushed off. The woman from WEIR stuck with me for about 50 metres until the crest of the hill but was pedalling gently at a family-ride-through-the-park pace. I struck up conversation with Abbie briefly; she had only landed hours before, dumped her bags at the hotel and come out on the road to find me. As the hill picked up and I dropped to the tri-bars, I pulled in front and urged Abbie to tuck in behind me, but was dabbing the brakes just for us to stay together. After a minute of this I gave up, released my brakes and pedalled on. The next time I looked back she was almost out of sight.

I was back in race mode, but this wasn't the euphoria of the mountain sprint, this was a red mist. It took about fifteen minutes for that to clear, and then my spirits started to lift. During that time I powered along at a completely unsustainable speed. I was riding like there was no tomorrow – and in my case, there wasn't.

Tim and Anton obviously loved this speed and they looked comical cuddled up on the scrambler as Tim tried to wield the camera in my direction. We stopped for five minutes at one set of traffic lights to attach a camera to my handlebars for the final miles, and while Tim was doing this I had time to reflect, just for a few minutes. I looked around and it was like a 20kg weight was lifted off both shoulders. I realized where I was. A daft thought went through my mind: if everything breaks right now I can walk it!

The rush-hour traffic was jammed up behind the lights and I was standing on the verge beside a wall covered in graffiti. But this wasn't some political statement; the most prominent words right next to me were HARMONY and SERENITY. In this mental rollercoaster of a finale those words seemed at odds, and yet apt. Because what I felt was inexpressible relief. I could now believe this mission was about to be over.

As we reached the suburb of Milnerton there was some confusion when a police escort joined us. I had been told for many weeks that this was happening and then in the final days that it wasn't possible. Only now, as I entered the final 20 miles, did news come in that the police were waiting for us. Except we missed them. In our haste we shot straight past them and it was only Frans, trailing way behind in the car, who spotted them. So we had to turn around and go back to find a police car and two police motorbikes. The officers seemed in no rush to get started and we stood for a few minutes by the side of this dual carriage-way, wondering what would happen next, wondering who was in charge. When we eventually set off, I looked across at Tim to see him beaming. I smiled back, feeling victorious at last.

But I wasn't there quite yet. All day, since the 4.30 a.m. start, I had been targeting a 5 p.m. finish. Apart from wanting to get every possible hour off the record, there was also the practical issue of not keeping the many sponsors, media and, most importantly, the British Ambassador waiting for too long. At the summit of Bainskloof this had seemed easily possible, but the unexpected hills and delays, along with the expected suburban traffic, had put this under pressure. I now realized that we were coming into Cape Town from the north-east and Mouille Point was in the south-west, and to get there meant reaching the Atlantic near Table View and skirting the bay all the way around.

We speed-weaved on and off the highways and cycle lanes, then as we approached the harbour on the outskirts of the city, the grey blanket of cloud hovering over Table Mountain suddenly cleared and shafts of golden light showered upon us. Tim pulled up alongside and shouted excitedly, pointing: 'Welcome to Cape Town!'

As predicted, we hit the rush-hour traffic at its peak. The traffic department cops worked wonders blocking lanes, guiding us through the city, past Green Point, alongside the World Cup stadium, and around the bay. This police escort definitely didn't win me new fans. The two motorbikes took it in turns to race ahead and cordon off junctions. This meant I never had to stop, but we compounded the already massive queues of traffic. As I raced onwards, I spotted quite a few raised arms and other exasperated gestures.

Skirting the bay on the cycle path was a fast game of dodgems. The motorbikes once again raced ahead and quite rudely, but very helpfully, told all other users to get off the path. On a few occasions innocent runners or walkers ducked off the path with surprise at the instructions of the police and then stepped straight back on in front of me. Yes I was in a rush, but I felt a bit embarrassed about throwing everyone out of my way on my blazoned final approach.

These last few miles really did take a while. As I dropped slowly on and off pavements, following the cycle lane as it meandered around the back of buildings, I was thinking there surely must be a more direct route to Mouille Point. Finally, on a pedestrian bridge, I called back to the motorbike one more time: 'How far now?'

Tim's smile said it all.

The path suddenly led on to a busy road and I was met by a huge finish-line banner, the sounds of music playing and a crowd of people. But as I pulled up to stop there were shouts of 'Keep going, go, go, around the lighthouse!' So I cycled on to the pavement, left this celebration behind and, feeling very confused now, carried on around a route flanked by more people urging me on. After clearing the lighthouse I had a view down the pedestrian walkway. Less than a hundred metres ahead, up a gradual hill, was a much bigger crowd and the finish, a tape being held across the path. And behind that, the Atlantic. Una was leaving no margin for error: I couldn't get much closer to the ocean for the finish line.

Rising out of the saddle for the last time and putting on a bit of speed, I rode to the finish. A wall of flashguns went off as I stood with the tape across my handlebars.

In truth it was all a bit confusing in those final minutes, so the smile wasn't how I felt. There was an indescribable sense of relief, but I wasn't feeling elated yet. Applauding strangers surrounded me, which was wonderful but surreal.

Then I saw Nicci, holding Harriet, standing some way back. She came forward as I beckoned her and we all fell into an embrace. There was another volley of shutters and flashes. Poor Harriet looked bemused but stayed perfectly calm. I was relieved she didn't howl in fright at her bearded, smelly daddy.

After that, I spotted Mum. It had taken some persuading and a last-minute decision on her part to get on the first long-haul flight of her life and leave base camp from where she controlled everything. It was a wonderful family moment, but I could tell Mum was also in the mindset of Una, project coordinator. She got straight down to business.

'Papers for us to sign . . . Chris, meet Mark. This is Chris.'

'Well done!' Chris Trott, smart in a suit, was looking as triumphant as I felt.

'Have you been waiting for ages?' I asked. 'Considering I said five o'clock, it's not too bad.'

'Haha – I was going to walk away if you weren't here by ten past five.' With that, he checked his watch. 'Right, so, 5.22 – 17:22.' He took the printed paper from the Embassy and started to sign and date it. 'I hope this works. Twenty-two . . . on the twenty-first . . . Oh dear, I'm going to have to find another pen!'

A minute later, Dr Theuns Vivian stepped forward. He was the Destination Development Officer for the City of Cape Town and had been hugely helpful, holding lots of meetings, getting permissions for the finish at Mouille Point and organizing the police escort. He'd even had his team out clearing away any litter for a sparkling finish. Dr Vivian asked for silence from a group of journalists and with much gravity heralded my arrival.

'On behalf of the City of Cape Town, we welcome . . . Chris, and his family, to Cape Town.'

There were murmurs from the crowd, but everyone still applauded – at least those who weren't holding cameras. I turned to the British Ambassador, who was standing beside me, and muttered, 'Welcome Chris.' He chuckled quietly as poor Dr Vivian continued.

'Chris, well done. As you know, we are very keen on cycling in Cape Town. We're keen to have you here, and have a wonderful stay in Cape Town. Thank you.'

Being the consummate professional, the real Chris broke

the confused silence. 'And on behalf of the British government, I should add that we're incredibly proud of what Mark has achieved. One of the straplines we use is "Adventure is Great Britain" and we think Mark has proved it. So, well done, Mark . . . fabulous new world record.'

There was over an hour of photos and interviews, but while this went on and I was busy with the media bubble, the cameras and the questions, my family were no longer celebrating, as it had become clear that poor Abbie was missing. I knew I had left her behind on the road but had assumed someone would look after her. She was at that very moment making her way through the townships of Cape Town without a phone, without money, on a bike, in a country she had just landed in for the first time. It was a daft situation, and the rising panic among those at the finish rightly distracted from the celebrations. Happily, hours later, after dark, Abbie made it back to the hotel, somewhat shaken and rather embarrassed, having had her own adventure.

Eventually almost everyone dispersed. Nicci went off to look for Abbie, and just a few sponsors and Mum remained. After the last interview I walked down to the main promenade and stood by the railings overlooking the crashing waves far below. A few ships dotted the horizon and behind me Table Mountain was glowing softly in the sunset. It was quiet at last, and the day was cooling fast. Or was that the adrenalin subsiding and the exhaustion hitting?

My bike leant against the railings. I gazed out at the Atlantic and soaked up the moment, the fiery orange skies and the setting sun. When I finally turned round, I realized Tim was filming me. I had been lost in my own world. So I went over, sat on a park bench and reflected on the finish. It was only just now starting to sink in.

Africa, solo, in 41 days, 10 hours and 22 minutes.

190,355 feet of climbing. 6,762 miles.

What an amazing place to finish. The actual finish line is such a mad scrum of cameras, people and . . . confusion. It's amazing just to stop. Because I've thought about this point for hours, and hours, and hours, and hours on the bike. I had no idea what it looked like. But, to be here, it's going to take a couple of days to sink in for sure. You always imagine that you are going to jump up and down and be excited, and . . . I think other people do that, definitely my family, but it's just relief, just incredible relief. Because there's a lot of pressure. I mean, that pressure comes from myself, but there is a lot of pressure on the road, and worry. It's exciting, and it's wonderful, and many good things, but there's pain, there's a lot of pain. I think it's hard to imagine, unless you've done ultra-endurance and big adventure stuff, just how much pain you go through, and I think if you remembered clearly what that's like each and every day . . . but you don't. In my wildest dreams, I thought forty-five, forty-six days. Never forty-one. So that takes over seventeen days off the old record. But I was never racing the record. I was never racing anyone else. I was racing myself; I was trying to push myself as fast as humanly possible. I've never really gone as hard or as fast as I could, mentally and physically. All the other expeditions I've pushed myself, but I've always come back thinking I could, I could, if I trained differently, if I had different priorities; there's always been things to juggle, whether it's filming or other things to do on the expedition. But this, this was an out-and-out race. This was just me, on my own, pure and simple, going as fast as I could. And I left everything out there. I really did. I don't care if another person goes and breaks that record. It doesn't matter. Because . . . I was on my own out there. It's incredible these days how you can share these stories, and the community around them, and that's a huge part of keeping me going; Una my mum, my wife Nicci, and everyone back home . . . there's no way I could do what I do without that team. Brilliant. Your arm must be falling off with that camera!

I laughed when I realized how long I had been talking. Tim's arm must have been aching.

Four hundred and thirty-nine hours in the saddle is a lot of pain and mental torment. Ultimately, though, you only ever remember the wonder, the awe, the friendship of strangers and the desire to get back on your bike and ride again.

easily to me. Bizarrely, and hopefully happily this time, Nicci is expecting the next addition to the Beaumont Clan on 19 May, the same day as this book is published.

In the autumn of 2015, Nick Bourne led the six-man CaroCap Team Time Trial. I was interested to see how fast they could go being fully supported. And I was able to help them in the months before they left, with information on road conditions and some border crossings, just like Nick had helped me with some of their research. Food poisoning and the extreme heat of the Sahara slowed them through Sudan, and they reached the equator in about the same time as me. Then David Kinjah and others had to drop out with injury and exhaustion. But helped by the same great conditions I'd revelled in through Zambia, Botswana and South Africa, Nick, Mark Blewett and David Martin reached Cape Town in thirty-eight days – a brilliant ride in aid of World Bicycle Relief and the Safari Simbaz Cycling Academy. Nick's words from day 34 of their ride bring back the harsh reality of the ride to me: 'Yesterday and today have nearly finished me off, suffering from heat: my body temperature hit 41°C whilst air temperature was 45. Now feeling exhausted and still battling headwinds – trying to hang in there one pedal stroke at a time.'

In the spring of 2016, Michael Strasser from Austria set out solo and supported from Cairo to Cape Town. He completed the ride in an incredible time of 34 days and 11 hours. Like Nick Bourne I was in touch with Michael throughout his ride, and knowing those roads it was fascinating to log on each day, as I wrote this book, to see the battle he was facing. At time of writing, Michael has not claimed the Guinness world record and I am not sure if he followed the criteria to be able to do so.

You may be wondering about the distinctions in category. 'Team' and 'Solo' world record attempts are normally, but not always, seen differently. There is an obvious advantage in riding as a group. However, there is not normally any distinction between supported and unsupported, as this is very hard to adjudicate. Is having packages sent ahead supported? Is having a camera crew with you supported? There is undoubtedly a huge difference between carrying your own kit on the bike and having a vehicle alongside you supplying the ideal food, hydration and a safe place to sleep each night. But I acknowledge that it is almost impossible to form clear criteria for distinct 'supported' and 'unsupported' rides.

When you are pushing yourself through ultra-endurance cycles, you aren't racing anyone but yourself. There is undoubtedly rivalry, but I also support and promote all these other rides. I certainly hope to look back in years to come on a change in the tide, a period when lots more people started looking seriously at the continent-wide world records and took ultra cycling to the next level.

I think it is inevitable that these world records, including the circumnavigation, the Pan Americas and the Cairo to Cape Town, will all become fully supported attempts. Going 'wildman' style is definitely tougher, and finding your own food, clean water and a safe place to sleep each night doesn't result in the fastest possible time. I expect the Cairo to Cape Town ride will be my last unsupported ride in the coming years. I really want to know how fast and far I can go, and that means those adventure cycling days are behind me now; the next challenges are all about pushing myself as an ultra-endurance athlete.

Family comes first so the tricky part is handling that healthy dose of obsession you need to push yourself as an athlete. My days of half-year expeditions are behind me for the time being, but there is no reason, by going faster and faster, why I can't still push these ambitions each year.

One thing I am certain of: I am loving life back on two wheels.

Acknowledgements

Africa Solo was a solo and mostly unsupported ride from Cairo to Cape Town, but in no way was it an individual effort. At my homecoming party, kindly hosted by Edinburgh Airport and Franck Arnold at the Balmoral Hotel, there were many people who had played an important role in the grand plan. It is my job to set the timescale and ambition of the expeditions, but there are many skillsets I don't have the ability and time for. So I hope it doesn't spoil the illusion of a solo man cycling the length of a continent to give credit and huge thanks to my hard-working team.

Life has different priorities in my thirties with a family from when I was in my early twenties pedalling off around the world. Nicci, my wife, has been with me through many long leaves of absence and moments of worry, but with Harriet now in our lives, that trust and support is taken to another level. Quite simply, I couldn't keep pushing these ambitions without her love and guidance. Thanks to her best friend Abbie Briscoe for taking a sabbatical, flying over and supporting Nicci while I was in Africa. Thanks also to friends at Glenalmond College for their support, in particular Gordon Woods.

Una, aka Mum, has been my expedition base camp since I was twelve years old, pedalling across Scotland. The ambitions have grown but her incredible attention to detail, skilled negotiations and level-headed decision-making were the biggest part of the success of Africa Solo, apart from actually turning the pedals! My family are a constant source of support and motivation, in particular sisters Heather and Hannah, parents-in-law Trish and Ron, my grandparents and father Kevin. Special mention also to cousin Catie, who is quite the adventure athlete herself and regularly sends her support.

Gaining sponsorship for expeditions is always the hardest part of reaching the start line, and there is no golden ticket, even with a public profile and strong track record. I have worked to build a network of companies that support my career in the long term rather than just for specific expeditions, who are invested in the values and the ambition. The longest-standing of these is LDC, for whom I have been Corporate Ambassador for over eight years. LDC stepped up to be the title sponsor for Africa Solo and I am proud of their long-term, loyal support. Special thanks to Sophie Reed, Sam Grey and Andrew Sanders.

For the same values and in support of the expedition charity Orkidstudio, my thanks to Drum Property Group, in particular Fife Hyland. The WEIR Group also donated considerable support to Orkidstudio and went above and beyond to help organize the finish celebrations in Cape Town. I'd like to thank Keith Cochrane, Raymond Buchanan and Kristofer McCue from WEIR and Gavin Dyer and Rene Calitz from WEIR Minerals Africa, and also Elena Synman from the Paper Daisy Company. This significant backing from Drum and WEIR has helped fund the construction of new and upgraded facilities for a remote health clinic on the Zambia/Democratic Republic of Congo border.

Thanks also to James Mitchell from Orkidstudio for his support throughout Africa Solo. Having worked with Orkidstudio for many years, I was delighted to bring James and the team onboard as the project's charity. You can read about their amazing work and ambitions on pages 329–33.

Sir Ian Wood, on behalf of the Wood Foundation and in partnership with their work with Youth Philanthropy Initiative (Scotland), generously sponsored Africa Solo. Martin Currie sponsorship organized by Willie Watt and Sheena Kelman was an extension of the work I do with them for their charity event the Rob Roy Challenge.

Endura, based out of Livingston, came onboard as kit and capital sponsors. I was proud to be partnering a Scottish brand, and their bespoke race suits, helmet and sunglasses were the perfect apparel for Africa Solo. Special mention to Jim, Pam, Alan and Michelle.

Lindsay Whitelaw and Derek Stuart from Artemis have been friends since my world cycle, and personally backed the Africa Solo expedition, with no request for recognition. Thank you for your kindness and belief in the ambition.

KOGA bikes were given a very new challenge to build the Africa Solo bike and it took months to fine-tune specifications and fit. Thanks to Pieter Jan Rijpstra and Aloys Hanekamp for their long-standing sponsorship. In support of this build a huge thanks also to Marc Meulmeester at Wheel-Tec and Jeroen Broekhuizen from Shimano.

In training I was given superb backing by Mark McKay, Kevin Stewart and Craig Burn at Scottish Cycling as well as support for testing from the Scottish Institute of Sport. Thank you to my mechanics Gavin Brough and Owen Cooper from Gamma Transport Division for the meticulous set-up (and cracking coffee).

For providing kit and supplies my thanks to Tori Fahey from Apidura, Helen Cussen from Trident Sensors Ltd, Wattbike for the training kit, Andy Hain from Leslie Bike Shop, George Bowie, Barry and Stephen from 2pure Ltd, Martin Kirkton at

Lyon Equipment, Ark Consultants for Nordisk tents, Saddleback for Stages Crank, Dalesman for Garmin. And special thanks to Arron Sinclair for organizing the flash new Infiniti QX70 that was waiting for me on my return from Cape Town. Online, I had Jason Waghorn volunteering on the data management and Jason Wagner from Ping Creates working on the website and social media.

During planning I gained a huge amount of support from Henry Gold and the Tour d'Afrique team – if you would like to cycle Cairo to Cape Town then contact them. Thanks also to Michael Kennedy, Chris Wrede from Oasis Overland, Ross Methven, Huw Thomas, Naomi Johnson, Philip Maciocia, Tamir Delf, Kevin Lyon, David Fox-Pitt, Rob Pendleton, Chris Blair, Craig Taylor and Kamal Omer. Thanks also to Corrinne Burns at Guinness World Records for her prompt and enthusiastic support for the world record verification.

Africa Solo was a challenging broadcast project and special thanks to the key players in capturing the story: Jeremy Sutton-Hibbert, Tim Chevallier, Colin Cosier, Robbie Wright, Antony Smyth, Alan Hill, Anton Crone, Alice Oldenbury, Sami Bala, El Tayeb and Glen Thomas. For fantastic logging and editing my thanks to Kevin Woods.

For logistical support on the road, my thanks to Ramy Nicola and the team from Lady Egypt, Claire Powell and George from Thorn Tree Safaris, Midhat and Mazar Mahir and Salah from Mashan Sharti. Ed Jarvis, Mark Windmill and Martin from Saladin Security Ltd, Duncan Higham from Ship Security International, Duncan Sutcliffe from Sutcliffe & Co. Insurance Brokers, Ahmed Naylor Mahmoud from GBI Egypt and Ayman from TFA, Mohammed Abouda, Mark Nightingale, Joshua Malanda and Jonathan Lamont. Jurgens Schoeman, Frans Groenewald and Elsabeth Miller from Live the Journey, David Scott from Sandbaggers, Ignatius Lindeque for the pedals in

Zambia, Dr Theuns Vivian from City of Cape Town Government, Corporate Traveller and the team at Protea Hotel Fire & Ice in Cape Town.

With regard to British Embassies and Consulates, a special thanks to John Hamilton, Stephen Hickey and Chris Trott, as well as David Kinna, Len Parr Ferris, Paul Lawrence, Gelilawit Damena, Rita Solomon, Jackie Brown, Raju Majithia, Dax Patel and Karen Van Boxtel.

Lastly, but brilliantly vital to the production of this book, many thanks to the belief of Giles Elliott, my editor, and his team at Transworld Publishers, Penguin Random House UK. Thanks also to Daniel Balado for his work on the book, Una for many read-throughs and checks, and to Stan, my literary agent from Jenny Brown Associates.

What a team effort – I share this world record with you all.

Orkidstudio and Africa Solo

by Mark Beaumont

James Mitchell set up Orkidstudio when he was nineteen years old. I heard about their work soon afterwards, on my return from cycling around the world in 2008. James is from Kilmacolm, a village outside Glasgow – the same village as Una, my mum. I could see the direct impact of Orkidstudio's work and through my travels I connected with this idea that buildings could be the pride of communities and so much more than just walls and a roof. While Orkidstudio have worked in four continents, their biggest focus is Africa, so when I decided to turn my attention and my bicycle in that direction, I realized this was the perfect project to put a spotlight on Orkidstudio.

A sincere thank you once again to Drum Property Group and the WEIR Group, whose sponsorship and names on the Africa Solo strip were wholly in support of Orkidstudio, and whose significant backing helped fund the construction of the medical centre in Zambia.

by James Mitchell, Director of Orkidstudio

The first drops of an approaching thunderstorm started to drum down on my head as I handed my bulky rucksack to one of the bus-station helpers, a young man sporting a dirt-stained football top and clutching a wodge of tear-out tickets. The chaos of African transport hubs stirred up familiar feelings as I made my way on to the bus, leaving the destiny of my luggage, as usual, to trust and hope.

On finding my pre-allocated seat, the only one still empty, I settled my head against the window and prepared for the long overnight journey ahead. As we set off, the storm soon found us and revealed a series of large leaks in the rubber window seals. I found little sleep that night, as the bus lumbered slowly southwards and the rainwater running down the inner face of my window soaked my entire left side.

Like many of you during Mark's cycle down Africa, I found myself frequently refreshing the GPS tracking website that marked his progress. Despite the continent's vast size, there are only a few possible routes down its full length, fewer if you wish to remain on well-surfaced roads. Mark's route picked up the main road linking Lusaka with its copper-mining towns around halfway, at a small intersection called Kapiri Mposhi. As I followed the GPS dot through this section I was reminded of my damp night trip along the same road. Even when I've travelled that route in better circumstances, it is a long, arduous stretch of tarmac with little to stimulate or disrupt the flat surrounding savannah except a stream of HGVs and large mining vehicles.

The dot moved with the customary speed that ultimately led to Mark breaking the world record by a remarkable margin. I was struck by the contradiction in pace relative to my own experiences. What I had considered to be a long, slow route, Mark was shrinking right before my eyes.

There are different ways of understanding or viewing a place. Racing the length of a continent affords you little time to explore the intricacies of the locale, certainly not much beyond a few yards off the main roads, giving a different though equally profound experience. When I spend time in Africa, speed and distance are frequently at the opposite end of the scale. I enjoy soaking up the local pace, often exploring without a map or destination in mind, just allowing my surroundings to guide me. Despite these different approaches, Mark's Africa, as you will have read in this book, is one of people, culture and place, and it bears a number of similarities to the Africa I know and love.

I first set foot in sub-Sahara Africa aged nineteen. I had two years of architecture school under my belt and just the right mix of confidence and naivety to carry me from the studio to a close-knit community on the eastern reaches of Kampala, Uganda. I had quickly grown disenchanted with the profession I had entered. Where I'd thought I'd find opportunities to help others and to apply my design ideas with my own hands on site, I found an industry in servitude to the wealthy and so removed from the realities of building that it seemed almost laughable. I later discovered that an estimated 1 per cent of the world's population has access to or lives in buildings designed by an architect. For me, it was time something changed.

In Uganda I discovered an architecture where people became more important than the building and where the building could mean far more for people than just a place to shelter or congregate. One young man, Milton Yada, who worked with us throughout the build, said some years later, 'But for us, when you reach here, this kitchen gives everyone the image of places that you're going to see in the future.'

Eight years on, that first build signalled the start of what is now Orkidstudio, an organization whose aim is to create change through building, enterprise and community. Informed by these early experiences, our projects focus on the process of design and construction rather than just the final product. We believe this process can be a powerful tool for affecting social change and empowering people through the sharing of skills and knowledge on site.

Yet the African continent is diverse and complex. Creating better buildings is only part of the story. For us, our work becomes far more than just a building, it is about people, and striving to create lasting change and development. Owen Kariuki is part of a community team that has worked with Orkidstudio on a number of projects in Nakuru, Kenya, over the past few years. Following one particular build, he commented, 'You help one person, that person you have helped goes and helps another person, that person goes and helps another, then by the end we will have helped millions of people.'

Owen's words, unprompted and encouraging, still resonate with me today. However, the 'teach a man to fish' theory isn't always a straightforward recipe for success. With teaching and training there also needs to be opportunity – to build livelihoods and self-sufficiency. There also needs to be that drive and motivation to succeed. At Orkidstudio our work is founded on four key principles: to inspire, to promote equality, to educate and to empower. In respect of the first of those, we believe that architecture has the power to inspire, excite and instil hope in people and communities regardless of background and circumstance. When dealing with those at the lower end of the global economic spectrum this subjective quality, the aim to inspire, is so often disregarded, even considered repugnant or extravagant. Yet most of us know from our own lives that the activities and interactions that engage and excite us the most are the ones we plough our energy into.

In Kenya we have worked with many women on site, including single mother of eight Hellen Nyambura Kamau. On being asked what it was like to work with Orkidstudio, she recalled, 'I felt happy, for it is not an ordinary thing. Never in my life would I have imagined this. I am used to tilling and washing people's clothes to earn a living but when I found myself working with men on the project, something that has never happened in Kenya, this made me feel very happy.'

When we look at world records smashed or far-reaching goals achieved, we feel inspired and it sparks something in us for a moment or a lifetime that we perhaps didn't expect. Milton, Owen and Hellen found inspiration in the projects they helped construct, and all three of them are an inspiration to me in different ways. Following Mark's journey down Africa inspired me too, and though I may not opt to cycle the length of Africa on my next trip there, the belief and determination that resonate through all of these ventures should be valued and cherished.

Appendix 1

Africa Solo Strava Data

Strava is a social-media platform for cyclists and runners where you can log your GPS data for rides/runs. The entire world is split into segments and you can see on a leaderboard your position on any one of them. This allows cyclists to get competitive even when they are cycling alone, as they are competing against anyone else who has ever cycled there and uploaded their data to Strava.

Detailed day-to-day information on my Africa Solo route can be found on my Strava profile, where you will see in the activity log each day's map, speeds, et cetera.

www.strava.com/athletes/8288853

Appendix 2

Africa Solo Kit List

Frame: KOGA Solacio 60cm

Groupset: Shimano Dura-Ace Di2 with bar end shifter, 50-34T and 12-28T

Bars and stem: FSA K-Force with PRO Missile Ski-Bend Clip On

Saddle: Selle SMP Pro

Lights: Exposure Race Mk9

Brakes: Shimano Di2 shifters suitable for hydraulic discbrakes (ST-R785), Shimano calipers (BR-R785) and Shimano center-lock discs (SM-RT99)

Tyres: Schwalbe Marathon Supreme – 28mm front, 32mm back

Rims: Pacenti SL25

Front hub: SON28, 100mm quick-release

Rear hub: White Industries CLD, 135mm quick-release, Shimano 11s

Spokes: 32x Sapim CX Ray + CX Sprint J bend black

Nipples: Sapim brass polyax black

Luggage: Apidura, total of 35-litre capacity

Cages: Salsa Anything

ABOUT THE AUTHOR

Mark Beaumont was born on New Year's Day 1983 and grew up in the foothills of the Scottish Highlands, where his parents ran an organic smallholding. When he was twelve, he cycled across Scotland from Dundee to Oban, then a few years later, while still at school, completed the 1,000 mile solo ride down the length of Britain from John O'Groats to Land's End. After graduating from Glasgow University in Economics and Politics, he decided against a conventional career and devoted himself full-time to adventures and broadcasting. Mark is the Rector of the University of Dundee, from where he also received an honorary degree. He is also Patron for a number of charities including the Saltire Foundation, Orkidstudio and the Winning Scotland Foundation.

Visit his website at www.markbeaumontonline.com

The Man Who Cycled the World

Mark Beaumont

On 15 February 2008, Mark Beaumont pedalled through the Arc de Triomphe in Paris, 194 days and 17 hours after setting off on a mission to cycle around the globe. He had travelled 18,297 miles solo and unsupported, averaging 100 punishing miles a day, and smashed the Guinness World Record by an astonishing 81 days.

The Man Who Cycled the World is the story of that incredible feat of endurance. After battling broken wheels in Europe, then the hostile mountains and deserts of Turkey, Iran and Pakistan, a saddle-sore Mark crossed Asia. In Australia, the heat and a ferocious headwind threatened his resolve, before a terrible crash in America nearly ended the journey.

By the time Mark had raced night and day to reach Paris again, he had completed a remarkable adventure. *The Man Who Cycled the World* tells his epic story and provides an insight into many of the world's cultures from a unique perspective.

The Man Who Cycled the Americas
Mark Beaumont

One year after he became The Man Who Cycled the World, Mark Beaumont set off on a second record-breaking endurance adventure. It would involve another huge distance: 15,000 miles from the wilds of Alaska to the windswept southern tip of Argentina. But this time he faced a new challenge: scaling North and South America's highest peaks. Mount McKinley, otherwise known as Denali: 20,320 feet, technical, extremely cold, very dangerous. Aconcagua: the highest summit outside Asia. Tough at the best of times. Even harder after eight punishing months on the road.

The Man Who Cycled the Americas tells the story of Mark's incredible journey down the longest mountain range on the planet and of both the dangers and exhilaration that it brought. Full of his trademark charm, warmth and fascination with seeing the world at the pace of a bicycle, it is a thrilling trip through the diverse cultures of our most fascinating continents.